EUROPEAN CONFERENCE OF MINISTERS OF TRANSPORT

Sustainable Transport in Central and Eastern European Cities

*Proceedings of the Workshop
on Transport and Environment
in Central and Eastern
European Cities*

28th-30th June 1995
Bucharest, Romania

ORGANISATION FOR ECONOMIC CO-OPERATION AND DEVELOPMENT

ORGANISATION FOR ECONOMIC CO-OPERATION AND DEVELOPMENT

Pursuant to Article 1 of the Convention signed in Paris on 14th December 1960, and which came into force on 30th September 1961, the Organisation for Economic Co-operation and Development (OECD) shall promote policies designed:

- to achieve the highest sustainable economic growth and employment and a rising standard of living in Member countries, while maintaining financial stability, and thus to contribute to the development of the world economy;
- to contribute to sound economic expansion in Member as well as non-member countries in the process of economic development; and
- to contribute to the expansion of world trade on a multilateral, non-discriminatory basis in accordance with international obligations.

The original Member countries of the OECD are Austria, Belgium, Canada, Denmark, France, Germany, Greece, Iceland, Ireland, Italy, Luxembourg, the Netherlands, Norway, Portugal, Spain, Sweden, Switzerland, Turkey, the United Kingdom and the United States. The following countries became Members subsequently through accession at the dates indicated hereafter: Japan (28th April 1964), Finland (28th January 1969), Australia (7th June 1971), New Zealand (29th May 1973), Mexico (18th May 1994) and the Czech Republic (21st December 1995). The Commission of the European Communities takes part in the work of the OECD (Article 13 of the OECD Convention).

THE EUROPEAN CONFERENCE
OF MINISTERS OF TRANSPORT (ECMT)

The European Conference of Ministers of Transport (ECMT) is an inter-governmental organisation established by a Protocol signed in Brussels on 17th October 1953. The Council of the Conference comprises the Ministers of Transport of 31 European countries.[1] The work of the Council of Ministers is prepared by a Committee of Deputies.

The purposes of the Conference are:

a) to take whatever measures may be necessary to achieve, at general or regional level, the most efficient use and rational development of European inland transport of international importance;

b) to co-ordinate and promote the activities of international organisations concerned with European inland transport, taking into account the work of supranational authorities in this field.

The matters generally studied by ECMT – and on which the Ministers take decisions – include: the general lines of transport policy. investment in the sector; infrastructural needs; specific aspects of the development of rail, road and inland waterways transport; combined transport issues; urban travel; road safety and traffic rules, signs and signals; access to transport for people with mobility problems. Other subjects now being examined in depth are: the future applications of new technologies, protection of the environment, and the integration of the central and eastern European countries in the European transport market. Statistical analyses of trends in traffic and investment are published each year, thus throwing light on the prevailing economic situation.

The ECMT organises Round Tables and Symposia. Their conclusions are considered by the competent organs of the Conference, under the authority of the Committee of Deputies, so that the latter may formulate proposals for policy decisions to be submitted to the Ministers.

The ECMT Documentation Centre maintains the TRANSDOC database, which is available on CD-ROM or accessible via the telecommunications network.

For administrative purposes, the ECMT Secretariat is attached to the Secretariat of the Organisation for Economic Co-operation and Development (OECD).

1. Austria, Belgium, Bosnia-Herzegovina, Bulgaria, Croatia, the Czech Republic, Denmark, Estonia, Finland, France, Germany, Greece, Hungary, Ireland, Italy, Latvia, Lithuania, Luxembourg, Moldova, the Netherlands, Norway, Poland, Portugal, Romania, the Slovak Republic, Slovenia, Spain, Sweden, Switzerland, Turkey and the United Kingdom. (Associate Member countries: Australia, Canada, Japan, New Zealand, the Russian Federation and the United States. Observer countries: Albania, Armenia, Belarus, Georgia and Morocco.)

FOREWORD

As central and eastern European countries continue their transition to market economies, cities in the region are struggling to cope with growing car ownership and use; rising motor vehicle traffic, chaotic parking; congestion; and consequent air and noise pollution. At the same time, municipalities are seeking ways to adapt their public transport systems to evolving requirements and severe budgetary constraints; national and local policy-makers pursue new policy approaches and stable sources of financing.

In June 1995, a Workshop on Transport and Environment in Central and Eastern European Cities was held in Bucharest, Romania to examine urban transport trends, related environmental, economic and social problems and possible policy approaches for cities in the region. The workshop was jointly organised by The European Conference of Ministers of Transport (ECMT), the OECD Centre for Co-operation with the Economies in Transition, the Urban Affairs Division of the OECD Territorial Development Service, the Non-Member Countries Branch of the OECD Environment Directorate and the Romanian Ministry of Transport and the City of Bucharest.

Drawing on the recently completed work of the OECD/ECMT Project Group on Urban Travel and Sustainable Development, the workshop participants -- more than 50 transport, environment and urban experts, public transport operators, ministry representatives and municipal officials from both central and eastern Europe and OECD countries -- explored lessons to be learned from the experiences of OECD countries, and discussed the problems and conditions specific to central and eastern European cities.

This publication is a collection of the principal papers presented at the event, preceded by a summary of conclusions based on workshop discussions. It is divided into five main sections:

- Mobility in Urban Areas
- Managing Traffic Growth
- Organising and Financing Urban Public Transport Services
- Implementing Urban Transport Policies
- The Case of Bucharest

The conclusions provide a synthesis of the predominant challenges facing central and eastern Europe in the development of their urban transport systems -- challenges to which many cities in OECD countries continue to seek solutions as well.

TABLE OF CONTENTS

EXECUTIVE SUMMARY

In Central and Eastern Europe, rapidly rising numbers of motor vehicles are crowding urban roads and city centres, causing congestion, serious air and noise pollution problems and safety hazards. Confronted with this situation, decision-makers in the region face difficult choices regarding the design and development of their urban transport systems. Saddled with the legacy of transport networks conceived under central planning, they must find ways to address the economic, social and environmental pressures caused by rapid growth in car use. At the same time, urban public transport authorities must reconcile a decline in demand for public transport with tight budgetary constraints and pressure to increase cost recovery through fare increases.

This publication, a collection of expert analyses on the urban transport problems facing central and eastern European cities, is a follow-up to the recently completed work of the OECD/ECMT Project Group on Urban Travel and Sustainable Transport. This group devised a policy plan for addressing urban transport problems that would promote "less congestion, reduced energy consumption, improved access for those without cars, higher environmental standards and reduced overall costs." OECD cities acknowledge that they have made mistakes in managing the evolution of urban travel, resulting in exponential growth of car traffic, congestion in city centres and serious air pollution. In order to attack these problems, substantial amounts of resources are now being committed to "un-doing" the mistakes -- to rethinking transport systems and influencing user behaviour. The countries in transition in Central and Eastern Europe now have the opportunity to learn from the mistakes of western cities -- as well as from the experiences of other cities in the central and eastern European region -- and move forward toward more economically and environmentally sustainable development of their urban centres.

Managing Traffic Growth

Since the economic and political reforms of the late 1980s, motor vehicle use has soared in Central and Eastern Europe. Under central planning, private car use was extremely limited because of restrictions on imported vehicles and minimal domestic car production. In 1980, automobile ownership in Warsaw amounted to 157 cars per 1 000 population. By 1989, however, this figure had grown to 247, and by 1992, to 322. As Wojciech Suchorzewski of the Warsaw University of Technology states in his paper, "Warsaw has already entered the vicious circle of more cars, more traffic, worsening public transport."

Because of this growth in car traffic, public transport use is declining. For example, Budapest has experienced an evolution in modal split from 80 per cent public transport in 1985 to 60 per cent public today. Existing urban road networks and parking structures have proven inadequate to handle the increasing volume of traffic and greater demand for parking space brought on by higher motorisation. Delays are worsened by traffic-control systems that are out of date. It has been difficult to obtain public and political approval of proposals for car traffic restraint, parking charges and public transport priority measures; as a result, traffic congestion and subsequent air pollution levels have reached serious proportions in regional city centres.

In OECD cities, where car traffic doubled between 1970 and 1990, parking control measures have been widely applied to address traffic growth. Charging for on-street parking and controlling development of new parking capacity have been instrumental in alleviating traffic congestion in city centres. In addition, parking fees have proven to be an important source of finance for municipalities, providing resources for improvements in the urban transport system and attracting private parking suppliers, thus relieving some pressure on municipal provision.

Enforcement is the key, however, to the effectiveness of these measures, and enforcement remains a problem in central and eastern European cities. With few controls in place, parking in many cities is chaotic. Unrestrained parking in streets and on pavements is common, partly because no policy exists for time limits or charges. Therefore, policies aimed at controlling parking -- such as the introduction of parking fees for use of existing space, assessing and enforcing fines for illegal parking, and limiting construction of new parking facilities -- may prove effective in addressing the traffic problem.

Determining the right level of parking supply is a major factor in effective parking management. Rolf Monheim of the University of Bayreuth explains in his paper that parking demand and supply are inter-related in a complex way: high demand for parking exerts pressure to increase supply; likewise, extensive parking supply encourages use of cars for travel. Monheim states that the supply of parking should be managed in such a way that demand adapts to the carrying capacity of the traffic system. Since parking supply cannot meet all demand, the different elements of demand must be prioritised; supply will meet only demand that is essential to the effective, prosperous functioning of the city centre: demand generated by business traffic, goods delivery, service vehicles, and to a certain degree, residents. This is known as "qualified demand". In Central and Eastern Europe, the need to increase parking supply -- currently under consideration in numerous cities in the region -- should be based on qualified, instead of total, demand in order to mitigate the effect of parking availability on traffic congestion.

Car restraint measures, including pedestrianisation of city centres and promotion of bicycle and pedestrian travel, also contribute to reducing traffic congestion, especially when coupled with parking management initiatives. Mr. Monheim asserts that parking management and pedestrianisation are two key elements of a strategy for sustainable traffic development; when pursued together -- in the context of overall transportation and land-use planning -- they can be highly effective in managing traffic. Road construction in urban areas should also be limited, by-passing dense residential areas where possible, or if not, introducing traffic-calming measures; and giving priority to public transport traffic.

A number of central and eastern European cities have already designed plans to use parking management and car-restraint measures to attack growing traffic problems. Among these cities, Krakow has pedestrianised its historic city centre and established parking zones to accommodate motorists. And Budapest is taking steps to restrict car traffic in the centre and castle districts. Pedestrian zones have been gradually added in strategic parts of the city, and week-ends are car-free in tourist areas.

Land-use planning contributes to traffic mitigation by providing a framework for medium- and long-term decisions on development of real estate sites, access to which would require travel by car. As Susan Owens of the University of Cambridge explains in her paper, the need to consider land-use planning and the transport system as a whole along with their environmental implications is increasingly recognised. Indeed, land-use patterns are influenced by transport infrastructure developments; likewise, patterns of urban development influence both the need for transport and choices among different modes of transport. If economic growth patterns follow those of many OECD cities, there will be increasing movement of commercial and residential development outside of city centres to areas that are easily accessible only by car. Decision-makers throughout the region will need to find ways to channel this development along lines that are compatible with existing urban public transport networks, or further develop networks where needed, so that links between urban, suburban and inter-city transport are better co-ordinated and the need for cars to access these areas is reduced. Rendering city centres more attractive to business, commercial and cultural activities will also help to reduce urban sprawl.

Pricing mechanisms can be effective in harnessing un-restrained car use and bringing traffic under control, as well. For example, a number of OECD countries are considering road pricing schemes (tolls) along with parking charges to reduce traffic congestion. Stockholm is planning to introduce road pricing using a toll ring around the inner area of the city in the context of the city's recent transport plan -- the so-called Dennis Agreement. Estimates are that city-centre traffic will drop by a third.

Using the pricing mechanism for fuel can be effective in mitigating the environmental and economic costs of traffic congestion. The price of petrol in Central and Eastern Europe is generally lower than in western European countries; however, it is high in relation to average personal income. Peter Güller of the Swiss consultancy Synergo suggests in his paper that increases in the price of petrol should be parallel to growth in personal income: maintaining the high ratio of fuel price to income is one way to internalise the external costs of transport (e.g. environmental damage, accident costs).

Organising and Financing Urban Public Transport Services

Public-transport operators, working under severe budgetary constraints, are seeking ways to remain competitive in the wake of rising motor vehicle use. Central planning left much of the region's transport infrastructure in poor condition, with fleet, facilities and accessory equipment dated or obsolete and suffering from frequent breakdowns, unreliable service, inefficient fuel consumption and heavy vehicle emissions. Current financing for improvements is inadequate; consequently, replacing vehicles and upgrading transport infrastructure is virtually impossible. Tramway systems are in jeopardy, although in the OECD area, cities such as Strasbourg and Grenoble are enthusiastically reintroducing this mode of transport.

Several historical factors are behind this situation: first, cost recovery was not an issue under central planning. Today, it is a principal pre-occupation of public-transport operators, and new management techniques are therefore required to ensure that cost-recovery practices are introduced. For example, public transport companies are being re-organised to concentrate exclusively on core activities, returning the social-support functions for which they have been responsible to date to social security and other public administrations, and increase efficiency. Privatisation of urban transport companies is also being considered; however, OECD experience in this area is limited as well (mainly U.K.), and for the present, privatisation of urban public transport does not appear to be a viable option in Central and Eastern Europe. Instead, some cities are considering contractual arrangements known as *concessions* (as in France) between the local authorities and service providers that increase accountability and efficiency of urban transport operations.

Second, under the former regime, fares were incongruously low relative to the real operational and administrative costs of public transport. In his examination of urban public transport financing in OECD countries, Méyère states that fares should increase at a rate at least equal to that of operating costs. The share of tariffs in total income can be increased, Méyère says, provided that the social exclusion effects which could result are considered.

Other financing problems include widespread fare evasion, which continues to deprive transport company coffers of needed revenues. And, as Katalin Tánczos of the Technical University of Budapest notes in her analysis of the situation in the Hungarian capital, servicing the large debt inherited from the previous regime has increased pressure on already limited financing sources.

A further complexity lies in the incomplete decentralisation of responsibility for urban public transport. Decision-making power has been transferred from central governments to municipalities, but without control over the sources of financing -- notably the fiscal system. As a result, municipalities have been left without the financial means to support their newly acquired responsibilities. Further, central governments often do not dedicate income from fuel taxes and other transport-related import duties to the improvement of transport and road infrastructure, instead considering these funds available for other uses. Indeed, central and eastern European cities often benefit very little from taxes paid to central governments.

Along with decentralisation has come a significant reduction in national subsidies for urban public transport. In order to offset the decline in subsidisation and improve cost recovery, fare increases have been regularly introduced. In Budapest, for example, fares have shot upward since 1989 to compensate for subsidy cuts; in that year, a new public transport tariff system increased fares by an average of 85 per cent (in nominal terms). Tariffs increased twice again in 1990 and 1991, by averages of 60 and 50 per cent respectively. (Inflation was running at 20 to 30 per cent at this time).

Throughout the region, however, fare hikes of this kind have been imposed without accompanying improvements in services. As a result, public-transport users are increasingly dissatisfied. Méyère points out that there is no urban transport system in the OECD which operates without some financial support. The trend is to bring the level of government involvement as close as possible to the user, i.e. to the local level. However, this is only possible if the local government has adequate financial independence and resources.

The lack of domestic financing for transport system improvements has led many central and eastern European countries to seek foreign credits for this purpose. One of the roadblocks to this financing, however, is a lack of legislation allowing sovereign guarantees for local credit schemes; the major international financing institutions are requiring these guarantees as a condition for loan approval. For example, as of August 1995, out of 38 transport sector loans approved by the European Bank for Reconstruction and Development in Central and Eastern Europe, only one concerned urban transport. This is primarily due to reluctance on the part of national governments to provide guarantees for urban projects. As a result, the international financing institutions are currently investigating alternatives to sovereign guarantees for municipal loans.

Transport policy-making structures and procedures in the region are in need of re-organisation. Co-ordination of transport policy and operations on local, regional and national levels is vital in order to overcome fragmentation and inefficiency of local initiatives. Likewise, short-, medium- and long-term planning for the development of different modes of transport should be a collaborative effort, so that long-term budgeting is possible. Local transport authorities can be established to handle the co-ordination of planning, development and operation of different transport modes.

Implementing Urban Transport Policies

Despite these challenges, public transport systems in many central and eastern European cities benefit from several important, positive features that could form the basis for long-term, sustainable urban transport development in the region; notably, a strong tradition of public transport use, extensive public transport networks, and land-use patterns that are conducive to public transport. In order to take advantage of these benefits, existing public transport should be rehabilitated, upgraded and restructured as needed. Development outside of urban areas should be based on existing accessibility by public-transport networks; and connections should be considered before, not after development occurs, as has been often the case in the OECD area.

Along with these initiatives should come a concerted effort to confront the car traffic problem. A combined "push-and-pull" strategy, as Mr. Monheim calls it, is one way to attack traffic congestion: this entails "pushing" or dissuading residents from excessive car use through parking management measures such as fees and time limits, and fuel pricing; and attracting or "pulling" users to public transport and other travel means by providing a safe and efficient public transport system, favourable conditions for walking and bicycling, and pedestrianising or rendering "car-free" sections of the city centre. This will likely require considerable political courage, as cars are often associated with newly acquired independence and prosperity; public transport is often associated with the old regime; and efforts to manage the growth of motor vehicle use might be perceived as a constraint on individual freedom.

For these reasons, it is essential that the public understand and support measures taken to enhance public transport and curb traffic growth. Effective communication with the public at large is the key to winning this support. The public must understand that traffic congestion has a negative impact on the urban environment; that citizens have a role to play in assuring the economically and environmentally sustainable development of their cities; and that the choices they make regarding transportation will have a direct effect on the future of this development. The experience of Sweden is particularly illustrative as concerns the winning of public support in transport policy development. Bo Peterson, Director of Stockholm Transport, describes in his paper the innovative initiatives taken in Sweden to involve public opinion in the development of the Dennis Agreement to solve traffic problems in the Stockholm area.

Krakow's 1993 progressive transport policy plan exemplifies how with political courage and effective public communication, positive, comprehensive initiatives can be taken to facilitate and enhance the sustainable development of urban centres. The plan sets specific objectives to counter increased motor vehicle use, declining public transport and rising congestion and vehicle emissions. It includes: priority investment for public transport; a commitment to improved public transport service in order to raise competitiveness relative to motor vehicles; the elimination of traffic from densely populated areas; the integration of suburban and urban transport systems; and the provision of park-and-ride facilities. In addition, the local mass media provided valuable support in favour of the sustainable urban and transport policies. Andrzej Rudnicki, one of the principal architects of the Krakow transport plan, sees the bold initiatives agreed by the Municipality of Krakow as the way to assure a sustainable transport future for the city, perpetuating its long tradition of public transport use and managing growth in car traffic.

The Case of Bucharest

The situation in Bucharest exemplifies the variety of urban transport challenges currently facing central and eastern European cities. Under central planning, Romania followed the rules of an exceptionally rigid, isolated form of command economy which tolerated virtually no external trade. As a result, urban public transport infrastructure, equipment and services are in a particularly distressed condition relative to many other cities in the region. And car traffic is on the rise.

The public transport situation in Bucharest is complicated by the lack of a specific public transport law establishing the responsibilities of authorities and passenger rights to mobility, as Constantin Popescu, General Manager of Bucharest's surface public transport company RATB points out in his paper. Moreover, urban public transport is not considered a priority issue among authorities, and there is a lack of co-ordination between local officials and transport operators, Popescu says.

In his analysis of the Bucharest metro, Octavian Udriste, Director General of the city's metro company Metrorex, traces the long history of the city's metro system from its beginnings in the aftermath of the First World War, through the dominance of the Soviet development regime, to today's challenges -- which like those of other cities in the region -- include aged equipment, frequent breakdowns and high operating costs. While pursuing answers to these problems, Bucharest Metro officials are also seeking to establish a regional railway link between the city and its populated suburban areas -- an idea which has long been discussed, but for which financial resources are lacking. Germany's regional railway system is an example to which Bucharest and other cities are looking for possible solutions. In her paper, Jutta Völker of the German Deutsche Eisenbahn-Consulting GmbH draws from the German *"Regionalisierung"* experience to make recommendations to central and eastern European cities examining regional railway solutions. In the short term, however, maintenance and upgrading of existing transport infrastructure and rolling stock should be the priority.

Despite the complexity of transport problems in Bucharest, the city possesses numerous advantageous features that may help it along the way to an improved, more-efficient urban transport system. These advantages include:

- an extensive public transport network;
- a long-standing culture of public transport use;
- a dense, mixed land-use pattern.

Investment is urgently needed to:

- upgrade and improve the reliability of public transport infrastructure and rolling stock;
- introduce road network improvements to safeguard investments and improve safety.

In addition, a combined land-use and transport strategy is needed for Bucharest to provide a framework for: growth in the city; land-use and transport policies; and cost-benefit analyses of investment in different transport modes. Components of a transport plan for Bucharest might include:

- policies and measures to give priority to public transport (e.g. separate bus lanes and tram tracks; priority at traffic lights);
- strong parking supply and management policies to respond to the growing problems caused by chaotic parking practices.

As in other cities in the region, public acceptance of new policies and measures could be facilitated by a concerted communication effort, possibly with public debate of the issues and choices involved. Users should be viewed as clients, whose patronage of the public transport system depends to a large extent on their understanding of the economic and environmental benefits of using public transport, and the issues and choices involved in the development of the public transport system. Likewise, political leaders and government officials must openly recognise the dangers of unmitigated growth in car use to the city. This may require considerable political courage, especially in the current economic climate.

Perspectives for Change

Political courage is needed in the development of urban transport policies in OECD member countries as well. Indeed, the majority of the world's car fleet and vehicle-related environmental problems are found in developed countries. In order to establish sustainable transport systems, the external costs of transport, which include environmental damage and accident costs must be paid for. Essential in attacking these costs are bold pricing mechanisms such as fuel taxation and enforced parking charges, initiatives which often encounter public resistance.

Clearly, a concerted effort is required of both developed and transitional economies to manage the growth of motor vehicle use and encourage use of public transport systems. Through comprehensive policy packages which include effective pricing and communication measures, urban transport systems in both the OECD and Central and Eastern Europe can follow a sustainable course of development. OECD countries recognise their numerous errors in dealing with urban traffic. The countries in transition of Central and Eastern Europe should seize the opportunity now before them to avoid these same mistakes.

I. MOBILITY IN URBAN AREAS

Urban Travel in East and West:
Key Problems and a Framework for Action

Peter Güller
Synergo
Switzerland

TABLE OF CONTENTS

LIST OF FIGURES

SUMMARY

This paper aims to pursue the East/West and East/East dialogue on urban transport issues by putting forth a series of questions which so far have not been raised forcefully enough and have not found satisfactory answers in political practice.

The first question relates to the common responsibility of both parts of Europe with regard to environmental damage and the growing dangers in terms of carbon dioxide (CO_2). The hypothesis is that the West must carry most of the responsibility for restraining motorised individual transport, and that on the other side, the transitional Central and Eastern European Countries (CEEC) should carefully conceive of an appropriate "development window".

The second question is of another nature: to what degree does socio-economic development depend on the car? What would a blueprint for prosperity on the basis of public transport look like? What, in particular, would be the answer for Central and Eastern Europe, with its still elevated share of public transport?

Third question: How can settlement and land-use policy support the development of environment-friendly modes of transport? How can the benefits of fairly dense housing in CEEC be reconciled with the perceived needs of a society on the eve of hedonism?

Fourth question: How can the internalisation of external costs of traffic be implemented in countries with low income levels and high aspirations for fast-growing individual mobility?

Fifth question: How can local governments acquire more responsibility and a stronger financial resource base for developing public transport? In what way can higher levels of government (provinces, national) support an economically, socially and environmentally sound local transport policy?

Finally, how do CEE cities and countries share information and search for pertinent solutions among themselves, learn from their common experiences and undertake innovation in a difficult economic context?

This paper tries to deal with these questions by confronting the OECD/ECMT approach to urban transport problems with transport-related development mechanisms in the CEEC. It portrays East and West as a community of fate and describes each area's specific ecological responsibilities. A strategy is outlined for the promotion of public transport; related support by land-use policy; and steps for keeping the price of motorised individual transport relatively high. The question of how satisfactory benefit/cost ratios and acceptability of individual measures and policy packages is examined. A final point is made that even if certain OECD cities have found answers to some of these questions, it must be recognised that the CEE context may require modified approaches.

1. INTRODUCTION

1.1 The OECD/ECMT approach

In its recently published final report, the OECD/ECMT Joint Project Group on Urban Travel and Sustainable Development presents an integrated policy approach for addressing transport problems in urban areas. The plan is comprised of three distinct strands:

- Strand 1: Best practice;
- Strand 2: Innovations;
- Strand 3: Sustainable development.

The first strand -- **best practice** in land use and transport planning and traffic management involves more-effective and wider use of measures such as parking controls; encouragement of public transport use; and traffic calming initiatives designed to reduce urban congestion and its effects on the environment. Along with these measures must come standards and targets relating to road safety, environmental quality and social welfare. In order to increase use of best practice, members of the international community can and must learn from each other. Even with best available practice, however, only limited effects in terms of environment-friendly transport can be achieved: the growth rates of congestion and car travel will only be reduced in urban centres, while traffic-intensive social and economic activities may shift to suburban areas that are less constrained by regulations. In addition, Strand 1 alone would have an only limited effect on climate change; it must therefore be used in combination with Strands 2 and 3 to form a coherent policy.

The second strand -- **innovations** -- means that the problems stemming from high mobility cannot be solved without bold and creative policy-making and a common effort to bring about change. Land-use planning must become more effective in influencing the location of jobs, homes and shopping areas so that dependence on cars for accessibility will decrease. Balancing demand and supply for road space entails measures such as bus and tramway priority in surface traffic; speed limits; congestion pricing; higher charges on parking in city and suburban centres and telematics for advanced traffic management. With effective application of these measures, traffic growth in urban areas might cease altogether; however, without the other two Strands, overall traffic levels, noise and CO_2 emissions would continue to grow.

With its third strand -- **sustainable development** -- the policy plan declares that not only should short- and medium-term policy initiatives be undertaken, but also that appropriate paths for achieving long-term sustainable development should be selected. The Intergovernmental Panel on Climate Change[1] states that CO_2 levels must be reduced by 60 to 80 per cent if atmospheric CO_2 concentrations are to be stabilised. A steadily increasing comprehensive tax on fuels -- the key element of Strand 3 -- will encourage development of environment-friendly technologies; and influence decisions of car buyers, travel behaviour and locational decisions for business areas, recreational parks and homes. An additional benefit is that most measures cited in Strands 1 and 2 would become more effective under a regime of higher fuel prices, and the pressure of regulatory measures would gradually be reduced at the same time.

The OCED/ECMT strategy reflects the need for action in OECD countries. The workshop was organised in order to examine this policy approach in the context of Central and Eastern Europe.

1.2 The CEE context: Heritage of the past; seductive force of the new

1.2.1 Socio-economic background

At the end of the 1980s, conditions and living standards in the West and East, especially with regard to the socio-economic sphere were very different. GDP per capita in the former was about 2.5 times higher than in the latter.

While the West during this period shows a slightly undulating growth of its economy as a result of recessional phases, the development curve of the CEEC is characterised by a much more drastic J-line development[2], initiated around 1989 (Figure 1): after generally slow economic growth until 1989, there was a strong setback, which amounted to as much as 20 to 25 per cent in Poland, Czechoslovakia and Hungary, and 30 to 40 per cent in Romania and Bulgaria. The former group is considered to have overcome the decline in the mid-1990s, whereas the transition phase in the latter group has been considerably longer. Characteristics of the transition period can be summarised as follows[3]:

In Poland, the crisis had already manifested itself at the beginning of the 1980s. Initial reforms were implemented in 1982. Transition after 1989 was characterised by "shock therapy", including a rapid decontrol of prices, promotion of export-oriented growth and rapid privatisation, cutting of subsidies, and reduction of public expenditure. At the same time, borrowing abroad increased heavily.

The Czech Republic experienced a gentler revolution, accompanied by a liberalistic policy which soon led to a situation of economic stability. The economic context of the Slovak Republic has been more difficult due to less-favourable structural conditions (unprofitable industrial background).

Hungary has been involved in a continuous reform process since before 1989, originating in reform communism (blend of socialism with market economy). The country is currently heading towards capitalism, similarly to Poland, but at a much more modest pace.

Romania's economy was destructured by the previous regime. It represented an extreme form of command economy, with little external exchange. Economic decline after 1989 was very strong. Reforms have been slow -- some tendencies towards liberalisation are still contrasted by a strong influence of the state on the economy.

Bulgaria's development has taken place in two phases: first, reform communism, then liberal orientation of government. The peculiarity of this country is that it had no industrial past and therefore no capitalist tradition before its integration into the economic system of the USSR.

Emerging from the transition phase must be supported by transport policy. An efficient transport system can facilitate interregional and international integration of markets. The difficulty is to link transport policy with initiatives targeting sustainable development in terms of environmental quality.

1.2.2   The challenge of urban transport

At the end of the 1980s, a large part of the transport infrastructure in Central and Eastern Europe was in desperate condition. Transport networks were primarily based on barter relationships within the Eastern Bloc. Heavy mass goods and raw materials were dominant, the railways being the most suitable means of transport. In the agglomerations, tramway and bus traffic played the key role, largely because of the low income level of the mass public.

With the collapse of the planned economy, it immediately became clear how uncompetitive many goods produced in the East were in the Western markets. The breakdown of employment was reflected in gross domestic income as well as in the poor condition of the public budgets.

Within this context (see Figure 2), conditions for the maintenance of the transport infrastructure and the rolling stock have deteriorated further. Central governments have passed responsibility for urban transport to municipal governments. However, this transfer of responsibility has not been accompanied by reforms in the taxation sector, which would have provided the necessary means for real commitment to local transport. The national governments have largely retained responsibility for the national railway and road networks, along with the underground systems and the large traffic arteries of the urban areas.

At the same time, initial steps towards rationalisation and reorganisation of the activities of traffic companies have been taken in most cities. Through service contracts between governments and transport operators, initiatives are being taken to formulate clear concepts of desired supply and determine the conditions for achieving transport efficiency. In addition, tendering has been opened to a broader palette of potential bidders including private franchises. To improve cost recovery within the companies, financial support from foreign donor institutions is often made conditional on fares being raised.

The impact on demand for public transport has been predictable: it has declined, while at the same time, individual use of vehicles has grown. Moreover, at the time of the planned economy, individual consumption was restricted. As markets opened to the West, the demand for goods and services was met with a huge -- very tempting if also expensive -- supply. As regards automobiles, the primary source of supply for CEEC was the second-hand market; therefore, cars imported to the region were often technically and ecologically outdated. International joint ventures for car production were not immediately a success.

In goods traffic, on the other hand, as previously restrictive conditions for road transport were loosened, a multitude of smaller companies rushed to join the emerging transport market. The call for better road conditions, network extensions and thus, connections to the West has therefore increased. International sources have provided necessary investment for these initiatives.

Again, for the previously so dominant public transport sector, the result of so much competition has been a significant drop in demand.

What can be expected if the course of events is not changed? If we extrapolate from the experience of many OECD cities, an increase in motorisation will reinforce and gradually help to fulfil the wish of city residents to live outside of urban centres. Communities will thus become more dispersed and poorly served by public transport. The decentralisation of work places and shopping centres will underline this trend.

Already, the increase in individual traffic has surpassed the capacity of the urban road network. Traffic jams abound, and the burden on the environment as a consequence of this traffic has increased. As people move out of cities, the drop in public transport use will exacerbate growth in deficits. External costs of traffic will rise on all fronts. On a local environment level, vehicle emissions such as Nitrogen Oxides (NO_x), particulate matter and lead must be reduced.

2. EAST AND WEST: A COMMUNITY OF FATE, A COMMON WELFARE

2.1 Applying the OECD/ECMT approach

When examining the OECD/ECMT recommendations in the context of Central and Eastern Europe, three questions arise:

2.1.1 Transferability of experience and know-how

To what extent are transport policy instruments, which have proved to be successful in one urban area, transferable to another, given that the latter has a different historical, cultural or political background, or is in another phase of economic development? Are there "best practices" which are convertible like currencies? If not, how and to what extent must one take account of specific circumstances?

2.1.2 Solidarity in the use of natural resources

What is the significance of solidarity among countries and regions with regard to the drain on world-wide available resources? Is there general agreement that every society has the right to its fair share of a universal heritage such as fossil energy reserves? And to what extent will developing or transitional economies need increasing amounts of resources? Would that imply a special allowance for related environmental pollution?

2.1.3 *Appropriate individual approaches*

Can we agree among ourselves that for all countries of the world, there is one common objective, that of sustainable development, and that differences can only exist with regard to the approach, the intensity and the time-schedule of actions? Can we also agree that sustainability in CEEC involves first of all social and political stability, and that for this purpose, the overcoming of the economic crisis must be a high priority for years to come? How then can the tensions that exist between the notions of sustainability and development and between environmental concern and the wish to build up efficient road networks be overcome?

These are challenging questions, and this workshop will most likely not provide answers to them all. They do, however, provide a framework for discussing common responsibilities of the West and the East -- conclusions to be drawn from the former, and specific approaches to and best practices of transport policies in the latter. Moreover, it will be interesting to see how Central and Eastern European cities and countries share information and search for solutions among themselves, learn from their common experience and undertake innovation in a difficult economic context.

2.2 Considering CO_2: Two models

The environmental impact of transport differs between the West and the East. At present, most of the world's car fleet, and most of the local and global environmental problems created by cars in cities, are found in OECD countries, where urbanisation has been resource-hungry. It may be a mere matter of time before CEE cities will be so too.

If it is assumed that total CO_2 emissions from traffic in the two parts of Europe should be reduced by half within the next 20 years (see the above cited IPPC statement of 1990; current policies are less demanding), two models for achieving this goal can be identified:

2.2.1   Proportional or "everyone-the-same" policy

The halving of the CO_2 emissions must be undertaken by all countries, irrespective of their levels of economic development.

2.2.2   Rapprochement or convergence policy

The well-developed economies of the OECD, which, when it comes to traffic also belong to the worst polluters per head, must reduce their emissions more than the transitional CEE states. At the same time, these states may claim a "development window" or "allowance" for further increase of fuel consumption during economic transition.

Convergence policy would offer the better basis for a co-operative dialogue between East and West.

2.2.3   Other elements of these models

Energy efficiency in the economy and in transport relates both to the vehicle production process and the fuel consumption of vehicles. It is widely observed that in CEEC, particularly great efforts in energy efficiency must be made. Pertinent potentials for energy efficiency in the West are smaller, as technology is more advanced. However, fuel consumption per 100 vehicle kilometres could in technical terms easily be brought down to 2 or 3 litres. Once this technical potential is reached, increases in price of fuel (as a result of a strong CO_2 policy) will no longer affect mobility. Yet certain sacrifices with regard to mobility are imperative in the West.

CEE governments, on the other hand, may want to find a transition path that includes further development of individual vehicle mobility, as pertinent requirements of the economy and society are still very high there. Moreover, CEE governments cannot be expected to ask for substantial sacrifices from their citizens, while the West, with its already high levels of mobility and fossil fuel consumption, has had difficulty making sacrifices on this level, as well.

3. PATHWAYS TO SUSTAINABLE URBAN TRANSPORT IN CEEC

It is necessary to keep in mind that both the East and the West share the common goal of a positive contribution of urban travel to sustainable development. At the same time, their socio-economic and political starting positions in this endeavour are different: in Western societies basic needs are satisfied, in CEE societies this is not the case. What then should be their respective paths to the future?

As concerns the West, the OECD/ECMT approach lays out the necessary steps. For CEEC, however, the steps to are less-clearly defined. In general terms, two paths toward sustainable urban transport development in the CEE region can be identified: first, a "short cut" to sustainable development, or second, a "detour" via the Western path.

3.1 The short-cut

The point of departure for CEEC is a high share of public transport in overall transport use. Factors behind this are a dense urban settlement pattern and a relatively low income level of the public-at-large. Of these two factors, the first should be preserved for the future. At the same time, the socio-economic context of this transport structure should evolve: more prosperity is needed, but environment-friendly forms of transport must be retained. One could label this development path a **short-cut**. The idea is that as an individual's prosperity increases, so does his or her sensitivity to the environmental problems of transport; this sensitivity is then incorporated into his or her behaviour relative to transport use.

Another aspect of the short-cut is the question of how the economies of the CEEC can be developed on the basis of a strongly improved public transport system. Herein lies the requirement for **innovation** in this region, Strand 2 of the OECD/ECMT approach: a blueprint for economic development based on public transport is needed.

Western transport policy aims to restore public and economic confidence in *S-Bahn*-type regional transport: with suitable accompanying financial instruments and incentives, *S-Bahn* systems can support land-use policies and could become the backbone of future settlements. Thus, the short-cut policy of CEE cities would have the same objectives as those in the West, but the starting position (dense settlement pattern) is more favourable in CEEC.

The bottleneck of this issue is the problem of financial backing for public transport development. The magnitude of the problem is illustrated by the example of roads: The World Bank estimates that in CEEC, at current level of expenditure, more than ten years would be needed just to cover the existing road maintenance and rehabilitation backlogs, without undertaking any significant upgrading or new construction programme[4].

3.2 The detour via the western way

The alternative path, namely the **detour via western development**, means that actual physical and economic limits for vehicle and goods traffic on roads will gradually disappear. Individual needs and the desire to open markets are satisfied, while external costs of vehicle traffic are not taken into account. At the same time, public transport is treated as a poor relation and declines. This has so far been the dominant path of transitional economies.

Regarding external costs, Zurich offers an alarming example: a relatively small agglomeration with 1 million inhabitants, Zurich's external costs of transport (environmental costs, time losses due to traffic jams, and transport infrastructure and operation deficits) amount to SF 1.5 billion or ECU 1 billion per annum. In order just to cover the external costs of private automobile traffic, the price of petrol in Switzerland would have to be more than tripled. And Swiss research has shown that these external costs grow disproportionally with increasing agglomeration size. One can imagine the results for the large urban areas of Central and Eastern Europe with more than 2 or 3 million inhabitants!

The Western path is thus one along which for many years the fruits of growth have been eaten without being paid for. Public transport deficits have grown to the extent that the situation now has to be topped with heavy investment and subsidies. An example of this is the relatively rich canton of Berne, Switzerland, which is facing difficulties maintaining its very extended road network: instead of over ECU 100 million needed for renewal per year, the canton has only ECU 30 million available. This is a price to pay for dispersal of settlements.

There are certainly a number of other possible development paths between the "short cut" and the "detour". CEEC may be limited in the development paths open to them, however, because of limited financial capacities. Aid from the international banking system is provided to accelerate development processes. At the same time, certain forms of development may be preferred over others within these institutions. And on the recipient side, powerful interest groups may significantly influence the development path taken; for example, by not considering the external costs of their activities, a "detour" via the Western path may result.

4. ELEMENTS OF A SUSTAINABLE TRANSPORT POLICY IN CEEC

Three crucial elements characterise the attempts to come closer to what mobility policy aims at in the East and the West:

- promotion of public transport;
- land-use policy;
- fuel pricing policy.

4.1 Promotion of public transport

In statistical terms, the share of public transport in total transport in CEEC is high -- though actually declining. It will be very important to maintain the share of public transport at a high-enough percentage to offset growth in vehicle use, especially if further development of individual transport should (and must) take place. Rehabilitation, upgrading and in certain cases, restructuring of public transport are of foremost importance. Urban development policy will define the need for gradual extension of the networks.

Apart from being beneficial in terms of environmental quality, public transport in CEEC should be the dominating factor in structuring the future development of settlements. As compared to the West, with its already dispersed settlement structure, this is an extraordinary opportunity. Many OECD cities are facing great difficulty in influencing their dispersed urban development pattern with public transport improvements.

4.2 Land-use policy

Dispersion of settlements and the quest for personal comfort and expansion of activity have been driving forces of mobility growth in the West. A substantial reduction of the demand for transport without taking the influence of the settlement pattern into account is hard to imagine. Thus, the West will have to make great efforts to arrive at more "internal community developments" and a better functional mix of work places, homes, shopping and recreational areas.

In CEE cities, however, extremely dense forms of settlement are the norm. As the society develops further, this settlement structure may prove inadequate.

The wish for attractive -- and this means less dense -- housing must certainly be accepted.

Yet on the basis of environmental grounds, decentralisation should not go as far as it has in OECD urban regions. On this level, as well, a convergency policy is necessary. Both societies -- Western and Eastern -- must find the way to quality living and working under medium-density conditions.

4.3 Fuel pricing

The price of gasoline in CEEC is low compared to OECD countries; however, relative to the personal income levels it is high[5]. If one assumes that for environmental reasons, this relationship should remain as it is today in CEEC, there should be parallel increases in the price of petrol as personal income levels grow.

In OECD countries, there has not been this parallel movement over the last decades. A look at the United Kingdom reveals that working-time to purchase one litre of petrol has decreased from 8 minutes to 5 minutes in the last 20 years. In the same period in Switzerland, the price of petrol remained almost the same, whereas average consumer prices rose by 75 per cent. Cheap mobility has produced excessive mobility. The external costs of transport have not yet been taken into account. It is for this reason that the West, with its large responsibility for world-wide CO_2 emissions, must accept a significantly higher increase in the price of its mobility than in the rise of personal income levels.

The increase in fuel price in OECD countries must thus, for years to come, be higher than in the CEEC. Only later, when the West is able to reduce its CO_2 emissions substantially, a convergence of the prices between West and East may be envisaged on common policy grounds.

4.4 Summary of issues

A brief summary of the questions that emerge from what has been said follows:

First, how large must the postulated "mobility development window" be for CEEC in order to support development objectives and respond to the demands of the population while avoiding that level of mobility which, in

OECD experience, has proven to be harmful to the environment? What consequences for transport policy will arise from this?

Second, how should it be understood that Western advisers and international banks make policy recommendations to CEEC -- one thinks of road or fuel pricing -- which go significantly further than those which OECD countries themselves attempt or are able to accomplish?

5. ACTION TO BE TAKEN: STRENGTHS DEVELOPED; WEAKNESSES ELIMINATED

In order to avoid the detour via the Western way and to preserve positive values in transport systems of CEE cities, a package of three main action lines is recommended:

-- rehabilitation and upgrading of the public transport system;
-- efficient housing and land development policy aimed at attractive and moderately dense settlements;
-- retention of the current relationship between fuel prices and average income growth.

A basic condition for the success of these initiatives is that municipal governments are not only provided with more responsibilities, but also with the financial resources necessary to carry out these responsibilities. They should be allowed to raise their own taxes; to receive adequate financial support for urban tasks from upper levels of government; and to contract directly for loans from the banking system.

5.1 Rehabilitation and upgrading of the public transport system

Long-distance transport of goods, which relate to increased international trade but also serves internal exchange, should a priori use rail. This would be in accordance with the efforts of the West to promote at least combined transport modes, with the rail as backbone. Long-distance transport of persons ought to be based on public transport as well, with rail and air traffic complementing each other: airports should be directly linked to intercity and downtown rail connections. Railway stations in towns and in suburbs may ideally become preferred areas for urban development.

Attractive regional public transport can fully profit from the condensed settlement pattern. Rail connections ought to serve both radial travel to and from town centres as well as tangential movements in the future suburban belt, i.e. around the cities. The role of local government in urban mass transport should be shifted from ownership to service contracting with public or private enterprises. Transport fare and subsidy policies have to take better account of profitability and the social function of public transport (splitting).

Financial aid from the international banking system or other external donors should be linked to the promotion of public transport, with urban road traffic remaining a secondary priority (except investments designed to increase personal security and speed of public transport).

Walking and cycling may be encouraged by a sufficient mix of urban activity and attractive and secure networks, including better access to public transport.

5.2 Efficient housing and land development policy aimed at attractive and moderately dense settlements

Development of working areas (from clean factories to business and research centres) should be geographically concentrated, so that public transport services are easy to install and cost-effective. The spreading out of housing and jobs should be discouraged in order to avoid investment in excessive infrastructural equipment.

5.3 Retention of the current relationship between fuel prices and average income growth

Car traffic in towns should be restrained so as to preserve quality of life and tourism opportunities. High accessibility to city centres of public transport and development of pedestrian zones is a key element of this "keep-business-in-town" policy. The provision of parking facilities downtown, both on public and private ground, should be handled with reserve. Parking charges both in city and suburban centres should complement this approach.

The internalisation of environmental costs of transport, from local to national levels, will reinforce the emphasis given to public transport.

6. SPECIFIC INITIATIVES AND MEASURES: A PLEA FOR POLICY PACKAGES

The three main action lines just described comprise a broad approach to coping with transport problems in urban areas. A more comprehensive view of initiatives to achieve sustainable urban development is as follows (see Figure 3):

6.1 Specific initiatives targeted

-- raising sensitivity to environmental and social effects of high mobility;
-- developing technical solutions to cope with air pollution, noise, accidents;
-- promoting environment-friendly means of transport: public transport, slow transport (pedestrian, bicycles);
-- land-use planning considering a decrease in travel demand;
-- calming of individual motorised traffic;
-- new modes of living in view of less dependence on mobility.

6.2 Policy measures available

-- information;
-- institutional and financial solutions;
-- infrastructure and operations;
-- incentives (positive and negative);
-- interdictions.

The matrix in Figure 3 is composed in such a way that gentler (promotive) measures are located in the top left corner, and hard (prohibitive) measures are located at bottom right. The Swiss sometimes associate the position of political parties to such a grid: Conservatives favour education as a means to cope with transport problems; Liberals favour technological inputs; and Socialists and Environmentalists feel there is virtually no other way than intervention and the internalisation of external costs.

6.3 Benefit/cost ratios of individual measures

It is important to understand the contribution which can be made by single measures, as compared to whole packages: a test to rank single measures with regard to their benefit/cost ratio was done for Zurich, as part of the Swiss National Research Programme "Urban Areas and Transport". This research has provided indicators for the economic and ecological benefits (effectiveness) and costs of each policy module. Figure 4 shows their ratios[6]. A substantial increase in fuel taxes generates the best benefit-to-cost ratio. Speed limit reduction, zonal traffic speed management in urban areas and considerable parking fees promise good benefit-to-cost-ratios as well. City access cards (*vignettes*) are next in ranking.

The common characteristic of all these measures is that their benefits, in terms of environmental quality, can be substantial. At the same time, their implementation is not costly. Moreover, a possible loss with regard to the consumer rent may not outweigh the benefits, especially as, for those people remaining in road traffic, there is less congestion. This may prove even more true if attractive alternative modes for travelling exist.

It may, at a first look, be somewhat discouraging that the promotion of public transport alone has a poor benefit/cost ratio, and that even in urban areas, policies for subsidising or for expanding capacity of public transportation appear less promising than policies which aim at optimising the use of existing system capacity first. The reason is that promotion of public transport without accompanying measures aiming at car restraint may bring about little change in traffic structure at high cost. A similar argument applies to the construction of road bypasses: if they are not accompanied by traffic calming measures within the zone around which they are built, the benefit/cost ratio is uninteresting.

Not surprisingly, however, the acceptability among politicians and drivers of these measures is another matter. The ranking can be reverse; for example: people may prefer to pay taxes for public transport development instead of paying more for petrol. And the problem with regard to the assessment of the benefits is that a clean environment is not seen as high priority by many. Another matter is that benefit/cost ratios for different measures can differ from one context to another; the result may not be the same for all cities.

6.4 The plea for packages

Practice of transport policy shows, however, that while all the policy instruments listed in Figure 4 can potentially be helpful, not one of them alone has the power to achieve the objectives of sustainable development: governments need to introduce packages of policies that are mutually reinforcing. In other words, governments would do well to find a co-operative approach where each party and interest group can contribute according to its conviction.

According to the International Union of Public Transport, there are two public transport strategies (subsidised or commercialised) and two vehicle traffic strategies (free or restrained flow) which must be combined. This results in four policy combinations, all of which have their advantages and disadvantages.

Combination 1: **Subsidised public transport and free car traffic**

Very negative budgetary consequences and continuing environmental impacts, yet few problems with political acceptance and no special social constraints.

Combination 2: **Commercialised public transport and free car traffic**

Very high external costs (congestion and environmental impacts), and politically divergent due to the social constraints involved.

Combination 3: **Subsidised public transport and car traffic restraint**

Interesting budgetary outlook due to the increase in demand of public transport and thus high coverage of respective costs. Some negative reactions from car owners. Strongly reduced environmental impacts.

Combination 4: **Commercialised public transport combined with car restraint**

Positive budgetary consequences and reduced environmental impacts, yet politically divergent as regards the poorer sector of the population due to increased transport fares.

It is difficult to compare the benefits and costs of such combinations on a concrete numerical base. An effort has been made in Zurich to this effect: for an investment of less than ECU 160 million or for about ECU 6.5 million of annual costs for depreciation, interest and operations, the whole tram and bus network of the Zurich Transport Company has been brought up to a high standard of speed, frequency and reliability. Comparison with other European cities of the same size shows that promotion of public transport on surface by giving it priority of space and green phase at traffic lights is almost by itself linked with some car restraint. In terms of the above discussed IUPT categories, the Zurich case is located somewhere between Combinations 1 and 3. Modal split in Zurich has achieved very positive values; the benefit/cost ratio is remarkable.

One factor behind the choices made in Zurich may be that Swiss cities have less access to "free" resources from national government for public transport investment than cities in their neighbouring countries. And as projects for subway systems have been rejected by popular vote in Zurich, the city has had to make the best of the situation.

This does not deny that subway systems can play an essential role in larger cities. However this raises a key point: the Zurich example shows in much broader terms that a certain autonomy on the local level, both in decision making and in financial resources, can play a key role in finding appropriate paths for transport policy development. At the same time, the local level should be supported by both regional and national levels in incorporating economic, social and environmental responsibilities in their transport policy.

7. CONCLUSION

This paper was designed to be used as a background presentation of issues to be discussed at the workshop. Seven principal areas have been raised for discussion. They are:

1. a convergence policy between CEEC and the West;
2. "short cut": a blueprint for socio-economic development based on public transport, from national to local level;
3. the key role of settlement policy;
4. maintaining fuel prices at least parallel to personal income development;
5. restrictive parking policy in urban and suburban areas;
6. benefit/cost ratios of single versus package approaches;
7. municipal-level revenue base with support from higher levels of government.

NOTES

1.   IPCC (1990), Climate Change, the IPCC Scientific Assessment, Intergovernmental Panel on Climate Change. Cambridge University Press, New York.

2.   HILFERINK, P., Recent Economic Developments and Forecasts in Central and Eastern Europe. In: *Comment définir des priorités en transport.* INRETS-DEST, Paris 1994.

3.   CHATELUS, G., In: *Comment définir des priorités en transport.* INRETS-DEST, Paris 1994.

4.   GASPARD, M., 1994.   Financing needs and means for transport infrastructure in Central and Eastern Europe.

5.   THE WORLD BANK. Poland Urban Transport Review, 1994.
      A litre of 98-octane gasoline cost Zl 9 000 in March 1993. In nominal terms this is equivalent to USD 0.53, approximately twice the US price but half of the French price, the latter typical of European Union countries. When multiplied by two to reflect the purchasing power of the zloty relative to the exchange rate, the price just exceeds the West European price. Indeed, this is quite expensive when measured against average wages in Poland: driving Polski Fiat 8 000 km per annum would take 11 per cent of each month's wage for fuel alone. In France the comparable figure is 2 - 4 per cent only.

6.   MAUCH, S. *et al.* 1992, Costs and Benefits of Internalisation Strategies: Case Study Zurich. In: Frey R.L. and Langloh, P. M. ed., The use of Economic Instruments in Urban Travel Management, p. 131, OECD workshop Basle.
      Under benefits are summarised: Reduced environmental impacts. Less uncovered capital, maintenance and operational costs. Gains in time and security.
      Under "costs" are summarised: Losses in travel time (reduction of consumer rent; excess burden). Costs of implementation (administration, control). Uncovered capital, maintenance and operational costs. Externalised environmental costs.

FIGURES

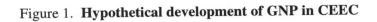

Figure 1. **Hypothetical development of GNP in CEEC**

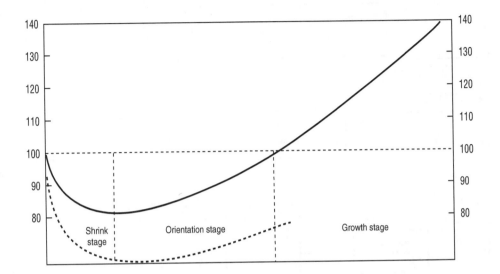

Source: Hilferink, P., Recent Economic Developments and Forecasts in Central and Eastern Europe. In: *Comment définir des priorités en transport*, INRETS-DEST, Paris 1994. Slightly adapted.

Figure 2. **Socio-economic and transport development in CEEC**

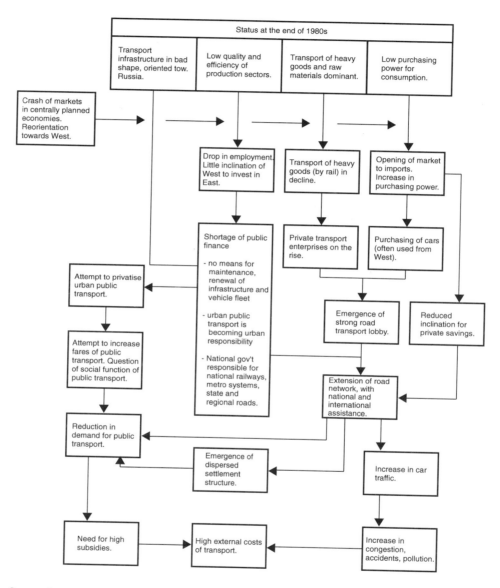

Source: Synergo.

Figure 3. Action lines and instruments in urban transport policy

Instruments \ Action lines	Raise environmental sensitivity.	Improve environmental technology.	Promote environmental transportation means.	Land-use planning.	Restrain individual motorized transport.	Adopt new modes of life.
Information, education.	Monitoring and information activities; media campaigns.	Technology fairs; technology education; clean vehicles in public service.	Infosystems and marketing of public transport slow motion campaigns.	Planning courses and guidelines; local participation.	Appeals, demonstration projects for environment-friendly mobility.	Basic education in new environmental ethics.
Institutional and financial arrangements.	Mobility consultancy; budgets for PR actions.	Research programmes; financial support for R&D.	Regional transport association; deregulation of subsidies.	Combined land use and transport planning; regional boards.	Consideration of external costs in road traffic accounts.	Local level involvement; more public/private partnership.
Infrastructure and services	Documentation centres; teaching materials.	Technological innovation centers.	Own right of way for public transport; pedestrian and cycle paths.	Attractive neighbourhoods; restrictive land development.	Traffic management; better urban integration of roads.	Decentralisation of infrastructure in support of smaller social nets.
Positive/negative (financial) incentives.	Rewards for ecologically sound behaviour; eco-labelling.	Pricing to influence vehicle design; eco-audits.	Attractive fare and tariff arrangements; eco-tickets.	Densification permits in areas well served by public transport.	Fuel price, variable motor vehicle tax, parking fees, road-pricing.	Ecological tax reform.
Regulation: commands, prohibition.	Environmental labelling codes, rules and legislation.	Emission and technological standards.	Priority to public transport on roads; car free zones.	Zoning for mixed land-use; urban containment.	Speed limits; parking standards, "Green" parking areas.	Pollution limits which guarantee sustainability.

Source: Synergo.

49

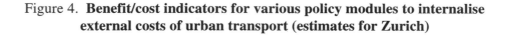

Figure 4. Benefit/cost indicators for various policy modules to internalise external costs of urban transport (estimates for Zurich)

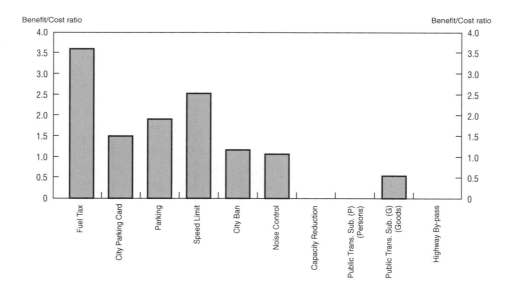

Source: Mauch, S. *et al.* 1992, Costs and Benefits of Internalization Strategies: Case Study Zurich. In: Frey R.L. and Langloh, P.M. ed., The use of economic instruments in urban travel management, OECD/ECMT Workshop Basle.

II. MANAGING TRAFFIC GROWTH

Parking Management and Pedestrianisation as Strategies for Successful City Centres

Rolf Monheim
University of Bayreuth
Germany

TABLE OF CONTENTS

LIST OF TABLES

LIST OF FIGURES

SUMMARY

This paper examines parking management as a vital tool for achieving and sustaining access to city centres, and pedestrian zones and "car-free" city centres as traffic management instruments within city centres. Both issues are discussed within a broader context that includes the role a society attributes to the centres of their cities and the lifestyles expressed by the city centres. The paper is based on a European understanding of city centres as focal points of activity for cities, regions and countries. It also evokes the necessity of defending the city centre from mounting car traffic problems.

Parking management as part of integrated strategies

City centres in European culture are considered to be the heart and the "living room" of their entire urban regions. For decades, western societies have tried to adapt their cities to the demand of car traffic, which was believed to represent economic progress and social freedom. Any questioning of this orientation was perceived to be ideologically backwards. The leading role of city centres can only be defended if car traffic is adapted to the limits of the urban environment. This requires combining policies for use of "green modes" of transport (public transport, cycling, walking) with traffic management tools designed to facilitate necessary car-use by reducing undesirable car-use. Further, traffic generation must be avoided through co-ordinated urban and regional planning.

Parking management has a key role in steering traffic development. The parking demand realised within a given volume of parking capacity primarily depends on how it is managed, with the number of cars parked per site and day ranging from about one car to 15 cars on legal and 25 cars on illegal sites. The legal conditions for a more effective parking management are only recently being developed. Parking management cannot be effective if it is not enforced. Yet, in most cities there is a high proportion of illegal parking. This is partly due to a widespread social acceptance of illegal parking (especially not paying fees).

City centres can defend their leading role only if they are easily accessible by all modes of transport. Their prosperity, however, depends most importantly on their ability to adapt themselves to the changing lifestyles of society.

Pedestrian zones and "car-free" city centres

Pedestrianisation, even more than parking management, has been influenced by changes in planning goals due to the development of post-industrial economies and societies. The success of pedestrian districts in European cities is illustrated by their rapid increase in numbers (more than 1 000 in Germany alone) and by their expansion in the more developed cases to networks of 3- to 8 km of pedestrian streets that often encompass more or less the entire city centre. This success is due to a feed-back process involving strategies designed to improve accessibility, the quality of public open spaces, the supply of retail as well as cultural and social activities and the development of new lifestyles. Several examples show how large pedestrian precincts developed despite numerous political controversies over a period of decades.

"Car-free" city centres do not really exist, with the exception of Venice and of some tourist resorts like Zermatt (Switzerland). The term describes city centres where access by car is limited to designated groups holding special permits: primarily residents, service vehicles, goods delivery and public transport (including taxis); permits are also sometimes issued for business activities. The main problem with this approach concerns the high demand for special permits and low compliance with access limitations. Strong enforcement measures are therefore necessary.

The process of adapting the city centres to new requirements for building and transportation structures is evolving in former socialist countries at a break-neck pace. Often this development is not controlled by established checks-and-balance systems, which have been instrumental in helping countries with a long tradition of democracy and citizen initiative (notably in Switzerland) to avoid mistakes.

Clear planning goals are of utmost importance. Their realisation requires a framework for national legislation and financing systems on national, regional and local levels. Developing liveable and attractive city centres requires the integration of vision with practical knowledge of how to get there and the patience to follow a long and often arduous path. There are many examples showing that such efforts are worthwhile in the long run.

1. INTRODUCTION

This paper[1] examines the results of parking management, pedestrian zones and "car-free" city centres as measures for sustainable traffic development implemented by municipalities in European OECD countries. It does not and cannot provide recipes, but attempts to explain the problems associated with these measures and strategies for their solution. There are no examples of ideal planning; some cities, however, are moving closer to achieving sustainable traffic development and, simultaneously, economic success than others. The current experiences of OECD Europe are discussed in the hope that others might learn from their successes and mistakes.[2] A few final comments on the situation in Bucharest may illustrate some of the problems encountered in attempting to apply these strategies and outcomes to a Central and Eastern European (CEE) context.

Every city centre is unique. In Europe, city centres are the focus of the entire city and its surrounding area. Often a region or even an entire country are represented by the centres of their leading cities. The prominent role of the city centre is determined by its accessibility from all parts of the city and its environs, as well as from other regions. This accessibility has facilitated the development of a wide range of functions that characterise the city centre, resulting in considerable economic opportunity. Along with this economic growth, however, has come strong development pressure and frequent traffic congestion.

The centre of a city not only has the highest concentration of activity, traffic and land values, but also is the focus of a city's historical and modern distinctiveness. Therefore, the needs of the city centre must be understood in terms of its cultural and social dimensions, as well as its economic and technological aspects. This makes planning for city centres an important task, where the right balance between the preservation of historically inherited features and the adaptation to new requirements must be achieved.

Traffic planning can play a key role in this process. For many years, traffic planning has been driven by the unquestioned needs of ever-expanding car traffic. This model was especially propagated in the United States: car traffic had to flow smoothly! Improvements for other means of transport were accepted only if they did not detract from car accessibility. Investments in public transport even improved the flow of cars, most notably when subways were built. Yet, it has become clear that over-dependency on car access has created manifold problems, which threaten the leading role of city centres. Furthermore, the limited availability of public finances has necessitated a focus on more cost-efficient strategies, instead of continuing the trend of dissipation caused by lack of decision-making.

In former socialist countries, exploding car traffic has put city centres under immense pressure within a very short time leading to catastrophic consequences. Dams against flooding by cars have broken down, even in those cities which had defended their vulnerable core-areas under socialism by controlling car-access and parking, as in the case of Prague. The tremendous expansion of car traffic is largely due to the belief that unrestricted car use represents new freedom and progress. It is also based on pressures of influential interest groups which tend to dominate the economy and society. There seems to be no institution which dares or is able to enforce limitations necessary to ensure sustainable development of the city centre and to prevent repetition of the mistakes that were made in earlier-motorised societies.

A new strategy for sustainable traffic development aims to maintain accessibility to the city centre from outside areas as well as the internal circulation of all transport modes, while ensuring that car traffic does not inhibit the effectiveness of other functions of the city. Parking management and pedestrianisation are two key elements of such a strategy. Yet, they are only effective if pursued and developed simultaneously within a broad framework that includes the overall transportation and land-use systems and, most importantly, the policy-making context. Therefore, planning for the city centre must be based on the co-ordination of engineering, economic enterprise and political leadership.

Transportation planning for city centres should distinguish two perspectives: "how to get to the city centre?" (Chapter 2) and "how to move within the city centre?" (Chapter 3). The first question should be addressed within a broader discussion of the relative importance of accessibility in comparison to other factors determining the prosperity of a city centre. Generally, the importance of accessibility, and especially the role of cars, is highly overestimated. Often it seems that complaints about poor car access to city centres are used to avoid discussing aspects of much greater importance: including, skyrocketing shop rents; speculation on the part of building owners;

ambiguous property situations, slow urban renewal, lack of enterprise among local retailers and aggressive agendas of national and multinational chain stores.

Accessibility by car cannot be understood from overall numbers. Rather accessibility for whom, when and under which conditions must be considered. Problems of accessibility are primarily caused by excessively high concentrations of traffic for certain purposes at certain times and in certain areas. Management and marketing ("public awareness") have shown potential as useful tools for improving this situation. Although these are relatively inexpensive methods, they are difficult to implement, due to the narrow agendas of certain interest groups which fear losing their advantageous positions.

The contribution of parking management to the accessibility of the city centre must be understood and developed within the broader framework of overall traffic demand. Certain problems of parking are only solvable through strategies that promote alternatives to the ownership and use of cars. The integrated "pull-and-push approach" (which also more illustratively can be called the "carrot-and-stick-approach") combines encouraging use of "green modes" of transport (walking, cycling, public transport) with discouraging car use.

A strategy that questions parking demand -- instead of simply fulfilling it -- requires more detailed information on demand structure than is normally used in traffic planning studies. The planning and management of parking supply also requires more precise information than under normal circumstances. The effectiveness of parking supply depends on how it is organised and used. This has to be taken into account especially if finances are restricted, as in the case of former socialist countries.

Supply and demand must be balanced according to general planning goals. There is a wide range of strategies and measures which must be implemented in an integrated approach. Isolated measures bear a great risk of failing.

Pedestrianisation has deeply changed the character of many city centres. Initially developed as a relatively isolated measure designed to solve traffic problems in narrow main shopping streets, pedestrianisation has since become a focal point of complex strategies for ensuring the prosperity of city centres. It has helped to defend central city zones against the negative effects of increasing car ownership and car use, and growth of suburban population, employment and retail. Pedestrianisation has also enabled city centres to take advantage of economic opportunities brought about by the increasing spending power of a large portion of the population and the decreasing size of families. Indeed, a large number of one- to two- person households in post-industrial societies exhibit a lifestyle characterised by strong market orientation, increasing leisure time and a preference for urban life.

The development of complex pedestrian zones will be discussed in a synthesised approach using pertinent examples. These examples are not unique. Special attention has been given to illustrating the gradual process of pedestrianisation, because it is impossible to simply copy the results. This process has to be understood as the outcome of many feed-back interactions, in which the "urban-system" has learned to adapt itself to changing conditions.

So-called "car-free" city centres do not exist. The term is used to characterise city centres that have an areawide limitation of access for designated groups during predetermined time periods. This approach is usually combined with pedestrianisation of the most valuable areas of the centre. It was first introduced and is most widespread in Italy, with Bologna and Florence as the most well-known examples. Due to the mixed structure of Italian city centres and the special character of Italian drivers, car traffic volumes within these areas were only effectively reduced in the short run, and have again reached levels that are incompatible with the character and needs of these historical centres. In Germany, Lubeck seems to have successfully implemented areawide access limitations, whereas Aachen, after a five-year attempt at implementing a "car-free" centre, has decided to use classical pedestrianisation and parking management for achieving areawide reductions of car traffic.

In summary, transportation planning and management for city centres have made some progress within OECD Europe over the last 20 years. Most cities are far from achieving their own goals, however. The process leading to sustainable traffic development still needs much support against the long-lasting opposition of car-oriented groups. These groups seem to be even stronger in former socialist countries, where criticism against car use is often rejected as ideology. It must be understood that transportation planning, as any kind of planning, is not a neutral engineering task. This is underlined by official German guidelines, which state that traffic planning must not follow the direction of "natural" traffic development; instead, society and politics must determine to what extent traffic should be developed (see: Forschungsgesellschaft, 1985).

An increase in car traffic is not necessarily a fixed destiny; on the contrary, it is both possible and necessary to "save" traffic in ways similar to those of energy-saving and waste-avoidance that do not endanger but instead reinforce economic welfare (Table 1). Europe is now learning that it can no longer afford continuous growth in traffic demand, nor that of energy consumption and waste production.

Table 1. **Objectives for a more environmentally compatible development**

Objectives	Energy	Waste	Traffic
1. reduction	less energy consumption	less waste production	less traffic generation
2. priority for environmentally compatible substances	fewer pollutant/ hazardous energy sources	fewer pollutant/ hazardous materials for goods, more recyclable materials	greater share of - walking - cycling - public transport (green modes)
3. safer use of unavoidable hazardous matter	make pollutant/ hazardous energy sources cleaner/ safer	clean up waste incineration and make waste disposal safer	make unavoidable car traffic safer, less noisy, less pollutant

There are several examples showing that the trend towards more car-dependency can be reversed. The initiatives for this reorientation towards sustainable development are being taken primarily in the wealthy sun-belt of central European OECD countries, e.g. Zurich or Basel in Switzerland, Graz or Salzburg in Austria, Strasbourg in France, and Freiburg, Karlsruhe or Munich in Germany. The reason is that citizens and decision-makers in these cities have understood the importance of quality of life for economic welfare and have a high ability to adapt themselves to new needs. Former socialist countries should use these regions as examples, instead of copying outdated models based on wasting limited resources. Socially, politically and environmentally responsible urban planning must dictate the future progression of traffic, rather than urban planning being determined by traffic expansion and increasing car dependency.[3]

2. PARKING MANAGEMENT TO IMPROVE ACCESS TO CITY CENTRES

The accessibility of city centres is an important, though insufficient condition for their prosperity. Accessibility can only be assured through strategies based on a rational balance between traffic demand and the supply of traffic infrastructure. In order to achieve this balance, planners and decision-makers must have a solid understanding of how road and parking infrastructure is intrinsically related to the overall patterns of traffic supply and demand. Traffic planning cannot be limited to the provision of infrastructure. Rather, planners must take into consideration how infrastructure is perceived and used and how it is interrelated with traffic behaviour.

2.1 Analysis of traffic demand

Traffic demand is generated by individuals carrying out activities within an urban area. Problems arise when demand exceeds the capacity of the urban system and hinders its effective functioning. This must be avoided by planning. The classical approach consists of adapting the system to the demand; the new approach for sustainable development aims to adapt the demand to the capacity of the urban system. The structure of parking demand is analysed in this section in relative detail because planning discussions tend to overlook the criteria determining for whom parking is to be provided and the potential associated with distributing limited capacities according to superior planning goals. A detailed knowledge of demand enables planners and politicians to develop strategies that maintain the flow of necessary car traffic and limit unnecessary car traffic.

2.1.1 Mode of transport used

Traffic in city centres depends to a large extent on the transport modes used to access the area. Traffic patterns are influenced by various factors, including: purpose and time of trip; size, economic structure, kinds of transportation infrastructure; local policy and lifestyle of a city. Discussions on the importance of cars to the accessibility of city centres are dominated by biased perceptions of the problems involved, especially among retailers who consider it essential that their customers be able to access the centre easily by car. They usually overestimate the share of car-users and underestimate the importance of alternatives to the car for the success of retail.

Inappropriate planning decisions can only be avoided if planners start with valid information on the share of car use relative to all modes of transportation. A statistical comparison of cities shows the various models that have developed in Central European OECD countries, where car use is much higher than in most formerly socialist countries. Therefore, discussion of the following statistics is mainly focused on structural aspects (e.g. mode and purpose of transport) and the results of political decisions on the development of urban traffic.

The Deutsches Institut für Urbanistik (DIFU), a body which conducts research on German cities, has frequently discussed the possibility of influencing car-traffic volumes through parking management. A survey published in 1990 shows that public transport clearly dominates trips to the city centre in cities with more than half a million week-day population (50 to 74 per cent of all trips and 43 to 76 per cent of trips for shopping and personal business). In medium-sized cities, the share of cars reaches the same or even higher levels (32 to 40 per cent of all trips and 32 to 49 per cent of shopping trips. (See Figure 2; and Apel and Lehmbrock, 1990).

Within this general framework, there are, however, some differences which result from urban structure and traffic policy. Munich, for example, has a stronger orientation towards public transport than Hamburg (especially for shopping), notwithstanding its smaller size; the same is true for Nuremberg as compared to Dortmund. The large cities in the other European countries have relatively higher shares of public transport and smaller shares of car-users. It is especially remarkable that in Amsterdam, a Dutch city of 1 million inhabitants, twice as many walk or cycle to the city centre than go by car. Non-motorised traffic dominates in the cities of Munster and Gottingen (38 per cent) which, especially in Munster, is due to very high bicycle-usage. This is even more the case in the Dutch city of Groningen, with 58 per cent of the city centre's visitors either walking or bicycling. The Swiss capital Bern has the highest share of public transport among medium-sized cities due to a good tram system and difficult access by car.

More recent, detailed and homogeneous data for a large number of cities have been derived from surveys commissioned by the cities themselves or by public transport companies as a basis for traffic planning and public awareness campaigns (Table 3).[4]

A comparison of individual visits to city centres for all purposes (without capture area) on all days in western and eastern Germany, shows that in western Germany, car-users (drivers and passengers) dominate slightly, whereas in eastern Germany, about two years after unification, car users have reached exactly the same level as public-transport passengers, non-motorised traffic accounting for 27 per cent in both cases. In contrast, those coming more frequently to the city centre for shopping use public transport, clearly surpassing the use of cars with 41 per cent compared to 31 per cent in the West, and 44 per cent compared to 27 per cent in the East. Nonetheless, polls among citizens, retailers, and decision-makers show that the perception is the opposite: all of them believe that car use for shopping is higher than the average of all trips to the city centre and even more for the average of all trips within the urban area.

A comparison of single cities shows a great diversity of traffic structures. A general trend is that the share of drivers normally increases and public transport users decreases as city size decreases. This trend varies from city to city depending on interrelated political and economic conditions.[5] Cities that are located in the Ruhr and Saar conurbations have much higher shares of car-users, especially as concerns the average of all trips to the city centre. This is primarily due to a type of decision-making that is generally less open to modern strategies of traffic planning and that does not question the role of cars. By comparison, cities with more service-oriented, post-industrial economies have much higher shares of public transport users, especially among shoppers. All of them have a definitive policy for limiting car traffic and all have quite prosperous and attractive city centres.[6]

To this point, only the residents of the city have been considered. However, the residents of areas surrounding cities (capture areas) -- whose numbers have been consistently growing due to suburbanisation, and who depend much more on cars because public transport is less accessible and less frequent -- are responsible for an increasing share of public transport problems. Of these suburban residents, car users dominate quite clearly, except in the largest German city, Hamburg, and the Austrian city of Innsbruck, where parking is extremely limited.

Table 2. **Mode of transport for trips to the city centre (1)**

Country/city		Week-day pop. (1 000) whole city(2)	Total trips to city centre (1 000)	Mode of transport (%)					
				All trips			Shopping, personal business		
				walk/ cyc	car (3)	pub. tr.	walk/ cyc	car (3)	pub. tr.
D	Hamburg	1 900	500	9	22	69	10	24	65
D	Munich	1 600	450	11	15	74	10	14	76
D	Stuttgart	800	300	10	30	60	10	30	60
D	Dusseldorf	800	300	13	33	55	15	40	45
D	Hanover	750	220	15	25	60	14	32	54
D	Dortmund	680	180	13	35	50	12	45	43
D	Nuremberg	650	230	15	25	60	14	29	57
D	Kiel	330	120	20	40	40	15	49	36
D	Munster	300	145	38	35	28	32	42	26
D	Kassel	280	115	20	40	40	18	46	36
D	Freiburg	270	120	30	33	38	31	33	36
D	Gottingen	170	90	38	32	30	41	32	27
I	Milano	2 100	400	15	13	73	16	10	74
A	Wien	1 800	500	15	15	70	16	11	73
NL	Amsterdam	1 000	350	30	15	55	27	14	59
S	Stockholm	950	280	10	18	70	10	21	69
CH	Zurich	950	300	15	17	70	15	17	68
CH	Bern	300	160	16	22	63	19	22	58
NL	Groningen	240	120	58	25	17	59	26	15

Notes: (1) trips within the city centre, trips back from the city centre and trips of city centre residents are not included;
(2) residents of the city and persons coming from the capture area for work, education, shopping, business and personal visits;
(3) including approximately 1 per cent motorbike.

Source: Apel, Lehmbrock, 1988, Tables 1 and 5, estimated figures based on different sources, reference year about 1988.

Table 3. Mode of transport for trips to the city centre (%) by city size

			All trips				Shopping trips			
	Year	R (1)	walk	cycl. (2)	car (3)	pub. tr.	walk	cycl. (2)	car (3)	pub. tr.
a. In average-sized cities										
Western Germany	1992	W	14	13	38	34	15	13	31	41
Eastern Germany	1992	E	18	9	36	36	19	9	27	44
b. In cities of more than 500 000 inhabitants										
Bremen	1991	W	6	13	33	48	10	10	21	58
Cologne	1992	W	8	11	44	36	16	13	33	38
Dusseldorf	1990	W	14	8	34	44	16	6	25	53
Essen	1990	W	28	7	46	19	39	3	35	23
Hamburg	1991	W	3	5	30	62	2	3	25	70
Hanover	1990	W	7	12	33	48	4	9	25	61
Leipzig	1990	E	22	3	25	49	25	4	21	50
Munich	1980	W	12	2	22	64	14	2	13	71
-	1989	W	10	7	19	64	10	7	9	74
-	1992	W	15	9	14	62	17	6	8	69
Stuttgart (4)	1981	W	14	2	37	47	18	1	26	55
-	1990	W	1	4	36	49	14	3	29	54
c. In cities of 250 000 - 500 000 inhabitants										
Bochum	1990	W	20	3	58	19	33	5	39	23
Gelsenkirchen	1991	W	27	3	57	13	39	9	39	13
Nuremberg	1989	W	13	12	35	40	11	10	25	54
Wiesbaden	1990	W	29	3	36	32	36	3	28	33
Wuppertal	1990	W	24	1	43	32	32	0	31	37
Zurich	1992	CH	15	7	11	67	14	6	6	74
d. In cities of 100 000 - 250 000 inhabitants										
Aachen	1990	W	32	13	36	18	40	10	30	19
Bottrop	1990	W	24	9	57	10	30	8	52	10
Erfurt	1990	E	12	7	44	37	17	4	35	44
Freiburg	1989	W	13	25	29	33	21	25	11	43
Graz	1988	A	26	15	27	32	26	12	19	43
-	1991	A	24	16	26	34	28	16	18	43
Innsbruck	1993	A	20	21	31	26	24	20	19	36
Kassel	1988	W	16	7	39	38	20	4	24	52
-	1991	W	13	4	42	41	14	1	32	53
Linz	1990	A	24	3	45	28	34	3	33	30
Neuss	1990	W	16	16	47	21	13	18	44	25
Recklinghausen	1990	W	28	10	53	9	29	4	52	15
Rostock	1992	E	15	3	35	47	22	0	25	53
Saarbrucken	1989	W	9	1	60	30	9	0	58	33
Salzburg	1992	A	19	26	29	26	17	31	18	34
Schwerin	1992	E	12	6	39	43	8	6	25	61
Ulm (5)	1992	W	26	6	40	28	35	7	29	29
Witten	1992	W	19	4	58	19	28	4	47	21

Notes: (1) Region: A=Austria, CH=Switzerland, E=eastern Germany, W=western Germany;

        (2) including 0-2 per cent motorcycle;

        (3) in the average of all cities, between 21 and 26 per cent of car-users are passengers;

        (4) 1981 shopping and services;

        (5) shopping trips include residents of the neighbour-city Neu-Ulm.

Source: surveys (home interviews) by Socialdata, separate reports for each city.

The above statistics, gathered from home interviews, show a monthly average of the modes of transport used for trips to the city centre. Average statistical figures, however, do not provide an appropriate measure for understanding access problems to city centres. Congestion does not occur on a continual basis, but only at periods of peak demand, especially on Saturdays and on the "service-Thursday", during which shops are open two additional hours in the evening. These two days bring about 19 per cent and 21 per cent respectively of all monthly customers of the major shops in the city centre.

Surveys taken among passers-by and shoppers respectively[7] show that the mode of transport used changes significantly during the week: on Saturday the share of car-users is highest and that of public transport-users is lowest (Table 4): the car, which during the week is mostly used for travel to work, is now available for family shopping. In addition, the share of out-of-town visitors is higher.

In eastern Germany, weekday car use is much lower and the increase in car use much higher on Saturday. This is due to very restricted car-access for women. The share of shoppers coming from out-of-town barely increases on Saturday as a result of the very weak position of traditional town centres in comparison to new large shopping facilities on the urban fringes of cities in eastern Germany.

Although serious problems of car-accessibility and parking in most cities are limited to a few hours on Thursday and Saturday, these short periods of congestion are the primary source of customer and retailer complaints. They repeatedly and short-sightedly demand the expansion of facilities that, in turn, encourages more people to use their cars and, consequently, results in more congestion at higher levels of traffic volume.

Table 4. **Mode of transport used by large retail store customers by day of week**

(in per cent)

	Walking	Bicycle	Public transport (1)	Car (2)	Out-of-town visitors (3)
Western Germany					
Thursday	16	4	34	45	38
Friday	17	5	34	43	36
Saturday	14	5	25	55	42
Eastern Germany					
Thursday	22	3	46	28	24
Friday	23	3	45	28	23
Saturday	21	3	32	43	26

Notes: (1) including park-and-ride;
(2) motorcycles are not included, their share is 0.5-0.8 per cent;
(3) proportion of all visitors.

Source: Surveys by Bundesarbeitsgemeinschaft der Mittel- und Großbetriebe des Einzelhandels (BAG) 1992.

According to the new, more-sustainable approach to planning, the transport system's capacity cannot be adapted to peak demand periods, because it would not be economical to do so (the same is true for energy supply) and would encourage traffic growth. Therefore, "normal demand" must set the standard, and congestion must be accepted as a measure for determining traffic volumes. This approach can be justified by the fact that the times of peak demand are much shorter than normal traffic periods.

Polls taken among department store shoppers in Germany confirm the results of the home-interviews presented above: the size of the city strongly influences the share of cars and public transport. Public transport use increases with the size of the city from 13 to 56 per cent and car-use decreases from 60 to 29 per cent on Friday, which is the day closest to a "normal" weekday. This results from a pull-and-push system: public transport improves and parking problems increase with the size of the city.

The statistical findings on modes of transport lead to two principal conclusions: first, decisions on traffic problems should not refer to the average traffic situation but should be focused on detailed information regarding trip purposes and on times of day when problems occur. Second, there is considerable opportunity for local policy to reduce car dependency, which is seen primarily in prosperous cities that have a greater ability to adapt themselves to future needs.

2.1.2   Purpose of trips

Discussions on problems of access to the city centre should always take into account the broad mix of different functions that characterise city centres: shopping and services, administration and business, culture and leisure and, to a certain extent, housing (the latter is mostly decreasing but politically it is considered an important element of a lively city centre). These functions attract different volumes and types of traffic, and traffic accessibility is of different importance for each (Table 5).

Among the purposes of trips to the city centre, shopping, leisure and personal business have an aggregate share of between one-half and two-thirds: in Gottingen, these activities account for 70 per cent of trips to the city centre; in Munich, 66 per cent; and Freiburg, 59 per cent -- all cities with very lively shopping areas.   Trips to work range between one-fifth and one-third, professional business trips one-tenth or a bit less. The proportion of educational trips varies greatly; it is highest where universities are located in the city centre (13 to 15 per cent). In other countries, shopping accounts for a relatively higher share (58 to 67 per cent), whereas work and business remain more modest.

Regarding car traffic problems, it is necessary only to look at those trips which have been made by car (in this case, only trips of drivers are considered in order to represent the number of cars parked). Due to long-term parking problems, the share of work-related trips decreases significantly (nearly all trips for education are made without private car and are not included in Table 5). Business trips, in contrast, are mostly made by car, thus, their share increases considerably; Munich is an extreme example of this, with an increase in business trips from 7 to 31 per cent of all car trips. The aggregate shares of trips for shopping, leisure and personal business increase in some cases, and decrease slightly in others.

Table 5. Purpose of trips to the city centre by mode of transport (1)

City	Week-day population whole city (1 000)	Trips by car (2) abs 1 000	Trips by car (2) per pop. x 100	All trips (in per cent) work	education	shopping (4)	profess. business	Trips by car (2) (3) (driver only) (in per cent) work	shop (4)/ leisure	profess. business
Hamburg	1 900	90	5	36	4	50	10	16	56	29
Munich	1 600	52	3	23	4	66	7	12	58	31
Stuttgart	800	68	9	30	10	50	10	22	51	26
Dusseldorf	800	73	9	31	7	51	10	12	62	26
Hanover	750	48	6	35	5	51	9	17	56	27
Dortmund	680	50	7	27	8	56	8	10	68	22
Nuremburg	650	45	7	22	9	62	7	13	67	20
Kiel	330	40	12	26	9	56	10	15	63	22
Munster	300	39	13	24	13	54	9	13	64	23
Kassel	280	35	13	30	13	47	10	17	57	26
Freiburg	270	29	11	18	15	59	8	14	62	24
Gottingen	170	20	12	13	9	70	8	10	65	25
Milan	2 100	33	2	23	6	63	8	9	45	45
Vienna	1 800	55	3	24	5	64	7	15	50	35
Amsterdam	1 000	43	4	22	7	63	7	12	58	30
Stockholm	950	40	4	27	7	58	7	8	65	28
Zurich	950	38	4	19	8	67	6	11	66	24
Bern	300	30	10	20	9	62	9	9	63	28
Groningen	240	22	9	15	17	59	8	5	64	32

Notes: (1) trips within the city centre and trips of city centre residents are not included;
(2) including 1 per cent motorbike;
(3) trips for education are not included;
(4) including personal business and leisure.

Source: Apel, Lehmbrock 1990, Tables 1 and 5: estimated figures based on different sources, reference year about 1988.

2.1.3   Structure of parking demand

The pressure of parking demand appears to be reflected by the often-chaotic -- if not illegal -- kerbside parking, along with high numbers of cars seeking parking facilities[8] and queues of cars at the entrances to centrally located parking garages, especially on Saturday. However, there is a general lack of systematic surveys showing the structure of the parking demand. Even existing surveys are often used superficially and do not fulfil the criteria of responsible planning for sustainable traffic development.

A widespread method used in parking surveys is the direct observation of parked cars. In this case, however, only cars parked on roads and parking places and in garages which are open to the public can be considered, whereas in many cities one-third to one-half of all parking facilities in the city centre are accessible only to employees or residents.[9] The on-street observations are normally made during on-foot rounds or at certain times of the day (morning, afternoon, night) or at regular intervals (every 30, 60 or 120 minutes). Such observations reveal how many parking sites are used by residents and employees for long-term parking and how many by visitors parking for shorter periods. They also can show how many sites are used for illegal parking.

Although the results of these detailed surveys provide some useful information on demand volumes and structures, they convey an inaccurate impression of real parking turnover, because they neither provide data on the total number of cars parked during the day nor on the parking volumes used by different groups. This can be illustrated from continuous observation in the small town of Sulzbach (18 300 residents). Most drivers park their cars for only a few minutes, whereas other drivers (much fewer in number) park for much longer periods (even where this is not allowed) and consume a very high proportion of the total parking time available. Continuous observation revealed a much higher turnover than that noted during hourly observation: in the area of one-hour maximum parking, the turnover was nearly threefold compared to that noted during hourly observation, and in the two-hour area, more than twofold.

Continuous observation provides demand figures in number of cars parked and parking duration. This is very important if one is considering the volume of demand in relation to the needs of an urban area served by the parking facility and the influence of parking management. Examples from the medium-sized city of Bamberg (70 700 residents) show that the volumes of demand realised at certain locations differ greatly. The highest turnover of parked cars is observed at locations where parking is not allowed, but where certain functions, such as the post office, attract many visitors who park for only a few minutes

(19 to 25 cars per day per site). Parking sites with a one-hour limit attract 15 cars per day, while those with a two-hour parking limit draw seven to 12 cars per day. Occupancy is highest where no fees are charged. The most important source of additional parking capacity -- in terms of the number of visits by car in a given street/ area -- is effective parking management.

The impact of the introduction of parking fees on parking demand can be shown with examples from Munich and Nuremberg.[10] In Munich, an attractive secondary shopping street close to the principal pedestrian district was studied (see: Beschel *et al.*, 1995). At the time of the first survey (Table 6), parking duration was limited to one hour on one side of the street and two hours on the opposite side. Parking was free of charge with use of a parking disk.[11] There were numerous exemptions from time limits for residents and public service vehicles holding a special permit. Only a few cars parked less than 15 minutes. More than three-quarters of parking capacity was used by cars standing for more than one hour (the majority for more than two hours).[12]

After introducing the DM 5.00/h fee (collected by ticket machines), the share of cars parking no more than 15 minutes grew to 52 per cent, with the highest proportion in the areas closest to the pedestrian district, due to fewer long-term parking residents. Thus, in comparison to the former two-hour zone, the share of cars tripled. The share of those parking for more than one hour decreased to half of its former level, notwithstanding a still high proportion of parkers holding a resident's permit which exempted them from fees and time limits.

Yet, if parking time consumed is considered, the result is much less impressive. The time-share of very short-term parking is only 9 per cent in contrast to 3 per cent of the previous average, whereas those parking for more than one hour still consume 65 per cent compared to 79 per cent. The main reason for the still low share of short-term parking is that a large proportion of car drivers have not yet accepted the high fares for kerbside parking. This is evident in the decrease in occupancy rate to 69 per cent, partly due to the city's failure to market the new regulation.

Table 6. Parking volume and duration in Munich's Sendlinger Strasse before and after the introduction of parking fees

	1992 (without fee)		1993 (with 5 DM/h fee)		
Max. parking duration	1h	2h	East (1)	West (1)	2h average
No. of sites observed	12	9	23	15	
Per cent of cars					
1-5 minutes	10	4	28	17	23
6-15 minutes	17	13	26	32	29
16-30 minutes	18	13	16	18	17
31-60 minutes	15	30	15	11	13
61-120 minutes		17	11	13	12
>120 minutes	}39	23	3	10	7
Per cent parking time					
1-5 minutes	1	0	3	1	2
6-15 minutes	3	2	7	7	7
16-30 minutes	7	3	11	9	10
31-60 minutes	11	16	20	11	16
61-120 minutes		18	32	25	29
>120 minutes	}79	60	27	46	37
Per cent occupancy (2)	93	96	59	79	69

Notes: (1) Eastern part = more central; western part = more peripheral;
(2) parking time in relation to available time.

Source: Observations 1992/1993 by Abteilung Angewandte Stadtgeographie, Universität Bayreuth.

Higher fees for kerbside parking relative to parking garages are necessary because of the limited amount of kerbside parking to encourage shorter parking durations. However, this could cause problems due to more cars being attracted to kerbside parking (a consequence stressed, for instance, by Topp 1991 and 1995).

To address this problem, parking areas not needed can be converted into bike lanes, wider pavements and urban greens. This has been done in Salzburg: after the introduction of a parking management scheme in the central part of the city, the number of cars parked per site doubled from six to 12 per day, but the number of parking sites was halved; as a result, the amount of cars attracted remained stable (see Koch, Wiesinger, 1994).

The reactions of city-centre visitors to the increase in parking fees from DM 2.00 to DM 5.00 per hour were investigated in Nuremberg. Among passers-by owning a car, 45 per cent did not modify their parking behaviour with the change in fee -- half continued to park at the kerbside and half neither parked at the kerbside before nor after the fee increase. Almost one-fifth uses parking garages more often that charge about half as much as kerbside parking (most drivers are not aware of this). Eleven per cent now park their car before they reach the city centre and walk longer distances ("park and go"). One-fifth uses other modes of transport more often for the trip to the city centre. Only 5 per cent stated that they now come to the city centre less often. The higher fees in half of all cases have reduced the pressure of car traffic on the city centre. Increased parking in the areas around the centre, however, may cause some problems for people living there.

Up to this point, the analysis has considered the number of parked cars and parking conditions. A more serious questioning of parking demand, however, requires data on the time volumes by trip-purpose as criteria for the necessity of car-use and parking provision. For this, several survey methods can be used. One possibility for relatively small areas with a limited number of access-roads is a survey among drivers as they leave a given district. The usefulness of information obtained in this way can be demonstrated through the example of Sulzbach (Table 7).[13]

Results of this survey showed that 41 per cent of all cars were parked for shopping and 15 per cent for work. However, when parking duration was considered, 16 per cent of parked cars were for shopping compared to 61 per cent for work. This is due to the fact that in such a small town, most shoppers park for only a few minutes. It can therefore be concluded that the volume of parking demand for shopping and services does not really cause parking shortage, even though parking may be concentrated in a relatively small area. A reduction in car use for trips to work (which are often over short distances) would open up space that could be used for parking for other purposes, or for other uses.

Table 7. **Parked cars and parking duration in the city centre by purpose of trip (%)**

No = number of cars Du = parking duration (minutes)	Shopping		Work (1)		Leisure		Other	
	no	du	no	du	no	du	no	du
City residents only								
Bremen	20	7	30	65	18	16	32	12
Gladbeck	46	27	23	50	14	11	17	12
Kassel	39	17	17	37	25	35	19	11
Lunen	37	17	20	49	21	19	22	15
Nuremberg	29	14	22	43	28	26	21	17
Stuttgart	22	9	24	53	24	19	30	19
Wiesbaden	39	24	22	48	13	15	26	13
Residents of city and capture area								
Dresden	32	18	17	52	21	18	30	12
Dusseldorf	27	14	26	58	15	12	32	16
Freiburg	25	16	23	54	23	19	29	11
Innsbruck	12	6	30	61	20	18	38	15
Saarbrucken	20	12	37	60	15	5	17	17
Schwerin	10	5	35	73	18	9	37	13
Sulzbach	41	16	15	61	8	5	37	18

Note:
(1) Trips as part of work are not included in the survey.
Year data obtained: Bremen 1991, Dusseldorf 1990, Dresden 1992/94, Freiburg 1989, Gladbeck 1989, Innsbruck 1993, Kassel 1991, Nuremberg 1989, Saarbrücken 1989, Schwerin 1992, Stuttgart 1990, Wiesbaden 1990.

Source: Surveys by Socialdata (home-interviews) separate reports for each city; Sulzbach: Lappe, Monheim, 1991 -- survey among car-drivers leaving the centre.

Information on purpose and duration of parking can also be obtained from mobility surveys using traffic diaries (Table 7).[14] If the purposes of trips made by car to the city centre are elaborated not only by their number but also by parking duration, it becomes clear that the impact of commuter parking on parking demand is drastically underestimated when the classical survey-methods are used (as in Table 5). If only the number of parked cars is considered, the share of those who work in the city remains relatively modest with 17 to 30 per cent of trips by the residents of the city and 17 to 37 per cent when residents of capture areas are included. If parking duration is considered, however, about half of all parking demand is comprised of those working in the city centre. The share of shopping in total number of parked cars is higher than that of work when only the local residents are considered; it is smaller by half in those cities where residents of the capture area are included in the survey. In comparison, only between one-sixth and one-quarter of parking duration is used for shopping. If those coming from the capture area are included in the survey, the share of shoppers sometimes drops to 5 to 9 per cent. It is especially significant that Schwerin (125 000 inhabitants), the capital of the State of Mecklenburg-Vorpommern in eastern Germany, has by far the highest share of commuters and the lowest of shoppers (73 per cent as compared to 5 per cent): its city centre is dominated by administration, and it has been difficult to attract shoppers.

Based on the findings of parking demand analysis, it can be concluded that in virtually all of the "motorised" world, there is a widespread inability to take decisive action for management of parking demand. This is due to the strong pressure of interest groups, which -- in both small and large cities -- often use fallacious arguments against parking demand management. Countries now facing increased motorisation should carefully monitor how the structure of their parking demand develops so that they can defend themselves against pressure groups. The only alternative is to develop, from the beginning, a parking management scheme based on politically established needs on the one hand, and affordable strategies for sustainable development on the other hand. Some cities in "motorised" countries have shown that this is not at all utopian. Rather, a politically based, rational parking management scheme is absolutely necessary and feasible for improving urban traffic, the environment, and the economy.

2.2 Analysis of parking supply

2.2.1 General principles

Parking demand and supply are interrelated. There is no simple challenge-and-response mechanism. Yet, it is clear that a strong demand exerts pressure to increase supply. At the same time, an extensive parking supply encourages car use for trips to the city centre and, consequently, tends to generate additional demand. Generally speaking, one can distinguish two contrasting planning approaches for determining the amount of parking supply in city centres:

-- maximising parking supply in the city centre in order to successfully compete commercially with other city centres and free-standing shopping centres;

-- parking management: designed to prevent the city centre from being overwhelmed by traffic congestion and, as a consequence, lose its attractiveness and competitiveness.

In most German cities, the volume of parking supply has increased continuously due to the political pressures of interest groups complaining about shortages in parking facilities. In numerous cases, the construction of additional parking garages was required by retailers as a condition for their consent to the introduction or expansion of pedestrian zones. The improvement of public transport was normally not accompanied by a reduction in car accessibility; on the contrary, car accessibility was often increased simultaneously as a strategy to strengthen the attractiveness of the city centre. There are, however, considerable differences in the parking capacities of different cities, as Apel and Lehmbrock (1990) have shown.

The total number of parking facilities can provide an initial -- but unrealistic -- idea of the accessibility of the city centre by car, essentially because of two factors: first, the effectiveness of each parking site depends on how it is managed; and second, the availability of a free parking site is largely determined by the demand pressure that, in turn, is influenced by the attractiveness of alternative modes of transport. Both aspects have to be taken into account in every evaluation of an existing parking system and in every planning proposal. The usual comparisons of only the volume of parking supply are quite misleading if one does not consider how the whole traffic system works.

The analysis of parking supply must distinguish parking facilities under several conditions, making it possible to discuss the potential for a more effective use of parking supply:

-- Who has access: private permit-holders only (residents, employees, tenants); or customers and visitors of the parking-lot owner; delivery and other business vehicles; or everyone who wishes to park?

-- Is the parking duration limited? (This is often the case for kerbside parking or in open places but rarely in parking garages).

-- Is there a parking fee? If yes, is it a) linear (same fee for every hour); b) progressive (increasing fee per hour with longer standing time, as for instance in Zurich with SF 0.50 for the first 30 minutes and an increase of SF 3.00 for every additional 30 minutes); or c) digressive (first hour DM 2.00, each following hour DM 1.50)? Is it higher for garages or for on-street parking? Does it increase from the periphery towards central locations?

-- How extensive is the enforcement of parking duration limits and fee-payment (probability of receiving a fine and amount of the fine in relation to parking fees)? Who is responsible for the enforcement?

-- What is the quality of the parking site, including its accessibility and its location in respect to the main destination area of the customers? Does the location cause problems on the access roads (congestion, noise or pollution)?

-- Do the regulations vary by period (e.g. fees only during shopping hours, higher fees on Saturday, reservations for residents holding a special permit during certain hours)?

-- How effectively is parking managed and marketed? Is there a guidance and information system? Do car drivers know and use it? Do garage-operators work together in managing the supply?

This paper will not address how these questions apply to specific situations (for more details, see Topp, 1992; a collection of examples of parking management and marketing has been edited by Monheim, 1989). Yet, some discussion on the most important measures of parking supply may illustrate the possibilities and risks with respect to developing a sustainable traffic infrastructure.

2.2.2 On-street parking in public spaces

A high proportion of public parking supply is on-street. This is especially true in small cities and in the peripheries of large city centres. Less-developed regions and economies often can only offer on-street parking because of a lack of funds for construction of garages. On-street parking is generally the most preferred type of parking, but causes the greatest problems: it requires decisiveness in defining user-groups, the fee-structure, and the strength of enforcement. These aspects are often heavily debated by interest groups, making difficult any effective action, even though a well-managed on-street parking system would contribute to the success of the city centre. Due to very limited public awareness of the problems and negative side effects caused by on-street parking among citizens, politicians and interest groups, it is still presumed that parking in open public spaces should be maximised. Every proposal for reduction meets heavy opposition. This is even more the case in former socialist countries, where parking space in garages is very rare and hard to finance.

The negative side-effects of on-street parking include: loss of open public space for other functions, especially biking, walking, standing, sitting and growing trees; visual encroachment, especially in historical zones; noise and air pollution and traffic congestion on access roads. A high proportion of all car traffic in the city centre is caused by cars driving around in search of favourable on-street parking space.

Any planning for on-street parking must balance the positive effects of car accessibility with its many negative side-effects on the urban environment. It also must consider that in most cities, a majority of visitors does not travel to the city by car, and therefore gains no benefits, but only disadvantages from on-street parking. This is even more the case in former socialist and developing countries.

Due to both the high demand for and negative effects of parking in open public spaces, plans for further development in this area must be made with particular care. Within the business district, priority must given to short-term parking and to goods delivery, as long as there is no need for pedestrianisation or other functions such as wider pavements, bike lanes or trees (e.g. on boulevards). Spaces should be reserved for taxi-stands and handicapped access with a special permit.

2.2.3   Public parking garages

The limited amount of on-street parking and conflicts with other town planning goals have led to considerable pressure for the construction of parking garages above or below ground. In Central European OECD countries, and especially in western Germany, a very high proportion of parking capacity is offered by garages that are either open to the public or are reserved for entitled groups like residents, employees, or hotel guests. Garages owned by department stores usually are accessible to everybody, although store customers are charged a reduced parking fee.

The provision of parking garages has many positive and negative implications for urban traffic, making an overall judgement impossible. The main positive effects are:

--   concentration of parking in a small area, allowing a higher density of functions in the inner city, with fewer open parking lot "holes" (typical in US/North American cities); reduction of on-street parking;

--   fee-evasion is eliminated by mechanical control (no exit without payment);

--   number of vehicles seeking free parking facilities is reduced (this advantage, however, is only theoretical, because in practice, many drivers prefer to search for on-street parking, which is generally preferred and often cheaper).

The primary negative effects of parking garages include:

--   concentration of parking may cause congestion problems on access roads, especially at peak-times (e.g. queues of waiting cars for access on favourite shopping days);

--   concentration may overwhelm the whole road system if it is not able to handle the volumes attracted;

--   provision of parking garages encourages more car-use for trips to the city centre, which adversely affects the other modes of transport;

--   location of parking garages on roads parallel to an often pedestrianised main shopping street deteriorates the appearance of those roads: a "backyard character" reduces the attractiveness of retail;

--   goal to build garages as close as possible to the areas of highest demand may come in conflict with future plans to expand the pedestrian district and create larger street-networks comfortable for pedestrians;

-- costs of building, maintenance, and operation are not covered in most cases by fees; fee increases are difficult to implement, because of the competition of the city centre with peripheral shopping offering free parking.

Building codes require a given number of parking facilities at the site of new buildings and for newly established businesses within existing buildings. If this is not possible, the city may waive this obligation for payment of a fee, which is normally far less than the construction price. The city has to use this money for the improvement of accessibility. Initially, use of the money was restricted for increasing parking supply; however, in some cities now, the money is also used for public transport, including park-and-ride in the urban fringe.

Those cities in which parking supply already exceeds levels sustainable by the city centre and which are accessible by public transport may enact a special statute which limits the number of future parking sites that can be built, taking into consideration accessibility to the city centre by public transport. This may go as far as 10 per cent of the parking volume normally required by law (e.g. *"Stellplatzbegrenzungssatzung"* applied in Nuremberg).

Establishing the appropriate parking volume required for garages is very difficult. Usually, there is immense pressure from interest groups to build as many garages as possible because of presumed shortages. Surveys, in contrast, show that these shortages are limited to a few hours during the week, to prime shopping periods before Christmas, and to the most-favourably located garages.

This is true even for large cities, as can be seen from the example of Munich, which is known to have the worst parking situation.[15] Even in Munich, however, parking garages in the city centre are filled to capacity only a few hours on Thursday evening and Saturday, whereas the normal maximum occupancy is only 80 per cent (Figure 1). There are three principal reasons why most garages are not completely filled: most importantly, the easy accessibility of the city centre by other means of transport, mainly subway and suburban trains; second, the still considerable amount of on-street parking; and last but not least, the widespread opinion that it is foolish to come to the city centre by car: most automobile owners never came by car to the city centre, whereas the few who did on the day of the interview were mostly regular, habitual car users.

Figure 1. **Extent of parking garage use in the city centre of Munich (only old town)**

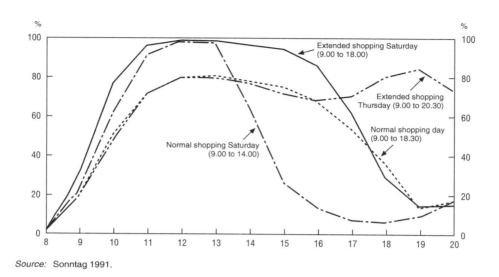

Source: Sonntag 1991.

One reason for the distorted perception of the parking supply is that car drivers remember often singular cases of frustration when a parking garage was filled to capacity. They forget that there is usually sufficient capacity. This is caused by the very uneven distribution of demand in time and space. There are several ways to best respond to such disproportion: the most attractive garages should charge higher fees than the less attractive. In times of peak demand (especially on Saturday) the parking fees could be higher, and public transport could offer more-frequent service and inexpensive group tickets (the city of Aachen, for instance, has introduced a "happy day ticket" along with its "pedestrian-friendly" city centre). On Thursday, public transport should provide longer hours of frequent service in the evenings.[16]

2.2.4   Park-and-ride

Park-and-ride is often considered an effective strategy for improving accessibility to the city centre from large peripheral areas where there is a weak presence of public transport. Two principal systems can be identified: the first entails parking at rail or light rail stations along the urban periphery or at further distances in the capture area. This system is most often found in metropolitan areas, as well as in some smaller cities with improved tram or light rail (e.g. Freiburg, Karlsruhe). The second system involves parking relatively close to the city centre at places with frequent bus service to the centre: this can be found in some large- and medium-sized cities. In most cases, park-and-ride is used primarily for commuting, because of the shortage of long-term parking within the centre. Some cities, like Aachen or Lubeck, have introduced park-and-ride specifically for weekend-shopping[17]. Several cities offer park-and-ride on Saturdays before Christmas when parking demand is highest (e.g. Gottingen).

The share of visitors using park-and-ride systems to access the city centre is always very low -- normally about 1 to 2 per cent; in large cities, the share sometimes reaches 3 to 4 per cent. Notwithstanding a widespread recognition of park-and-ride benefits, a critical evaluation shows many problems: one is the high cost of construction and operation of parking facilities, especially garages, and the negative effect on the environment surrounding the station. Another is that park-and-ride diverts public transport riders from the system of feeder-buses to the peripheral train stations; before parking was improved, a large proportion of those driving to the station came by bus. There is particular criticism of proposals that implement park-and-ride only in cases of road congestion. This is due to the extreme economic inefficiency of additional, but irregularly used rail stock. Finally, it can be observed from several surveys that the knowledge of park-and-ride systems among car drivers is poor.

Further details regarding park-and-ride systems will not be examined in this paper.[18] However, one can reasonably conclude that the contribution of these systems to the accessibility of the city centre is generally overestimated, and the problems involved underestimated.

2.2.5   Home delivery by city-centre shops

It is often argued that the city centre should be easily accessible by cars for shopping because of the high volumes of purchases that are made there. Several surveys show that this is true only for a very small number of all shoppers (about 5 per cent), and that this proportion is similar among visitors coming by public transport. These small proportions are primarily due to a division of labour, where bulky goods are normally bought in the outer areas or in the shoppers' own neighbourhoods. Public discussions often ignore the fact that many shops deliver bulky goods, of a certain value, to customers' homes, free of charge or for a modest fee. Shops do not advertise this, however, because this service is highly subsidised.

In some cities, models of a more-effective home delivery service, offered jointly by the retail community, are being developed as part of new efforts to achieve a better organised city-centre management. At the moment this is still in its initial stages (see Komming, Klewe, 1994). These attempts to establish co-ordinated delivery services are part of a general rethinking of goods delivery to the shops. Presently, this is done in a very inefficient way, with producers and distributors using their own vehicles, creating congestion problems -- especially in the large pedestrian zones where access is limited to a few hours in the morning (delivery is often made for practical reasons only between 9.00 and 10.30). In addition, vehicles are inefficiently used. This, along with the closure of many city centres to trucks of more than 7.5 tons, has led to the establishment of goods distribution centres at the periphery of the city: incoming goods are collected and stored and their distribution within the city managed.

2.3 Balancing supply and demand

As emphasized earlier, there is a complex interrelationship between parking supply and demand. Traditional transportation engineering was primarily oriented towards expansion of the technical supply ("hard policy"). It has since become clear that this approach generates greater demand ("law of persisting traffic congestion" due to the tendency of the system to fill up to its capacity limits). Therefore, it is necessary to manage the supply in such a way that demand adapts to the carrying capacity of the traffic system ("soft policy"). This requires, first of all, the political definition of the "qualified demand" which has to be fulfilled in order to ensure a vital city centre. Second, a broad set of managing and marketing techniques must be used in order to promote appropriate behaviour among car drivers.

2.3.1   *"Qualified demand"*

Due to the limited capacity of city centres to accommodate car traffic (driving and parking), plans for parking supply cannot aim to meet all demand (as once was believed); priorities must be set. These priorities should be based on: political decisions regarding the importance of a variety of activities to a well-working city centre; the dependence of each activity on car accessibility; the tolerable volumes of car traffic in a liveable city; and the amount of money available for expansion and operation of parking and road capacities.

The most important part of any strategy for balancing parking demand and supply is determining how much parking is needed, for whom, at which locations, and under what conditions. This inevitably causes controversy, but if no decision is made regarding these issues, the damage to the whole urban system will be worse. If possible, the decision should be reached through round table meetings, where planners and interest groups discuss possible alternatives and their consequences. This mediation-process should also be used to create greater public awareness of related problems and to challenge the domineering approach of some interest groups[19].

Parking for professional business, goods delivery, service vehicles and, to a certain degree, housing, is generally agreed by all responsible parties as "qualified demand", to which priority should be given.[20] There is debate over to what extent the demands of shoppers and those visiting private and public services can be fulfilled. In most cases, some limitations are inevitable.

Since the early 1970s, it has been generally agreed that parking for city employees should be strictly limited (Innenministerium Baden-Württemberg, 1974), because the normally long duration of parking and the density of traffic flow during short rush-hour periods reduce accessibility of the city centre for the qualified demand. According to studies on parking duration and purpose of trips, however, most cities have not taken action to reduce city-employee parking. One explanation is that a significant number of commuters park in the private parking lots of their employers -- in most cases, without charge.[21] Another reason is that in and around the city centre, there are many parking sites without fees and time limitations, especially in residential areas, which are invaded every morning by commuters. Moreover, some drivers treat illegal parking like a lottery; it seems more economically interesting to park illegally than to pay the legal fees, because the fines and the risk of paying fines are perceived to be low.

2.3.2   Management with fees, time limitations and access restrictions

Parking demand can be adapted to limited parking supply through use of instruments that are designed to influence car user behaviour. Some measures use market economy principles (fees); others put legal limitations on the parking duration or purpose. All management measures, however, are only effective if they are clearly communicated to the car-drivers through appropriate marketing strategies (Chapter 2.3.3).

The main objective of parking management is to maximise the efficiency of the limited parking supply so that the parking needs of activities most necessary for the smooth functioning of the city are served first. This entails reducing demand in cases where parking supply is insufficient, for instance: reducing parking for commuters to free up parking capacity for shoppers; or reducing parking for shoppers to maintain quality of living for the city centre.

The city's authority to set fees and parking time limits is primarily related to parking facilities on public property. Many German cities operate their own parking garages through public transport agencies or special organisations under the control of the city. In large cities, there are numerous private parking facilities, in which case, the city has no influence on fees and conditions for leasing.

Determining the right amount of parking fees leads to a fundamental dilemma: on the one hand, fees are designed to control the volume and structure of car traffic by more than just a "symbolic" price (the case for decades, especially in smaller cities where fees are still nominal). On the other hand, those car-users whose business is necessary for the success of the city centre should not be deterred from accessing the area. Retailers are especially concerned about this, fearing that large out-of-town shopping facilities will seduce customers with free parking. This fear is heightened by the widespread desire of car drivers to exercise their "civic right" to park where they want, with low fees or none at all. For many years, this approach was upheld by the law, which, in Germany, was only recently changed to promote more-efficient parking management in open public spaces. In some cases, retail owners have reacted to the attitudes of customers by paying for their parking fees. (The restitution of public transport fees was rejected for a long time and remains quite rare). The money necessary for fee-restitution, however, is taken from all customers, which means that car-users are in effect subsidised by those coming by "green" modes.

The dilemma in finding the right price level is complicated by a general preference for on-street parking over garages. The fee for the latter is relatively high due to enormous construction and operation costs. The fees for on-street parking should not be lower, as has been, and still is the case in most parts of the world. This results in overcrowded kerbsides and heavy traffic in search of on-street parking around under-utilised parking garages (see Flade *et al.*, 1988; for search traffic see Boltze, Puzicha, 1995).

A demand-oriented structure of parking fees follows the principle that the price level is related to the attractiveness of a given site; that is, the fee range is related to the pressure of parking demand: higher for on-street parking than in garages and higher at central locations than in the periphery. The top fee for on-street parking in the most central streets with highest demand pressure is now about DM 4.00 per hour in many European OECD countries. In the periphery of large city centres and in smaller cities, the fee is usually DM 2.00 per hour. In the more distant, smaller suburbs, the fee may decrease to DM 0.50 to DM 1.00 per hour. Many small- and medium-sized cities continue to charge no parking fees at all.

Fees for parking garages vary considerably due to the fact that some garages are privately operated and others publicly operated. Thus, there is no systematic fee strategy.[22] In most cases, it is DM 1.00 to DM 2.00 per hour. In larger cities and very attractive locations, the fee tends to be around DM 3.00 to DM 5.00. The fee structure is most-often linear: an equal price is charged for every hour. If shorter parking durations are encouraged, a progressive fee can be applied: the hourly price increases with parking duration (e.g. DM 1.00 for the first hour, an additional DM 1.50 for the second hour, resulting in a total fee of DM 2.50 for two hours of parking). If longer parking durations are desired, a digressive fee may be used (e.g. DM 2.00 for the first hour and DM 1.50 for every additional hour).[23] At locations of highest demand or at peak times (e.g. on Saturdays) a minimum fee for two hours sometimes must be paid, even if one parks only a short time. In the evening or on Sundays, fees in garages are normally much less because of lower demand (during these times, kerbside parking is usually free).

Even though there are good reasons for using a demand-oriented fee system, according to the general principles of a free market economy -- where rare goods carry higher prices -- the effect of fee differentiation on parking behaviour should not be overestimated. Among the various aspects determining the car-user's choice of a certain parking facility, the amount of the fee is of relatively low importance (except in the case of free and unlimited parking which is generally highly preferred). Most car-drivers have a very limited knowledge about fee conditions. Moreover, the cities and the operators of parking garages often employ a very poor marketing policy, making it difficult for drivers to be informed. Yet, there are widespread complaints among car-drivers who believe that fees are too high, even though they do not know the price.

Fees are often highly subsidised and cover only part of parking site construction and operation costs. The subsidies may come from federal or state programmes (especially for urban renewal), from cities or from business (e.g. as part of the investment and operation costs of a department store which are distributed among all customers). The subsidies may also come from a fund collected/accumulated by the city from compensations of those who have constructed new buildings and were not able or allowed to build the parking facilities required under building laws on their own site.

The fee for open-air parking is often paid at ticket-machines, which can serve larger areas. The car-driver deposits the fee into the machine for the time he wants to park, and then displays the parking ticket in the front windshield of his car. The end of his parking time is shown in large numbers on the ticket. The ticket should have a coupon serving to remind the driver of the place where the car is parked and the end of the parking time.

A previous system involved mechanical parking metres located immediately beside the parking lot. Coins were "fed" into the metre, which displayed the remaining parking time available. This system was easier to control, but more difficult to adapt to changing conditions; more intrusive in an historical environment, more expensive to maintain and operate; and a greater obstruction on the pavement.

Parking fees can also be assessed through prepaid tickets, as is done, for instance, in Singapore and Austria; fees are requested all over the city, including residential areas. Helsinki started the same system in 1994, when parking fees were introduced throughout the central area (more than 20 km²). The month, day, hour and minute of arrival is marked on the tickets. Each ticket is valid for a certain fee which corresponds, for example, to 30 minutes in the central area and up to one hour in the peripheral areas. For longer parking times (if permitted) more tickets can be used. No expenditures for machines are required for this system. There is no risk of money being stolen from parking machines, and the tickets can be sold in kiosks, shops or fuel stations.[24]

One important advantage of both prepaid tickets and individual parking tickets is that the city has no expenditures for the equipment and its maintenance and for the collection of coins. Further, both are flexible to changing conditions; the development of smart cards useable for a bundle of services like parking, public transport or telephone is now under way.

The time-limit for on-street parking in most cases is one or two hours (in Austria often 90 or 180 minutes). In special situations (e.g. in front of a post office or railway station), it may be 15 to 30 minutes, whereas in areas with predominantly residential functions, time limits may be increased up to four hours. There are also examples like Copenhagen, where due to a lack of parking garages in the old town, one can buy weekly or monthly tickets. The rate however is high, seemingly affordable only to business-people who need their cars close to their work.

Special parking regulations should be established for residents of a given area. These can include reserved access for residents holding a special permit, as is the case in city centres with limited access. Such limitations may only apply to certain time periods, e.g. the weekend (as in Lubeck) or during the night (as in a section of Nuremberg where the concentration of pubs adversely affects living conditions).

Reserved parking for residents can be implemented through different rules:

-- reserving certain areas exclusively for residents, the advantage being that others do not drive through these areas in search of a parking lot; this is known as "hard separation";

-- reserving areas for residents during designated hours, again, to prevent commuters from using these streets in search of parking (e.g. no parking for non-residents before 9.00);

-- issuing a special permit to residents which frees them from paying parking fees throughout the day or at certain times (e.g. between 17.00 and 9.00 the next morning); this is known as "soft separation".

The choice of regulation type depends on whether shopping, service, and business areas must be rendered accessible to cars; or whether the objective is only to prevent commuters from invading residential areas close to the city centre.

Residents pay a certain fee for their parking permits which must be renewed annually. In Germany, cities by law are allowed only to charge an administration fee -- normally between DM 35.00 and 80.00 per year. In

Austria, the city of Vienna has introduced a permit fee of Sch 2 000 (about DM 285.00) per year in some central areas. The number of permit-holders is normally higher than the number of parking spaces available; therefore, the permit does not guarantee a free parking space. Permits are released only to permanent residents who have no parking facilities on their own property. Special permits are sometimes given to local firms, to social services or to hotel guests.

Parking permit systems are not an appropriate solution, however, if residential densities are high in and around the city centre; if there is high parking demand both inside and outside of the area; and if there is virtually no provision for residential parking. This is the case in eastern Germany, where socialist planning models called for a high proportion of residential functions in city centres. Construction and operation of parking garages is extremely expensive, and, in most cases, cannot be financed. Therefore, parking will probably be possible only on peripheral sites, as is the case in some new "car-free" residential developments in Germany and in some Asian cities. In most western German cities, a parking permit system is less of an issue, because the number of residents in city centres has dropped considerably.

Responding to residents' demands for parking in central areas becomes nearly impossible when car ownership explodes. Efforts, therefore, should be primarily oriented towards slowing down the increase in car ownership. This complicated policy will not be discussed in the context of this paper; however, it should be noted that levels of car ownership vary considerably within European OECD cities. In some cases, car ownership has not increased for many years (e.g. Basel and Copenhagen); in others, it has even decreased (e.g. Freiburg and Kassel) (see ECMT, OECD 1995).

A special need for parking in city centres exists for vehicles delivering goods to shops and businesses. Given the volume and weight of the goods, parking must be available as close to the destination as possible. Within pedestrian districts, delivery is permitted in the morning and sometimes also in the evening. Outside pedestrian areas, delivery becomes difficult if all regular parking sites are occupied. Therefore, a certain amount of kerbside parking should be reserved for goods delivery, which must be carried out quickly and without interruption (these loading bays are, however, severely affected by illegal parking). In addition, better management can also alleviate delivery problems: it has been shown, for example, that distribution of goods can be carried out by fewer trucks, if operators work together. Co-ordination even increases their competitiveness. More-effective delivery-systems are increasingly being discussed and tested.

2.3.3   Parking enforcement and marketing

Parking supply management does not guarantee adequate accessibility to the city centre, if parking regulations are not enforced and communicated to car-drivers. As mentioned above, awareness of and compliance with traffic laws among car-drivers is very low. The lack of attention given to these aspects by administrative groups -- in particular, those which only address technical issues -- is a major cause of widespread parking disorder. The problems of marketing the appropriate use of limited parking supply are even greater in former socialist countries, where newly found freedom is often misconstrued as the right of the driver to behave as he likes, and where controls are stigmatised as relics of socialism. Therefore, the effective operation of on-street parking requires not only technical, but also "diplomatic" initiatives, such as achieving the right balance between parking needs and those of walking, cycling, public transport and the urban environment. This balance is the most decisive task involved in developing a sustainable urban transport system.

The efficiency of regulations for on-street parking in most European cities is adversely affected by an extensive amount of illegal parking. Several surveys have shown proportions of 30 to 60 per cent illegally parked cars, even in cities where effective traffic management would seem of particular importance, like London.[25]   Amsterdam has taken drastic measures to reduce illegal parking. However, in most cities, politicians are fearful of confronting the problem due to the power of the car lobby, which considers the regulations too rigid and therefore, unjust. Illegal parking is widely misunderstood as peccadillo or even a sport: who is most clever in fee-evasion?

Illegal parking should be stigmatised as improper behaviour, damaging the efficiency of the car-traffic system and the image of the city. Through adequate marketing strategy, enforcement can be transformed from a negative experience for drivers to a positive public service: enforcement provides the chance for the driver to find a legal parking space when and where he needs it.   A psychologically-oriented, "diplomatic" marketing strategy must clearly show that the chance for the driver to find parking at the location he needs and at the price he is willing to pay is highest if effective enforcement guarantees general compliance with established rules.

The main purpose of controls should not be to obtain income from illegal parking fines, but to assure maximum use of limited parking capacity. The economic benefits for the city are: directly, the income from parking fees (payment for which would be less without enforcement), and indirectly, the prosperity of the city centre and the image of a well-organised city.

Originally, the state police was responsible for parking enforcement; however, occupied with many other urgent duties, they could not effectively monitor parking. In many countries, therefore, on-street parking control was transferred to city governments. In Austria, for example, parking enforcement is managed by private firms in 29 per cent of the cities.[26] In Germany, legal stipulations still do not allow the transfer of this "governmental task" to private organisations; for the moment, private organisations may only notify illegal parkers and communicate their identities to the city for prosecution. The city of Berlin, which only introduced fees for on-street parking in the city centre in 1995, has transferred all parking management (including the use of equipment, but excluding the enforcement of measures against illegal parking) to two private entrepreneurial groups (one for the eastern and one for the western central area), which have worked very efficiently as far as economic outcome is concerned.[27]

The number of attendants needed for parking control depends on the proportion of illegally parked cars. If the observance is bad, a high presence will be needed. If the car drivers have learned that they have little chance not to pay, or are charged much higher for attempting to avoid paying fees, the proportion of illegal parking will decrease and the area which can be monitored by each attendant will increase. The income generated from enforcement -- first of all, by the higher proportion of parkers who pay the required fee, and second through the fines -- is greater than the salary expenditure, making staff increases relatively easy. Even so, the number of attendants, in most cities, is still limited due to political reasons.

Parking guidance systems should help to locate the right parking area. In most cases, static information tables are adequate guidance mechanisms. Several large cities have established dynamic parking guidance systems showing the numbers of free parking sites, despite enormous construction- and operation costs[28].

Some cities have divided their centres into sectors as part of traffic calming strategies; if one wants to drive from one sector to another, the ring-road around the city centre must be used (see, for instance, Nuremberg). In this case, it is especially important to inform car-drivers before they enter the city centre, so that they can take the right "entrance" for their destination. Each sector should be denoted by a certain name or colour (for example: "east-sector," "cathedral-sector" or "red-sector") which may facilitate explanations and assist the driver in choosing and finding the appropriate parking sites.

The operation of a parking system in the city centre generally requires considerable advertising[29]. In surveys it was found that most car-drivers had little knowledge about fees, parking sites and conditions. Many prefer to park at the location with which they feel most familiar.

The marketing of parking regulations has been emphasized in this paper, because up to now, these aspects have been largely ignored by administration officials preoccupied with technical concerns. This lack of attention is one of the major reasons for the widespread disorder in parking systems and for the failure of many parking initiatives.

2.4 Salzburg: Example of traffic management success

Even though there is no "traffic paradise", some cities -- such as Strasbourg, Freiburg, Basel, Zurich, Graz and Salzburg -- have proved that persistent efforts to move toward sustainable development can be successful. Salzburg is particularly exemplary in its management of parking.

In Salzburg (population 140 000, capital of the State of Salzburg, Austria), the reorientation of transportation and urban renewal policy began in 1982 with the success of a "green" citizens list in local elections against the traditional parties, all of which had advocated a car-oriented growth policy. The existing transportation plan, which was based on the premise of a strong increase in car traffic, was immediately suspended. This policy change brought with it political controversy that lasted approximately ten years.[30]

The new system of parking management was introduced in four stages from 1990 to 1992 as part of an overall reorientation towards sustainable transport policy (Figure 2). The plan covers 5.2 km² with 26 300 residents and 38 900 employees (43 per cent of all employees). Before the new system was implemented, 7 110 on-street parking facilities existed within the area of parking management, out of which 70 per cent could be used free of charge and without limitation; 11 per cent served short-term parking needs; and 17 per cent goods delivery.

Figure 2. **Parking management in Salzburg**

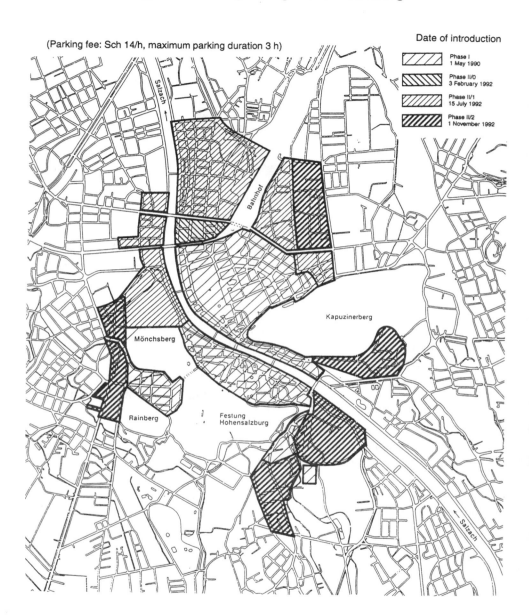

(Parking fee: Sch 14/h, maximum parking duration 3 h)

Date of introduction

Phase I
1 May 1990

Phase II/0
3 February 1992

Phase II/1
15 July 1992

Phase II/2
1 November 1992

With the new system, on-street parking has been reduced by 26 per cent (to 5 290 sites), and parking for delivery purposes by 40 per cent. Areawide time limits (mostly three-hour) and fees (Sch 14 per hour, payable with rechargeable smart cards) are now in effect between 9.00 and 19.00 (initially 8.00 to 18.00) and on Saturday between 9.00 and 13.00. Parking on Sunday is free. (By comparison, in most garages, the fee is Sch 25 per hour). Within this area, 5 200 special permits for unlimited and free parking were distributed to residents (80 per cent), business (16 per cent) and employees (4 per cent).

As a result of these measures, parking duration has decreased, albeit with great divergencies in the areas observed. Overall occupancy levels dropped with the introduction of fees (notwithstanding the reduction in parking supply); later, they increased again, because car-drivers became accustomed to the fees (the occupancy of parking garages remained stable on average due to their relatively high fees). Turnover during a 13-hour period doubled from six to 12 cars per space in retail and mixed-use areas with high demand. In most of these areas, parking facilities were halved, and the amount of parking therefore remained unchanged. Half of all cars parked have special permits. Some long-term parkers have moved to areas without parking management, causing increases in parking duration and occupancy rates; others have switched to other modes of transport. The impact of areawide management on on-street parking has been considerably reduced, however, by the fact that it concerns only 21 per cent of the area's parking supply; 18 per cent of the supply is in public garages and 61 per cent on private land. Relative to total parking supply, the reduction was only 5 per cent.

Despite the low share of on-street parking, the bundle of measures implemented along with the new parking management scheme has clearly improved the overall traffic situation in the city centre: within three years, car traffic to the central area has decreased by 11 per cent (compared to no change in average in the rest of the city), whereas the number of public transport users to the city centre increased (local bus: +5 per cent, regional bus: +20 per cent, regional train: +48 per cent). In addition, bike use has more than doubled (+115 per cent) due to the strong promotion given to this mode of transport in Salzburg.

A survey of the effects of the Salzburg parking management scheme states in its conclusion that all essential goals were achieved (Koch, Wiesinger, 1994, p. 70), including:

--   improvements in necessary car traffic by facilitating search for parking sites;

- reduction in unnecessary car traffic (primarily commuters);
- improvements for the local population (less car traffic, shorter search for parking facilities);
- liberation of residential areas from long-term parkers.

There are, however, still some problems: the area not included in parking management has been facing a higher demand pressure from displaced parking. The use of public parking garages has stagnated due to persistently low fees for kerbside parking. Nevertheless, development of a more sustainable traffic structure throughout Salzburg, particularly in and around the city centre, has been facilitated by the parking management scheme. In this respect, Salzburg is a good example of successful application of integrated strategies.

2.5 Conclusions on parking management

2.5.1 *Combining push-and-pull strategies*

In OECD Europe, most planners and decision-makers now agree that it is neither possible nor desirable to adapt cities to the needs of car traffic; on the contrary, car traffic should be adapted to the city. It is imperative that existing car traffic be evaluated in light of the requirements of the whole urban system. Many surveys have shown that a large proportion of trips made by car could also have been made by other means of transport without difficulty. The objective of traffic management within city centres can no longer be to sustain the flow of all car traffic; planners must now focus exclusively on the needs of necessary car traffic. This can be achieved only if unnecessary car traffic is avoided by "push" strategies, which allow for shortages in street and parking supply in order to create a certain resistance to car use, and to enable planners to distinguish necessary from unnecessary car trips.

This is a very difficult task because it seems to contradict a slogan used especially by the car lobby: "free ride for free citizens". Such a misunderstanding of freedom leads to chaos and causes problems for both the economy and society. Restrictions need not be totalitarian. They can and must be compatible with a free society and (social) market economy. The compatibility of car traffic restrictions with economic prosperity, however, is a matter of even more serious controversy for interest groups and their political allies who claim "no parking = no business" and "car-free city = dead city". Therefore parking management strategies should be based on the co-operation of all groups involved and should be explained to the citizens in a public-awareness marketing campaign (see Rinsma, 1995).

Every push strategy must be accompanied by "pull" strategies that emphasize attractive alternatives to the use of cars. These include:

-- An attractive and modern public transport system, always more economically efficient than expanding car traffic.

-- Favourable conditions for bicycling, which may require infrastructure improvements (especially when biking conditions are jeopardised by growing car traffic). In addition, the image of biking must be transformed from that of a mode of transportation for the poor to an act of freedom and responsibility towards society and environment: opinion leaders and politicians can set such a trend by personal example, as in the case of several Austrian, Dutch, Danish, Swiss and German cities.

-- Pleasing conditions for walking, the most endangered mode of transport. Walking has decreased in western Germany and, after unification, dropped in eastern Germany. In the United States, walking as a means of transport has virtually disappeared.

This paper will not examine the details of these strategies; however, it should be emphasized that they are economically and socially the most effective contributions to solving and preventing parking problems within a co-ordinated pull- and push-strategy.

2.5.2   *Political perspectives*

Due to political pressures and strong ideological and emotional perceptions of parking, the application of strategies for an effective parking system is still very difficult. Obstacles can be found on all political levels in all countries.

For a long time, German federal and state laws were primarily oriented towards facilitating car use and adapting cities to the need of cars. This is illustrated by the building code which requires parking provision with every new building, as well as by laws regulating fees and parking enforcement. Enforcement is often very weak, and penalties for illegal parking have been, and in some respects still are -- too low, especially if compared with penalties for fee-evasion in public transport. It is not widely understood that the damage of illegal parking is much worse than that of illegal rides on public transport, because the former, unlike the latter, negatively impacts the entire system.

Federal, state and municipal governments have highly subsidised the construction of parking garages, often as part of urban renewal schemes. Private enterprises have provided free parking for their employees but not free rides on public transport, even though this would be much cheaper.[31] Retailers often refund portions of parking fees or offer free parking, but oppose the idea of refunding portions of public transport fees (this was only allowed after a long struggle). For decades in Germany, money collected from parking had to be used for improvements in car accessibility (this is no longer necessary). Normally, deficits of public parking garages are not known. In contrast, deficits of public transport are annually discussed as a great sacrifice. It is not understood that public transport is an essential condition for ensuring the fluidity of car traffic in the city.

Parking facilities are considered to be somewhat of a "sacred cow". In most cases, it is very difficult to eliminate a parking site, regardless of how many new facilities have been built in previous years. Conservative politicians try to maximise the volume of parking by arguing for further increases in motorisation. The negative effects of parking are generally grossly underestimated.

It could be said that everyday practices of "motorised" countries inhibit their ability to provide sound advice regarding parking to newly motorising countries. This, however, is too simplistic. One reason is that the car orientation model, first developed in the United States and later copied by all other free-market economies, still has strong appeal and is propagated by powerful interest groups, especially in those nations that have yet to experience its seeming "benefits". There is a great danger that outdated planning models are transferred to newly motorising countries through "western" planning arrogance and paternalism, as has already happened in many developing countries. Indeed, newly motorising countries now have the opportunity to scrutinise and pursue strategies for development of more sustainable traffic systems, better suited to their situations. The willingness to follow more sustainable paths to traffic development may be encouraged by the model of several regions that have been "motorised" for many years and have successfully changed direction:

-- Several cities have stopped adding parking facilities and now redistribute existing parking supply according to general planning goals. Some have even reduced parking supply.

-- Laws have been changed, enabling cities to guide development of car traffic and parking volumes and to enforce parking regulations more effectively.

-- Public transport has received greater support from the political and business communities. Recent initiatives include the introduction of job tickets at a more-or-less reduced price. These tickets are often subsidised by employers who, in turn, reduce parking at their sites and sometimes charge their employees for parking, revenue which in turn can be used to subsidise the job tickets. Other efforts include those to encourage civic pride in the quality of public transport (the slogan in Zurich is: "We are No. 1").

-- The liveability of a city centre is increasingly acknowledged as a higher priority than that of maximum car accessibility.

3. PEDESTRIANISATION AND "CAR-FREE" CITY CENTRES

Large pedestrian zones and city centres with calmer traffic are the most visible signs of a new orientation in urban and transport planning. In many cities, such initiatives have considerably improved the perception of the city centre as "liveable" and economically prosperous. The main purpose of pedestrianisation, however, as compared to access- and parking-management discussed in the previous chapter, is not the reduction of car use, but the reduction of conflicts caused by cars within the city centre. This entails fewer car trips within the city centre through more efficient management of internal circulation and parking. These measures do not reduce accessibility of the city centre by cars; on the contrary, car accessibility -- as well as that of public transport -- are, in many cases, simultaneously improved by these measures. The principal aim of pedestrianisation is to create a more attractive urban environment. Support for this objective has grown, and the concept has spread as its positive effects have been shown.

3.1 Shopping-mall concept as first stage

The first examples of pedestrianisation in Germany date to the 1920s and 30s (e.g. Cologne, Essen) and to the reconstruction of heavily damaged cities after the war (e.g. Dresden, Kassel, Kiel, Stuttgart). The most well-known example of this kind of post-war reconstruction is Lijnbaan in Rotterdam (Netherlands), where Germans had completely demolished the town centre at the beginning of the war; in 1956, a new retail area was built in the centre away from road traffic with an environment especially adapted to pedestrians. In 1961, the League of German Cities (*Deutscher Städtetag*) recommended the pedestrianisation of main shopping streets as a means to protect their attractiveness against the pressures of rapidly growing motorisation. A boom in pedestrian malls began in the mid-1960s, with Cologne and Essen as models.

This early stage can be characterised as an attempt to adapt cities to the demand of car traffic following the model of the American shopping centre (Victor Gruen, an American/Austrian architect and town planner, is the most famous advocate of this concept for the United States). In no way did pedestrianisation put car accessibility at a disadvantage; it was an integral part of a concept to improve accessibility by car. New ring roads or roads parallel to the traditional shopping streets and multi-storey parking garages were seen as the condition for creating the "mall", along with delivery roads located behind the main shopping street. Essen and Kassel are typical examples of how historical city centres that had been heavily damaged by the war were transformed.

Secondary shopping streets with smaller numbers of pedestrians and squares of only historical or social functions for the city were not included in pedestrianisation plans at this stage: it was believed that they were not important enough. Following the architectural model of the American shopping centre, it was also a general belief that streets wider than about 10-12 metres could not be pedestrianised, because pedestrians would "feel lost" and could not see the window displays on both sides simultaneously.

This understanding of pedestrianisation is still typical in a great number of German cities, but even more so in many other parts of the world -- especially in the United States, where pedestrianisation has experienced a relatively modest development and even some failure, due to the weakness of retail in the city centres relative to suburban shopping centres.

3.2 Pedestrian zones as urban cores

3.2.1 Development of new lifestyles

In the 1960s, an increasing orientation toward the service sector characterised the transformation of western economies from industrial to post-industrial. Economic progress enabled growth in personal income and reductions in working time. In socialist economies, this transformation was impeded by the ideologically rigid position of traditional industry and by the inefficiency of the centralised economy, which resisted modernisation.

The changing character of western economies and society has led to new lifestyle preferences, including an increase in self-indulgent values.[32] As a result of these changes, the role of the city centre has evolved, with pedestrian zones increasingly being used and expanded. Visiting the pedestrian zone as an urban core or "living room" means much more than just going shopping: the pedestrian area is appreciated as one would a theatre, where the shopper is the spectator and actor at the same time. This is the new merchandising principle of a society for which the purpose of shopping is not primarily to procure the goods one needs, but to take on a particular lifestyle by buying goods one does not need. This approach requires an appealing environment such as that of American shopping centres, which have evolved into large entertainment areas (one of the most prominent is the Edmonton Mall in Canada and the Mall of America in Minneapolis).

Well-preserved historical city centres such as those of Bonn and Heidelberg, and city centres that were reconstructed after the war, according to the historical specifications of streets and buildings (e.g. Aachen, Freiburg or Nuremberg), are ideal for this new shopping lifestyle (see Friedrichs, 1992). They have increasingly developed in this direction by adding secondary and more specialised shopping streets and arcades to the pedestrian district and providing islands of relaxation and entertainment (see Florian, 1990). Arcades characterise the Hamburg city centre and the famous Dusseldorf Boulevard "Kö", that still allows car-access. Munich and Leipzig have an especially long tradition of developing arcades and are again expanding this system from arcades to shopping centres. In Germany, planned downtown shopping centres in most cases are well integrated into the overall pattern of the city centre (see Heineberg, Mayr, 1995) and therefore do not detract visitors from the surrounding streets as often happens in North-American cities. These "naturally evolving" city centres can adapt more easily and gradually to changing demands, whereas monolithic shopping centres are at greater risk of becoming outmoded and shabby and therefore require expensive remodelling with time.

Recent lifestyle changes are not limited to shopping and spare time; they include a more critical awareness of the negative impact of car traffic on the physical environment. Political support has grown for initiatives aiming to reduce traffic congestion in city centres. Broader planning goals (see Monheim, 1975) and new lifestyles have formed a mutual feed-back process, with the gradual expansion of pedestrian areas and the abolition of through-traffic in the city centre. This can be understood as a social and political learning process leading to the rediscovery of old values of urban life in public open spaces.[33] The following examples of pedestrianisation illustrate the development of pedestrian zones as core areas for urban life.

3.2.2 Munich

The most prominent German city to adapt this new lifestyle model is Munich (population: 1 241 000). In the 1960s, Munich became the "unofficial capital" ("*heimliche Hauptstadt*") of Germany, where most Germans expressed a desire to live and work. The city used the Olympic Games in 1972 to reinforce this position. The two most extensive infrastructure improvements for the Olympic Games were the upgrading of public transport with the construction of a subway and suburban railway network and the pedestrianisation of the most prominent urban axes. The secret of Munich's success was not so much the extension of pedestrian streets, but their new character: the main shopping street was quite large (in some places more than 30m wide)[34] with a varied ground-plan and prominent squares at each side (Stachus and Marienplatz). The setting for this site comprised historical buildings such as churches, the old and new town halls, and a medieval town gate at the entrance, camouflaging the highest concentration of big department and chain stores along this road.

The Munich pedestrian district soon became a model throughout Germany, if not world-wide. Its great success -- notably economic -- led to its gradual expansion beyond the main shopping mall. Pedestrianisation increasingly included secondary shopping streets, such as the famous Farmers Market ("*Viktualien-markt*") and areas of historical and tourist value (e.g. "Platzl" in front of the Hofbräuhaus). It also put an end to the remaining possibilities for cars to drive across the historical city centre.[35]

In the beginning, despite broad support for pedestrianisation from citizens and visitors, there was recurring opposition from shopkeepers and car-oriented lobby groups. Many shopkeepers feared decreasing business. Others feared that the increasing attractiveness of the area would accelerate the already-strong displacement of local small- and medium-sized retailers by national and international chain stores due to an explosion of shop rents which the smaller retailers could not afford. As a result, when the political majority changed in the city council in 1978 from the Social Democrats to the conservative CSU, plans for further pedestrianisation were curtailed. One "casualty" was Sendlinger Straße, an important secondary shopping street which carries 3 000-5 000 pedestrians per hour. Instead of the planned pedestrianisation, redesign was limited to making the street more pleasant without banning cars. Even when in 1984 the political majority changed to "red-green" (Social Democrat-Green parties), plans for further pedestrianisation remained more modest than they were in the middle of the 1970s, and in 1994, were completely dropped for tactical reasons. In 1992, however, an extensive plan for a much larger car-ban was surprisingly proposed by the powerful car manufacturer BMW, which is located in Munich. (See Janssen, 1993 and Schlütter and Schwerdtfeger, 1993).

In 1995, the Munich pedestrian district was comprised of approximately 7 km of streets and squares complemented by a large number of arcades (Figure 3). This pedestrian area has now reached a certain maturity, even though further extensions are well imaginable. However, the attractiveness of the area has resulted in exploding shop rents, that have, in turn, led to the expansion of chain stores to the detriment of shops with local identity and originality. This is a problem common to virtually all successful shopping streets in European OECD countries that have been pedestrianised.

Another problem accompanying the success of the main shopping streets is that the numbers of pedestrians at peak times have grown beyond capacity, with more than 20 000 per hour on Saturday, more than 100 000 per day on normal days (see Monheim, 1987), 150 000 on Thursday and more than 200 000 per day at Christmas time. As a result, the city has had to remove much of the street furniture which originally had been considered necessary in order to prevent the feeling of emptiness in the broad street. Furthermore, the pavement had to be replaced after 25 years because of ageing and wear caused by delivery trucks. These efforts were made in order to preserve the key role of the city centre in urban life.

3.2.3 Nuremberg

Another example of the development of a pedestrian district into an areawide system is the city of Nuremberg (population 499 000). Its large old town (1.4 km², 14 000 residents) is still surrounded by the medieval town wall and moat. Eighty per cent of the buildings were destroyed during the war. Nonetheless, citizens rejected proposals to adapt the old town to modern traffic needs in contrast to many other cities. They continued their local building traditions without copying the historical buildings, with the exception of some churches and public buildings.[36]

Figure 3. **Pedestrianisation in Munich**

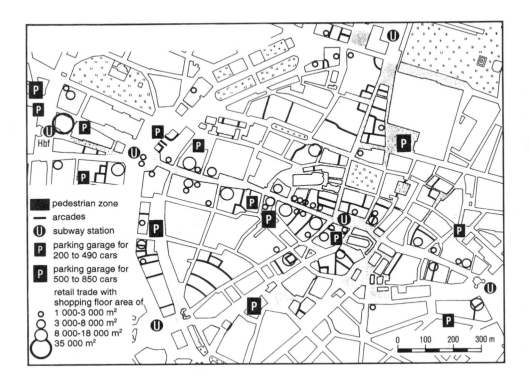

Pedestrianisation began in 1967 with a narrow shopping street. In 1972, a newly elected and progressive city council with a Social Democrat majority, knowing that a sizeable majority of citizens wanted an extensive enlargement of the pedestrian district, decided to close the main roads running north-south and east-west through the central shopping area. City planners were in opposition, because they were sure that the roads surrounding the city centre would not be able to carry the additional traffic. To the surprise of all, only about one quarter of the former traffic was added to the remaining roads (Table 8). The main reason for this was probably a decrease in numbers of cars seeking parking facilities and a drop in the number of short-distance trips within the city centre, as car drivers now use the garage most convenient for them and do all their business on foot within the city centre, given the good walking conditions.

In the following years, pedestrianisation continued without major event. The next "big push" came in 1988, when the last through-road in the northern part of the old town was discontinued, leading to strong controversy with the business community and their conservative allies. Retailers displayed posters in their windows complaining that access to the city by car was interrupted, and that Nuremberg would become a provincial, backwater village. However, surveys carried out before and after demonstrated that business was not damaged and that additional car traffic appearing on the remaining roads was only 29 per cent of the former volume (some residential areas were hurt, however).

In 1992, the remaining possibilities for driving through the southern part of the city centre were blocked. This led to a subdivision of the city centre into five segments. Cars driving from one segment to the other had to use the ring road. This again caused the business community to complain, especially since delivery and service-vehicles were hindered. The number of cars entering the old town decreased by 13 per cent (-15 650 cars in 16 hours) from 1991 to 1993, exclusively due to the abolishment of through-traffic, whereas the traffic for which the city centre was the destination remained unchanged. This can be concluded from the number of cars parked in public garages, which increased by 6 per cent, and the constant income from on-street parking fees. The reduction of traffic volume within the city centre was more noticeable: on those streets where through-traffic was considerable, nearly half as many cars were counted as before (-48 per cent and -47 per cent; together -11 000 cars). On the three tangential main thoroughfares, traffic increased by 15 per cent (+ 7 200 cars) and 6 per cent (+ 2 000 cars) respectively and remained unchanged on the third. Speed is now limited to 30 km/h throughout the city centre. The number of traffic accidents with persons injured or heavy damage decreased by 23 per cent, both within the city centre and on the ring road in contrast to the 11 per cent average for the whole city.

Table 8. Traffic dislocations in the Nuremberg city centre after pedestrianisation

Streets closed to cars	Years of elevation	Hours of elevation	No. of cars before street closure	Additional cars in parallel roads after street closure	
	before/ after				added cars as % of former cars
Museumsbrücke +Fleischbrücke	1972/ 1973	24h	22 500	+5 400	+24
Karolinenstraße + Kaiserstraße	1972/ 1973	24h	20 900	+5 400	+26
Bankgasse/ Adlerstraße	1982/ 1983	24h	8 400	+1 700	+20
Rathausplatz	1988/ 1989	16h	24 600	+7 100	+29

The pedestrian district is now more than 8 km long, with arcades and footpath connections (5 km) along the river and the moat. Its effect on traffic reduction covers the entire old town. Access by public transport to the old town is good, with the railway and tram stopping at the entrances of the old town and two subway stations in the centre of the main shopping area. There are also improvements for cycling and walking to the city centre from the surrounding areas. Regardless of the restrictions for driving through the centre, access by car is still very easy due to parking garages located in each segment. There are 3 700 spaces in public garages; 1 100 metered and 1 200 non-metered spaces accessible to visitors on road; 1 700 spaces retained for residents in areas where housing is still important; and 6 900 spaces on private property (5 100 for business). On-road parking demand has been reduced by raising the fees to DM 5.00/h. In order to protect residents from car noise, non-resident cars are excluded at night from an area near the castle where pubs and restaurants are concentrated (total length: 1 km).

The success of the pedestrianised city centre in Nuremberg is evident in the high number of shops that have been modernised and new shops established, as well as in increases in pedestrian traffic. On normal shopping days, for example, the number of pedestrians has grown from 25 400 to 39 000 during the period 6.00 to 22.00, and from 40 000 to 49 100 from 1975 to 1993 in two principal shopping streets. Even more spectacular increases have occurred on Saturdays before Christmas: in the main shopping street leading to the Christkindels-Market, the number of pedestrians grew from 8 000 to about 23 000 in one hour; in other main shopping streets, numbers of pedestrian shoppers grew from about 6 000 to 13 000 in one hour. This increase, cannot be explained exclusively by pedestrianisation, however; it is the result of a feed-back process including improved quality of life of the city through pedestrianisation; reduced car traffic; urban renewal; better accessibility to the area by public transport, cars, cycling and walking. In addition, enhanced economic attractiveness due to investments in the retail and services sectors has resulted in a success-story for the city centre. Even the long-lasting attacks of the business community on the city administration finally seemed to give way to more positive discussions of models for a successful future of the city centre (Stadt Nürnberg, 1995).

3.3 Traffic-calmed streets

Pedestrianisation always entails complete exclusion of private cars, even though delivery trucks are usually allowed at certain hours and, in some cases, access to a garage or a hotel within the pedestrianised area permitted. One possibility for expanding benefits for pedestrians to a larger area without banning cars is the traffic-calmed street. There are two alternative models for traffic calming:

-- mixing principle: pedestrians and cars have equal rights and may jointly use the whole street. Cars must be driven at walking speed and can be parked only at specifically designated sites; normally, it is assumed that the maximum number of cars per hour should not exceed 200, but there are several cases in which this number is more than 300 cars/h;

-- separation principle: pavements remain separate from the carriageway, but the speed is limited areawide to 20 km/h or, in highly sensitive areas, to 10 km/h.

These regulations are sometimes implemented in order to protect streets surrounding the pedestrian district and sometimes instead of pedestrianisation. The former is true in Günzburg (19 300 residents), where the central market street was first traffic-calmed but later had to be closed definitively because of persistently high numbers of cars. The latter has been implemented in the old town of Dinkelsbühl (11 300 residents), where the medieval urban structure has been preserved, and tourism is considerable on weekends. After several trials, an areawide speed-limit of 10 km/h was introduced in 1989, immediately after this was made possible by modification of the federal traffic code. In addition, the old town is closed to cars on Sunday from 11.00 to 17.00 between May and October (both examples are explained more in detail by Monheim, 1995a).

In some cases, traffic-calmed streets alternate with a pedestrian street every day, allowing car access during the morning and excluding it in the afternoon when the numbers of pedestrians increase and passers-by want to stroll at a more relaxed pace (one example is the town of Marktredwitz, population 20 000 -- see Monheim, 1987).

The examples above and others presented by Monheim (1987) show that the areawide implementation of traffic-calming regulations in city centres is typical for small and medium-sized cities (this is not the case when traffic-calming regulations are used for residential areas). One reason is the weaker retail structure and the lesser willingness of car-users to walk longer distances from parking sites to shops: they still expect to park immediately in front of the shop door. Empirical surveys have shown, however, that this is in part a prejudice, and that attitudes can be changed if the environment is appealing. The other -- and probably more important -- reason is explained by the local political climate: due to the smaller size of the city, retailers can more easily pressure city counsellors and impede decisions they do not support, which they are less able to do in larger cities.

3.4 Areawide access-management for city centres

The areas surrounding pedestrian districts in many cities suffer from increased car traffic due to delivery trucks and cars being diverted from the pedestrian zone and access to parking garages. There are several examples where this problem is being tackled by strategies of areawide access control.

3.4.1 Bologna

There are many traffic-restricted zones (*"zona a traffico limitato - ZTL"*) in Italy.[37] The most well-known example of areawide access control is the city of Bologna (population 450 000). The city's medieval town centre is very large (4.3 km²), well preserved, and clearly defined by its former ramparts (8 km). Urban renewal programmes have been implemented to preserve the lively character of the old town, where 54 000 Bologna residents live and

80 000 work. Since 1972, initiatives have been taken to reduce traffic volumes resulting from high car ownership levels and the low carrying capacity of the road network. In a 1984 referendum, 70 per cent voted for limiting access to the area. The "traffic-restricted zone", in effect from 7.00 to 20.00, was introduced definitively in 1989. However, the numerous exemption permits which have existed from the beginning of this initiative have limited its effectiveness. There are 10 000 holders of private parking spaces, about 25 000 resident cars and 15 000 vehicles for delivery, firms and services. The resident permits allow unlimited parking (only in the area in which one lives), and business vehicles can park for a maximum of 1/2 hour. Visitors from outside the Bologna region and hotel guests can drive into the centre, but only a very limited number of parking spaces with a maximum standing time of 90 minutes is available.

The pedestrian zone encompasses the intersection of the two main axes, the main square and some smaller streets (about 2 km). Accessibility to the city-centre was assured by improved public transport, including park-and-ride facilities in the urban periphery and some parking close to the ramparts. The volume of car-traffic in 1989 was reduced significantly, if only private cars are considered: by 60 per cent compared to 1981. At the same time, public transport use increased. Since 1989, however, car traffic has risen again due to the enormous number of exemptions and permits along with weak enforcement. According to Topp (1994), it has reached *"perhaps 90 per cent of the original levels";* therefore, *"new plans are being prepared to secure traffic reduction in the old town".*

3.4.2   Lubeck

In Germany, Lubeck (population 215 000) was the first city to test a "car-free" city centre that, in reality, is an area of limited access by car. The old town is located on an island (14 500 residents, 1.2 km²). Its medieval character has been well preserved, despite some destruction caused by war and street expansion to accommodate the then-perceived needs of car traffic. In 1988, it was named to the UNESCO list of world cultural heritage sites.

Pedestrianisation began in 1963 but made little progress, due to a very conservative and traditional decision-making process (in 1989, only 1.4 km had been completed). Great efforts were made to improve accessibility, first by car and later by bus. The traffic situation worsened so much, however, that in 1989, after lengthy discussions, it was decided to test a "car-free" city centre on six Saturdays with long shopping hours (10.00-18.00) once every month. Public transport, including federal rail and park-and-ride, was improved, all multi-storey garages remained accessible and the number of open parking areas

111

close to the historical area was increased (Figure 4). This resulted in even better accessibility. Public transport, taxis and handicapped were given free access from the beginning; later, delivery vehicles, residents and hotel-guests were also granted free access. If a car passed the access gate before 10.00, it was free to circulate until it left the restricted area.

The "car-free" centre experiment proved to be a great success. After nine months, due to large numbers of tourists, the initiative was introduced on all weekends (Saturday and Sunday); and in May 1995, the decision was taken to expand it in 1996 to all days of the week.

3.4.3   Aachen

The purpose of areawide access management, in contrast to pure pedestrianisation, is the protection of areas around the main shopping district -- primarily the residents of these areas, who make an important contribution to the livelihood of the city centre -- from the negative effects of car traffic caused by visitors. One of the main problems with access management, however, is controlling access. The willingness of car drivers to acknowledge access restrictions in most cities is weak. Therefore, attendants must be present to ensure that only authorised vehicles enter the area. The example of Aachen demonstrates the problems of marketing an areawide access control and, in this case, the necessity of applying a sector system and parking management in order to reduce traffic.

Aachen (population 245 000) has a very large old town (2.2 km² within the ring of boulevards), a considerable part of which has remained residential (35 000 residents). Parts of the old town are dominated by retail, offices and the Technical University; others are mixed or primarily residential.

Aachen was heavily damaged during the Second World War. Post-war reconstruction was successful in recreating the city's historic atmosphere, especially in the older and more central part; however, unlike Nuremberg, much more room was given to the then-perceived needs of car traffic, by widening the inner ring road and thoroughfares through the old town. Some of these plans date, in fact, to the 1930s.

Pedestrianisation began in the 1950s with some small streets and the closure of the main shopping street (at that time, a tram route) during the afternoon (15.30 to 19.00). It was gradually expanded to historical lanes and squares around the old town hall and cathedral. Even though the network finally totalled 3.3 km, serious conflicts remained because the cohesion of the different

Figure 4. "Car-free" city centre in Lubeck

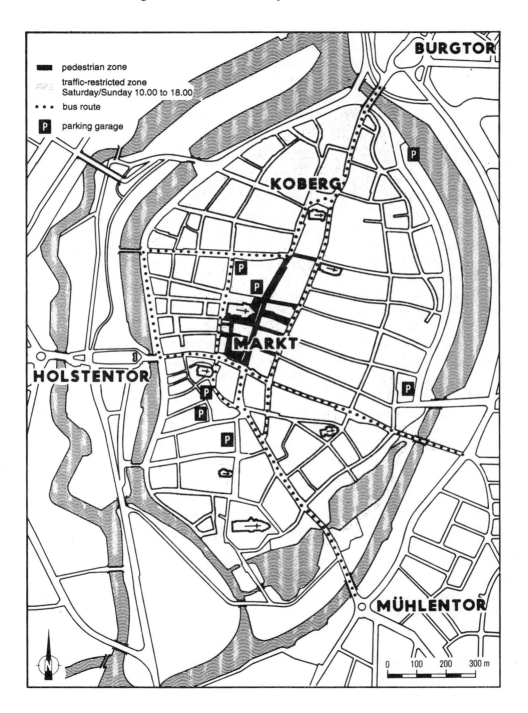

sections was undermined by the main thoroughfare and queues of cars that were backed up at the most central parking garages on weekends (Figure 5).

Official town planning in the 1970s and 80s did not question the thoroughfare. The majority in the city council changed in 1989 from conservatives to a "red-green" coalition. Shortly thereafter, a decision was made to close the thoroughfare and to preserve the residential areas around the shopping district from car traffic by restricting access for cars.

The new traffic management scheme was widely debated among all interest groups including retailers. A compromise was reached, and the new scheme was introduced in 1991 as a six-month experiment (Figure 5). It was limited to Saturdays (smaller traffic volumes), and was in operation only between 10.00 and 15.00 (17.00 on the first Saturday of every month). Access to parking was allowed on designated roads, except for two garages that created too many problems. On-street parking was allowed only to residents who were exempted from restrictions. Park-and-ride was established at six locations in the urban periphery, with frequent bus service to the city centre; its use, however, remained modest.[38] In addition, public transport was improved and made more attractive by a "happy day" group ticket (DM 5.00).

Even though access to the city centre by car remained very good and was improved for all other means of transport, there was widespread confusion about whether or not the city centre was accessible by car on Saturday: barriers had been placed around the area of limited access; politicians were urging visitors not to come to the centre by car; and retailers were complaining about the access limitations. Retailers were outraged by the drop in business on Saturdays, despite the fact that such decreases were largely outweighed by increases on other days of the week. One reason for the fluctuation of commercial activity was the general extension of service-hours on Thursday until 20.30 and the reduction of service-hours on Saturday morning by many shops. In any case, as a survey in the capture area showed, only a very small group of customers changed their preferred shopping area to other locations.

The attacks of retailers against the initiatives of the town planners and the "red-green" city council continued; however, in the 1994 elections, the majority in the council did not change. Finally, in May 1995, an agreement was reached, whereby the thoroughfare dividing the central shopping area would be closed definitively to private cars in 1996 and the street redesigned according to the needs of pedestrians and buses. Access to the surrounding areas will no longer be limited; however, there will be no through-traffic. The movement of pedestrians will be facilitated by additional pedestrian streets. Pedestrian

Figure 5. "Pedestrian-friendly" zone in Aachen

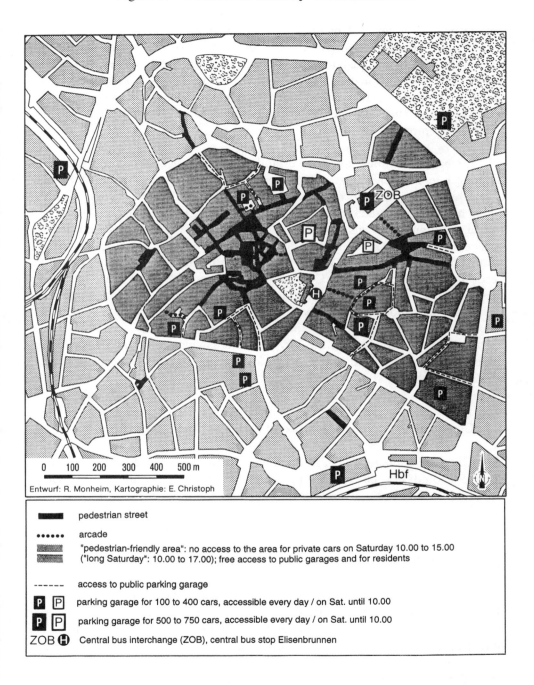

▬▬	pedestrian street
••••••	arcade
▨▨	"pedestrian-friendly area": no access to the area for private cars on Saturday 10.00 to 15.00 ("long Saturday": 10.00 to 17.00); free access to public garages and for residents
------	access to public parking garage
P ⊡	parking garage for 100 to 400 cars, accessible every day / on Sat. until 10.00
P ⊡	parking garage for 500 to 750 cars, accessible every day / on Sat. until 10.00
ZOB ⊕	Central bus interchange (ZOB), central bus stop Elisenbrunnen

Entwurf: R. Monheim, Kartographie: E. Christoph

underpasses will be replaced by surface crossings. Parking will be reorganised in the long run: of the two least accessible garages, one will be converted into long-term parking and the other replaced by a shopping arcade. New garages for up to 1 000 short-term parkers will be built at sites that are more easily accessible. Public transport will be further improved. The proposal to re-introduce the tram that had been removed in the 1960s is supported by the business community. It is hoped that this agreement will help to overcome the negative image caused by the long-standing disputes and bring investments back to the city centre.

In conclusion, the attempt to establish areawide access-control (limited to Saturday) in Aachen failed. This was not caused by problems of reduced accessibility. Rather, the barriers around the area of limited access -- each of which had to be enforced by guards -- created a hostile appearance. Attempts to find a solution were unsuccessful due to political divergencies between the conservative business community and the more- progressive city council and administration. As a result, it was not possible to create and market a positive, "pedestrian-friendly" image. Compromise occurred only after the elections for the city council confirmed the existing coalition. The new solution is similar to the Nuremberg model: it will be in effect all days of the week. Rather than erecting "artificial" barriers to the area, pedestrian streets will function as "natural" barriers, protecting the city centre areawide from car traffic through the introduction of traffic zones and parking management that gives priority to residents.

3.5 Conclusions on pedestrianisation and "car-free" city centres

The development of pedestrian zones, traffic calming and areawide access control should not be viewed as simply traffic engineering tasks, but as important factors in the overall development of the city centre, if not the entire city.[39] Comprehensive discussions on planning models for the city centre are necessary, and must be repeated every 10-15 years according to changes in the social, economic, and political climate and the results of measures already taken. The cities of Gottingen and Nuremberg are good examples of this process[40].

Traffic in city centres can be reduced considerably without jeopardising their accessibility and prosperity. In fact, favourable conditions for pedestrian movement in a city centre have proven to be the best condition for success. The attractiveness of the city centre depends on its ability to offer something special: for example, a wide range of functions (shopping, business, services, entertainment, public and private administrations) and a distinctiveness of urban design -- defined by a variety of streets and squares, and old and new, small and large, private and public buildings. Cars, therefore, should not dominate, but instead integrate into the urban fabric: measures to effect this integration include traffic-calming with limited, low-speed car access.

The extent of pedestrianisation, traffic calming and access limitations cannot be determined through fixed rules. Such is dependent upon the individual structure of the city centre and a vision for the future. In principle, it is necessary to first envision a gradual development towards long-term goals, a process in which every measure and strategy is carefully tested along the way. Planners must be sure to avoid any intermediary step that diverts resources from pre-established goals. There are many examples, however, in which this principle has been ignored, resulting in unnecessary expenditures and delays, or the complete abandonment of the goal.

4. RECOMMENDATIONS

The following recommendations present elements of a new traffic policy for city centres. There is no simple formula. Above all, it must be clear that it is impossible to solve problems with isolated measures; the only reasonable approach is an integrated strategy combining pull-and-push measures in all areas of planning.

The first and most fundamental goal, yet probably most difficult to achieve, is to minimise the growth of motorisation. The pressure for increasing motorisation is often exerted by the development of suburban housing areas with relatively low densities, poor local service infrastructure, limited employment opportunities, and unattractive public transport. Another stimulus for motorisation is the establishment of large free-standing shopping centres. In eastern Germany, shopping centres have become the symbol of the new prosperity. Their number and size have grown explosively to the detriment of the old established city centres. It is important to control these developments by urban and regional planning. This requires mechanisms for balancing interests between the city and its capture area.

There are different strategies for minimising the growth of motorisation. Several countries such as Denmark, Singapore and Hong Kong impose very high taxes on the purchase of cars. In other countries, car-buyers are required to provide evidence of the availability of a private parking site, as is the case in some Japanese conurbations. Car sharing (the ownership of a private car by a co-operative or similar organisation) provides a car for a larger group of persons, making it unnecessary for each member to buy -- and thus to park -- his or her own car. In Zurich, the public transport company initiated a car-sharing programme in 1995 as part of the public transportation system.

A high-quality public transport system that can compete with the image of the private car, also contributes to the alleviation of pressure to buy and use cars. This includes not only a good infrastructure and service, but also attractive fees -- especially monthly tickets such as "job tickets" -- and public awareness campaigns, which provide information and create positive associations with public transport: pride of a new bus or tram should be as strong as the pride of a new car.

Last but not least, it is important to increase public awareness of the problems caused by motorisation. Car ownership is very closely linked to a feeling of freedom and economic well-being. This ideological foundation causes the society to ignore the high price it pays. City centres are the areas most vulnerable to chaotic traffic conditions. Parking management (as a push-strategy) combined with favourable conditions for walking, cycling and public transport (as pull-strategies) are the most effective means for assuring the accessibility and "liveability" of city centres.

Parking management requires primarily parking fees and time limits combined with special regulations for residents. The fees should be set according to the market value of parking based on demand and supply, with maximum fees in the most central areas. Payment of fees and time limits should be enforced, otherwise, parking management is ineffective (if goods are not paid for, a business will not survive).

The provision of on-street parking must be compared to the other requirements of public open spaces. Shopping streets and squares of important historical and social functions should be gradually freed of cars in order to ensure that they fulfil their true purpose.

Most parking garages do not pay for their investment and operation costs, and the justification for public subsidy of garages is a subject for debate. One alternative source of funding might be revenues collected from on-street parking and private builders, in particular, those unable to build the parking lots required for new constructions at their sites. Private investment in parking garages might also be a solution, as long as the site is carefully chosen in order to avoid creating congestion on access roads. Parking garages are most successful if they are close to the prime shopping area. However, there is a high probability for conflict within this immediate area, which often includes historical streets and buildings, and with plans for expansion of pedestrian zones and traffic calming schemes for the city centre. Therefore, the location of parking garages must be decided very carefully.

Pedestrianisation and "car-free" city centres must be integrated into broader planning concepts if their aim is to achieve sustainable urban development and not merely the exclusion of cars from the central shopping area. These measures are most effective if they embrace the entire city centre with a gradual reduction of car accessibility. It is neither possible nor desirable to pedestrianise every street within the city centre. Thus, pedestrian streets can function as a strategic network connecting all relevant parts of the city centre (not only from a shopping point of view, but also from historic and urban design perspectives) and can forestall through-traffic with a system of traffic zones.

The development of pedestrian zones, similar to that of the transportation system, is the result of a political process. The widespread public support of pedestrianisation and traffic calming in the long run renders possible the success of these measures, despite the usual opposition from business and car lobbies. This essentially explains why in a period of about 30 years, cities in Germany and several neighbouring countries were able to develop comprehensive systems for traffic calming in their city centres -- systems which continue their development today. Their experience must be seen within the context of more far-reaching measures to reduce dependency on car accessibility.

In conclusion, it should be emphasized that isolated actions should be avoided: a broad strategy must be developed with interdependent, mutually reinforcing measures. The greatest danger for the city centre is the belief that more cars mean more prosperity, a path that has been followed for decades in "western" societies (and is still followed in most countries throughout the world). Transportation planning has been misunderstood for too long as an engineering task to facilitate the easy flow of motorised traffic. It is now being acknowledged that planners and engineers have to carry out/orient their work towards political goals set by society, and that the primary goal has to be the sustainability of the urban system.

5. COMMENTS ON THE TRAFFIC SITUATION IN BUCHAREST

Bucharest offers today's visitor a glimpse of the city's splendour during the first three decades of this century, when it developed its reputation the "Paris of Eastern Europe": this heritage can serve as the basis on which to revive civic pride and a sense of the city's uniqueness. Bucharest is greatly threatened, however, by unrestricted growth in car traffic. The boulevards, essential strategic elements for the recreation of the historic splendour of the city, and the city's historic buildings, many of which are under restoration, are increasingly suffering from traffic congestion and air and noise pollution. Pedestrians are not enticed to stroll leisurely and enjoy the city. A policy for sustainable traffic development, the most economically efficient development policy, must be adopted for Bucharest, based on a mixture of mutually supporting strategies that includes:

1. priority for public transport: this includes bus lanes and separate tracks for trams wherever possible, priority at traffic lights, and systematic co-ordination with the metro;

2. favourable conditions for walking and cycling: the latter is often said to be nonsensical in large cities, however, through decisive policy, the very attractive city of Munich, was able to double the share of bicycle trips from 6 per cent to 12 per cent within approximately ten years and to further increase this share to 15 per cent;

3. parking management with fees for visitors, special regulations for residents and goods delivery and virtually no parking within public areas for commuters: these initiatives help not only to reduce traffic congestion at peak hours, but also to maintain the accessibility of cars to the city centre.

4. pedestrianisation of some historic areas, i.e. the small streets and squares of the city centre that might attract shoppers, strollers, and tourists; areawide traffic calming (speed limit 30 km or less) in all central areas with the exception of the main thoroughfares, which should be upgraded as tree-lined boulevards with good pavements.

The implementation of such a policy requires an intense process of information dissemination and mediation. All interested groups should be included in this process. In many cities, the creation of an attractive urban environment has proven to be an ideal instrument for fostering optimism among the population. Such developments are of special importance in former socialist countries, which otherwise will have even more difficulty in mobilising the enormous resources necessary to move forward. This is true especially for a capital like Bucharest, which serves as the point of reference and as a model for all of Romania.

NOTES

1.   I am deeply grateful to Kristal Edwards, University of California at Santa Cruz, who corrected the English of my first and second drafts and who has also intensely discussed the contents of this paper.

2.   The limited length of this paper allows only a short overview. The references quoted provide a wide range of titles, enabling the reader to further explore the issues presented in this paper.

3.   The controversial discussions on increasing mobility, especially, on increasing trip distances and share of cars, has recently re-emerged in German transportation journals with a contribution by Topp (1994b) and comments by Cerwenka (1994), Schaaff (1995) and Willeke (1995).

4.   The design of these surveys has been developed by Socialdata, a private research institute directed by Brög, which has achieved a leading role in research on mobility and related policies.

5.   Among very large cities (more than 500 000 residents), high public transport use and low car use can be observed in Hamburg and Munich, and, to a certain degree, Bremen, Hanover, Leipzig and Stuttgart. The opposite is seen in Essen, the most important city in the old industrialised and now relatively depressed Ruhr-conurbation, where car users clearly dominate, especially as concerns the average of all trips to the centre (46 per cent compared to 19 per cent public transport).

    In slightly smaller cities (more than 250 000 residents), the highest dominance of public transport can be found in the wealthy Swiss "financial capital" of Zurich, which is famous for its excellent public transport, based mainly on trams: 67 per cent on average and 74 per cent among shoppers; only 11 per cent and 6 per cent respectively travel by car, which is much less than walking and cycling (22 per cent and 20 per cent). In western Germany, Nuremberg has the highest share of public transport and the lowest of cars. Again, two cities from the Ruhr-area, Gelsenkirchen and Bochum, respectively, have the strongest car-orientation. On top is Gelsenkirchen with 57 per cent on average and 55 per cent (shoppers) compared to only 13 per cent travelling by public transport.

High public transport use is also observed in the smaller eastern German cities of Schwerin and Rostock, as well as in the western German city of Kassel: all have good tram systems. The lowest shares can be found again in the Ruhr-area, with Bottrop and Recklinghausen "on the bottom". The highest share of car users can be found in Saarbrücken, the capital of the Saar-State, another old, industrialised and now depressed area, with 60 per cent on average and 58 per cent among shoppers. Very low shares of car users, especially among shoppers, can be found in the Austrian cities of Graz, Innsbruck and Salzburg and in the western German city of Freiburg (11 per cent and 19 per cent respectively).

Apel and Lehmbrock, 1990, have shown in more detail that prosperous cities are less dependent on car use.

Table 4 is based on surveys which are conducted regularly by the Association of Large and Medium-sized Retailers in Germany (BAG). Even though the latter does not represent all customers, but only those visiting these types of stores (mainly department stores), they are a useful source for observing structures and trends. The survey includes all visitors, whether they live in the city, the capture area or at greater distances.

In Germany, it is very often said that cars seeking parking spaces may account for up to 70 per cent of total traffic in city centres, however, there is no clear statistical evidence of this. A study on the effectiveness of the parking guidance system in Frankfurt a.M., by Boltze and Puzicha (1995), has revealed detailed data for the day and the rush hours: on a "long" shopping Saturday, out of all traffic in the city centre, an average of 13 per cent is seeking parking facilities (7 per cent of which park on the street) and 20 per cent during the rush hours (9 per cent of which park on the street).

9.   See Apel, Lehmbrock 1990, Table 1. Very low shares of private parking can be observed in Milan (17 per cent), Amsterdam (20 per cent) and Bern (25 per cent) which have historical and very densely constructed centres.

10.   Munich and Nuremberg are presently the only cities charging the maximum fee of DM 5.00/h, which is allowed by state law in Bavaria. In other German states, DM 4.00/h is the maximum.

11.   Previous parking fees of DM 0.20/h were abolished in 1982 as a populist action by the then conservative Lord Mayor, despite very high parking demand. Many other cities at this time had increased fees to DM 1.00/h.

12.   Out of all cars observed, 27 per cent parked no longer than 15 minutes in the one-hour zone and 17 per cent in the two-hour zone. Thirty-nine per cent parked longer than one hour in the one-hour zone and 24 per cent longer than two hours in the two-hour zone, many of them (but not all) holding a resident permit. Out of the theoretically available parking capacity, 95 per cent was used (average occupancy). That means that the chance to find a free parking site was very low, resulting in a high proportion of unsuccessful search-traffic.

13.   Throughout the day, cars leaving the centre on the three main access roads were counted and drivers were asked randomly for the purpose and duration of their stay. The answers were weighted for each hour with the total numbers. This makes it possible to say how many cars were parked for how long and for which purposes (Table 7, last row).

14.   Up to now, Socialdata has been the only research group to provide such information systematically; see also Chapter 2.1.1 above.

15.   In Munich, there are nine public parking garages for 2 600 cars within the historical city centre (20 more are located in its perimeter) (Sonntag, 1991). The parking capacity in relation to the size of the conurbation is relatively small (half that of several cities with about 500 000 residents). Nonetheless, in these nine garages during the week, the maximum occupancy averages only around 80 per cent, except Thursday at 19.00 when it reaches 85 per cent (Figure 1). Only

on Saturday is the entire capacity filled from 11.00 onwards. Some garages, however, are more often occupied to full capacity, especially a garage belonging to a department store. A short overview of Munich's parking strategy is given by Tehnik (1995).

16. For more details on planning, construction and operation of public parking garages, see the paper edited by *Bundesverband der Park- und Garagenhäuser e.V.*, 1994.

17. A special example of park-and-ride has been realised by the BMW car-factory on the outskirts of Munich: on weekends and evenings, the employee parking garage, which is located close to a subway station, can be used by the visitors of the city centre. Up to now, however, the number of users remains far behind expectations despite extensive advertising.

18. See Suchy, 1992 *and Vereinigung für Stadt-, Regional- und Landesplanung* 1995.

19. The necessity to win public support for parking policy and the success obtained with such a strategy (at a difference to the failure of former policies "from above") has been illustrated convincingly by Rinsma (1995) with the example of Enschede, Netherlands.

Following completion of this paper, a detailed study on "resistance against the implementation of areawide parking management concepts" was published by Schuster (1995). It starts from experiences with implementation of a parking concept in Frankfurt and develops a broad view of the political process among the groups involved (the author worked with a private consultancy in charge of developing the concept). The book also contains an extensive bibliography.

20. The necessity to orient parking policy for the city centre towards "qualified demand" has already been stressed in 1973 by a special commission of the German State Ministries on Building, Housing, and Town Planning (ARGEBAU): see Innenministerium Baden-Württemberg, 1974, and Monheim, 1975, p. 5.

21. The parking policy of public and private employers in Austria, Germany, and Switzerland has been surveyed by Krumm *et al.* (1993).

22. Comparisons should always take into account the particular circumstances of each garage, often not done in surveys (this is the case for surveys carried out regularly for all German cities by the Bundesverband der Park- und Garagenhäuser e.V., last conducted in April 1995).

23. The system of very low fees for cars arriving early in the morning and parking all day ("early bird fees"), widespread in American and Australian cities as a means of attracting commuters, does not exist in Germany.

24. The city of Helsinki has also introduced a specially developed parking machine that can be bought by the driver (about DM 145.00) and is operated by a rechargeable smart card similar to a telephone card (in some other Finnish cities, it can also be used for the telephone). The machine displays the charged parking time. If the parking ends earlier than originally planned, the unused fee can be recovered on the chip card. Users of these parking-machines receive a 20 per cent reduction on their fees.

25. See the survey by TEST (Transport of Environment Studies) 1981: "Park now, pay later?".

26. See Sammer, Wernsperger, 1993.

27. A short description of this effective Public-Private Partnership model is given in "Parkraum-bewirtschaftung in Berlin / City West" (1995).

28. Boltze and Puzicha (1995) recently have shown the effectiveness of a parking guidance system with the case of Frankfurt: the amount of time spent looking for a parking space and the length of tailbacks at preferred garages were reduced at times of peak demand, even though only a small proportion (3 per cent of all drivers on average) entrust themselves entirely to the parking guidance system. For more information on parking guidance systems see ADAC (1989), Forschungsgesellschaft (1993), Körntgen (1993), Polak *et al.* (1990).

29. See, with the example of Cologne, Creative Communications Concept (1989).

30. This has been vividly described by Strasser 1990 and by Voggenhuber 1988.

31. A similar distortion, in England, company cars have increasingly been provided free to employees as additional benefits.

32. See *"Auto, Verkehr und Umwelt"* 1993, p. 194-223.

33. These have been analysed in great detail by Crowhurst Lennard and Lennard (1995), Gehl (1987), Moudon (1987), and Project for Public Spaces (1984).

34. Many experts argued for this reason that pedestrianisation would not work because pedestrians would feel lost. Streets of similar size include the Frankfurt "Zeil", which was widened for car traffic after the war, and the Stuttgart "Königstraße".

35. A through path for cyclists remained open, which caused continuous controversies with conservative politicians and the police.

36. This approach can also be found in Aachen and Freiburg. It differs greatly from what has been done in Danzig (Poland), where the old town was reconstructed as a museum.

37. For pedestrianisation and ZTL in Italy see Lombardi and Meini, 1995.

38. See Monheim, in *Vereinigung für Stadt-, Regional-u. Landesplanung* (1995).

39. A very detailed overview of objectives involved in pedestrianisation is found in Monheim , 1975.

40. The city of Gottingen published its first planning model for the city centre as a discussion paper in 1970; it was adopted in 1974 and renewed in 1989 (see Stadt Gottingen). The city of Nuremberg published its first concept in 1972 and is now discussing a third model (see Stadt Nuremberg).

BIBLIOGRAPHY

ADAC (ed.) (1988), *Abschlußbericht zur Parkuntersuchung in Würzburg im Rahmen der Kommunalen Verkehrsüberwachung, Ruhender Verkehr II,* Nuremberg.

ADAC (ed.) (1989), *Schneller parken mit Parkleitsystem, Erfahrungen aus der Praxis, Empfehlungen für die Praxis, Ruhender Verkehr 1,* Munich, 2nd edition.

ADAC (ed.) (1993), *Verkehr in Fremdenverkehrsgemeinden. Eine Planungshilfe für Ferienorte mit praktischen Beispielen,* Munich.

AERNI, K. *et al.* (1993), *Fußgängerverkehr Berner Innenstadt, Schlußbericht, Geographica Bernensia* p. 28, Bern.

AMMERMANN, U. (ed.) (1988), *Parken in der Innenstadt, Tagungsbericht Fachkolloquium, Berichte und Protokolle des Münchener Forums 88,* Munich.

ANDRÄ, K., R. KLINKER and R. LEHMANN (1981*), Fußgängerbereiche in Stadtzentren.* Berlin (GDR).

APEL, D. (1992), *Verkehrskonzepte in europäischen Städten. Erfahrungen mit Strategien zur Beeinflussung der Verkehrsmittelwahl, Difu-Beiträge zur Stadtforschung 4,* Berlin.

APEL, D. and M. LEHMBROCK (1990), *Stadtverträgliche Verkehrsplanung, Chancen zur Steuerung des Autoverkehrs durch Parkraumkonzepte und -bewirtschaftung, Deutsches Institut für Urbanistik,* Berlin.

APEL, D. (1995), *Stadtstraßen als öffentlicher Raum. Grenzen stadtverträglicher Belastbarkeit mit Kfz-Verkehr, in Archiv für kommunalwissenschaften I,* pp. 90-118.

APPEL, H. P., R. BAIER and C. PETER (1988), *Parke nicht auf unseren Wegen, Handlungsleitfaden für die kommunale Praxis, Der Minister für Stadtentwicklung, Wohnen und Verkehr des Landes Nordrhein-Westfalen (ed.), MSWV informiert 5/88*, Dusseldorf.

APPEL, H. P., R. BAIER and A. WAGENER (1993), *Leitfaden Parkraumkonzepte, Berichte der Bundesanstalt für Straßenwesen, Verkehrstechnik* Fasc. V 1, 2nd edition, Bergisch Gladbach.

ARNDT, K. (1994), *P+R-Potentiale, in Handbuch der Kommunalen Verkehrsplanung*, Ch. 3.3.6.1, Bonn.

ATZBERGER, C., J. M. NEBE and H. SCHAD (1992*), Notwendige Schritte für eine fußgängerfreundliche Planung am Beispiel der Trierer Innenstadt, Trierer Forum e.V.* (ed.), Trier.

AUTO, VERKEHR UND UMWELT. Cars, Traffic and Environment. Automobiles, Circulation et Environment (1993), ed. by Rudolf Augstein GmbH & Co KG, Hamburg.

AXHAUSEN, K. W. and J. W. POLAK (1990), "The implications of parking search behaviour for parking demand management", Oxford University Transport Studies Unit (TSU) Working Paper 573, Oxford.

BAIER, R., A. MORITZ and K.-H. SCHÄFER (1984), *Parken in der Stadt, Schriftenreihe "Städtebauliche Forschung" des Bundesministers für Raumordnung, Bauwesen und Städtebau 03,109*, Bonn.

BAIER, R., H. HENSEL and P. A. MÄCKE (1981), *Ruhender Verkehr in citynahen Wohngebieten, Schriftenreihe Landes- und Stadtentwicklungsforschung des Landes Nordrhein-Westfalen 'Stadtentwicklung - Städtebau'* Vol. 2.041, Dortmund.

BAIER, R., W. DRAEGER, and C. PETER (1992), *Flächenhafte Verkehrsberuhigung, Auswirkungen auf den Verkehr, Forschung Stadtverkehr*, fasc. 45, Hof 1992.

BEERMANN, H.-J. (1990), *Rechtliche Aspekte der Kostenerstattung für Fahrkarten, in Vereinigung der Stadt-, Regional- und Landesplaner e.V.* (ed.) (1990), *Umweltorientiertes Verkehrsverhalten - Ansätze zur Forschung der ÖPNV-Nutzung, Bochum*, pp. 179-186.

129

BESCHEL, R. *et al.* (1995), *Verkehrskonzepte für Randlagen von Fußgängerzonen, Verhalten und Einstellungen von Besuchern und Einzelhändlern am Beispiel der Sendlinger Straße in München, Arbeitsmaterialien zur Raumordnung und Raumplanung 143, Bayreuth.*

BLECHINGER, W., W. BRÖG and D. ZUMKELLER (1986), *Wirksamkeit von Maßnahmen zur Steuerung des ruhenden Verkehrs - Alternativen, Möglichkeiten, Chancen, Forschung Straßenbau und Straßenverkehrstechnik 473*, Bonn.

BMW (ed.) (1992), *City-Konzept Blaue Zone München*, Munich.

BOEMINGHAUS, D. (1977), *Fußgängerzonen. Arbeitsblätter zur Umweltgestaltung 3, Institut für Umweltgestaltung*, Aachen, Stuttgart.

BOESCH, H. (1992), *Die Langsamverkehrs-Stadt, Bedeutung, Attraktion und Akzeptanz der Fußgängeranlagen. Eine Systemanalyse, ARF/ADP* Vol. 14, Zurich.

BOLTZE, M. and J. Puzicha (1995), "Effectiveness of the parking guidance system in Frankfurt am Main", in *Parking Trend* Vol. 7, Fasc. 1, pp. 27-30.

BOREL, R. (1995), "Cars kill cities, but without cars, the cities die", in *Parking Trend* Vol. 7, Fasc. 1, pp. 19-20.

BROCKELT, M. (1995), *Erreichbarkeit innerstädtischer Einzelhandels- und Dienstleistungsbereiche - untersucht am Beispiel der "Fußgängerfreundlichen Innenstadt" Aachen, Arbeitsmaterialien zur Raumordnung und Raumplanung 88,* Bayreuth.

BRÖG, W. (1992), *Entwicklung der Mobilität unter veränderten Bedingungen der Bevölkerungs-, Siedlungs- und Verkehrsstruktur, in Verkehr und Technik 45,* fasc. 1, pp. 3-8, fasc. 2, pp. 57-62.

BRÖG, W. and E. ERL (1993), *Die Bedeutung des nichtmotorisierten Verkehrs für die Mobilität in unseren Städten, in Verkehr und Technik 46,* fasc. 10 and 11.

BUNDESARBEITSGEMEINSCHAFT DER MITTEL- UND GROßBETRIEBE DES EINZELHANDELS (BAG) (ed.) (1988), *Verkehrsberuhigung, Fußgängerzonen, Arkaden- Passagen- Galerien, - Für und Wider, Schriftenreihe der BAG*, 4th edition, Cologne.

BUNDESARBEITSGEMEINSCHAFT DER MITTEL- UND GROßBETRIEBE DES EINZELHANDELS (BAG) (ed.) (1990), *Parken und Handel, Schriftenreihe der BAG*, 2nd edition, Cologne.

BUNDESARBEITSGEMEINSCHAFT DER MITTEL- UND GROßBETRIEBE DES EINZELHANDELS (BAG) (ed.) (1991), *Handel und stadtgerechter Verkehr - Perspektiven von Innenstadt und Einzelhandel -, Schriftenreihe der BAG*, Cologne.

BUNDESARBEITSGEMEINSCHAFT DER MITTEL- UND GROßBETRIEBE E.V. (BAG) (ed.) (1992), *Standortfragen des Handels*, 4th edition, Cologne.

BUNDESFORSCHUNGSANSTALT FÜR LANDESKUNDE UND RAUMORDNUNG (ed.) (1988), *Verkehrsberuhigung und Entwicklung von Handel und Gewerbe, Materialien zur Diskussion, Seminare - Symposien - Arbeitspapiere*, Vol. 33, Bonn.

DER BUNDESMINISTER FÜR RAUMORDNUNG, BAUWESEN UND STÄDTEBAU (ed.) (1978), *Siedlungsstrukturelle Folgen der Einrichtung von verkehrsberuhigten Zonen in Kernbereichen. Schriftenreihe "Städtebauliche Forschung"* 03.065, Bonn.

BUNDESMINISTERIUM FÜR RAUMORDNUNG, BAUWESEN UND STÄDTEBAU and Bundesministerium für Verkehr, für Umwelt und Reaktorsicherheit (eds.) (1992), *Forschungsvorhaben Flächenhafte Verkehrsberuhigung - Folgerungen für die Praxis*, Bonn.

BUNDESVERBAND DER PARK- UND GARAGENHÄUSER E.V. (ed.) (1994*), Hinweise für Kommunen für die Planung, den Bau und den Betrieb von öffentlichen Parkhäusern*, Cologne.

CERWENKA, P. (1994), *Kritische Hinterfragung - Mobilität zwischen Empirie und Engagement (Diskurs über „Weniger Verkehr bei gleicher Mobilität?"), in Internationales Verkehrswesen*, Vol. 46, pp. 654-655.

131

CREATIVE COMMUNICATIONS CONZEPTE (1989), *Das Kölner Parkleitsystem - Bekanntheit und Nutzung, Ergebnisse einer Passantenbefragung in der Kölner City*, Cologne.

CROWHURST LENNARD, S. H. and H. L. LENNARD (1995), *Livable cities observed*, Carmel, CA.

CULLINANE, K. and J. POLAK (1990), *Illegal parking and the enforcement of parking regulations: causes, effects and interactions*, Oxford University Transport Studies Unit (TSU) Ref. 519, Oxford.

DÖRNENBURG, K. and J. STINTZING (1994), *Einsatzmöglichkeiten und Grenzen von flexiblen Nutzungen im Straßenraum, Forschungsreihe des Eidgenössischen Verkehrs- und Energiedepartement, Bundesamt für Straßenba 306*, Bern.

EIR, B. (1994), "The bicycle as part of a healthy traffic plan for Copenhagen", Paper presented at the 7th International Velo City Conference 6-10.9.93 in Nottingham, Copenhagen.

ENTWICKLUNGSPERSPEKTIVEN FÜR DIE MÜNCHENER INNENSTADT (1985), *Eine Untersuchung der Infratest Sozialforschung GmbH, Munich, in Zusammenarbeit mit dem Referat für Stadtplanung und Bauordnung, Arbeitsberichte zur Stadtentwicklungsplanung*, Vol. 16, Munich.

FACHGRUPPE FORUM MENSCH UND VERKEHR (1989), *Beeinflussung des Verkehrsverhaltens durch Öffentlichkeitsarbeit, Vereinigung der Stadt-, Regional- und Landesplaner e.V.* (SRL) (ed.), SRL Arbeitsberichte, Bochum.

FIEBIG, K. H., B. HORN and U. KRAUSE (1988), *Umweltverbesserung in den Städten, H. 5: Stadtverkehr, Ein Wegweiser durch Literatur und Beispiele aus der Praxis, Deutsches Institut für Urbanistik* (ed.), Berlin.

FLADE, A., K. SCHLABBACH and F. DIECKMANN (1988), *Parkhaus oder Straßenrand? Eine Studie zum Parken in der Innenstadt von Darmstadt, Institut Wohnen und Umwelt*, Darmstadt.

FLORIAN, A.-J. (1990), *Passagen. Ein Beispiel innerstädtischer Revitalisierung im Interessenkonflikt zwischen Stadtentwicklung und Einzelhandel, Kölner Geographische Arbeiten 53*, Cologne.

FORSCHUNGSGESELLSCHAFT FÜR STRAßEN- UND VERKEHRSWESEN, Arbeitsgruppe "Verkehrsplanung", Arbeits-ausschuß "Sonderfragen des Stadtverkehrs" (1990), Flächendeckende Parkraumkonzepte für innerstädtische und innenstadtnahe Wohn- und Mischgebiete in Groß- und Mittelstädten, FGSV-Arbeitspapier No. 23, Cologne.

FORSCHUNGSGESELLSCHAFT FÜR STRAßEN- UND VERKEHRSWESEN (ed.) (1991), Empfehlungen für Anlagen des ruhenden Verkehrs (EAR 91), Cologne.

FORSCHUNGSGESELLSCHAFT FÜR STRAßEN- UND VERKEHRSWESEN, Arbeitsgruppe Verkehrsplanung, Arbeitsausschuß "Sonderfragen des Stadtverkehrs" (1993), "Autoarme Innenstädte" - Eine kommentierte Beispielsammlung, FGSV-Arbeitspapier Nr. 30, Cologne.

FORSCHUNGSSTELLE FÜR DEN HANDEL (FfH) (ed.) (1978), Die Bedeutung der Fußgängerzonen für den Strukturwandel im Handel. Bearb. R. SPANNNAGEL, Berlin.

FORSCHUNGSVERBUND LEBENSRAUM STADT (ed.) (1994), Mobilität und Kommunikation in den Agglomerationsräumen von heute und morgen, 6. Vol., Berlin.

FREY, R. L. and P. M. LANGLOH (ed.) (1992), "The use of economic instruments in urban travel management", Wirtschaftswissenschaftliches Zentrum (WWZ) der Universität Basel, Basel.

FRIEDRICHS, J. (1992), Haben traditionelle Fußgängerzonen Zukunft? in BAG-Nachrichten, Fasc. 5-6, pp. 18-19.

GEHL, J. (1987), Life between buildings, using public space, New York.

GEHL, J. et al. (1991), Bedre Byrum (improving urban spaces in Denmark), Dansk Byplan Laboratoriums Skriftserie No. 40, Copenhagen.

GOUT, P. (1990), Beschränkung des Autoverkehrs in Bologna, Monatsbericht des Instituts für Landes- und Stadtentwicklungsforschung des Landes Nordrhein-Westfalen, 11/90, Dortmund.

HALL, P. and C. HASS-KLAU (1985), "Can rail save the city? The impacts of rail rapid transit and pedestrianisation on British and German cities", Gower, Aldershot.

HASENSTAB, R. (1995), *Parkbauten im Zentrum der Stadt, Verkehr Spezial* Bd. 2, Dortmund.

HASS-KLAU, C. (1990), *The pedestrian and city traffic*, London.

HASS-KLAU, C. (1993), "Impact of pedestrianisation and traffic calming on retailing." *A review of the evidence from Germany and UK, in Transport Policy 1*, fasc. 1, pp. 21-31.

HATZFELD, U. (1994a), *Die Erreichbarkeit der Innenstädte - Perspektiven für den Handel, in Bayerisches Staatsministerium für Wirtschaft und Verkehr* (ed.), *Die Erreichbarkeit der Innenstädte - Perspektiven für den Handel -*, Munich.

HATZFELD, U. (1994b), *Moderne Strukturen in Handel, Freizeit und Verkehr - großmaßstäbig und "auto"matisiert? in Institut für Landes- und Stadtentwicklung des Landes Nordrhein-Westfalen 126* (ed.), *Urbanes Leben - mobil im Umweltverbund*, pp. 34-64, Dortmund.

HEIKKILA, M., T. SANTASALO and B. SILVERBERG (1994), *Ponjoismaisia Kävelykeskustoja* (pedestrian precincts in Scandinavia), *Selvitys 5*, Helsinki (with detailed maps and statistics).

HEINEBERG, H. and A. MAYR (1995), *Großflächiger Einzelhandel im Ruhrgebiet, Berichte des Arbeitsgebietes "Stadt- und Regionalentwicklung" am Institut für Geographie der Westfälischen Wilhelms-Universität 6*, Munster.

HEINZE, G. W. and W. SCHRECKENBERG (1984), *Verkehrsplanung für eine erholungsfreundliche Umwelt: ein Handbuch verkehrsberuhigender Maßnahmen für Kleinstädte und Landgemeinden, Veröffentlichung der Akademie für Raumforschung und Landesplanung, Abhandlungen 85*, Hanover.

INDUSTRIE- UND HANDELSKAMMER zu Köln (ed.) (1988), *Problematik der Verkehrsberuhigung. Negative Auswirkungen der kommunalen Verkehrspolitik*, Cologne.

INNENMINISTERIUM Baden-Württemberg (ed.) (1974), Erlaß zur Einführung der 'Hinweise der ARGE-BAU für die städtebauliche Planung von Parkbauten für Kernbereiche' vom 8.1.1974, Stuttgart.

INNENSTADTVERKEHR UND EINZELHANDEL: Einfluß von Innenstadt-Verkehrskonzepten mit MIV-restriktiven Maßnahmen auf den Umsatz und die Struktur im Einzelhandel, (1994), FOPS-FENr. 77365/93 BSV Büro für Stadt- und Verkehrsplanung DR.-ING. R. BAIER und Institut für Handelsforschung an der Universität zu Köln, unpublished report, Aachen and Cologne.

JANSSEN, C.J. (1993), City-Konzept Blaue Zone München, in Internationales Verkehrswesen, Vol. 45, Fasc. 4.

JUNKER, R. and W. SCHULTE (1992), City-Management Hamm, in Der Städtetag, pp. 659-663.

KANZLERSKI, D. (ed.) (1988), Verkehrsberuhigung und Entwicklung von Handel und Gewerbe: Materialien zur Diskussion. Seminare Symposien Arbeitspapiere 33, Bonn.

KEMMIG, H. and H. KLEWE (1994), Zustellservice - wer trägt oder fährt welche Waren zu welchem Preis wann wohin und warum? Institut für Landes- und Stadtentwicklung des Landes Nordrhein-Westfalen. Aufgabenbereich Verkehr (ed.), Monatsbericht, November/December, Dortmund.

KIRCHHOFF, P. and P. STÖVEKEN (1990), Besseres Verkehrsangebot im ÖPNV oder/und Restriktionen für den Pkw? Einflußgrößen auf den Modal Split in großstädtischen Bereichen, in Der Nahverkehr, Fasc. 3, pp. 34-40.

KLEIN, G. (1989), Akzeptanz von Tiefgaragen, Einfluß von Funktion und Gestalt, Fachgebiet Verkehrswesen, Universität Kaiserslautern, Grüne Reihe 9, Kaiserslautern.

KLOSS, H. P. (1991), Parkraumbewirtschaftung Salzburg, Ergebnisse einer Befragung 1990, Mag. Abt. 9/01 Amt für Stadtplanung, Salzburg.

KNOFLACHER, H. (1994), Verkehrs- und Parkraumuntersuchung Saarbrücken unter besonderer Berücksichtigung der künftigen Verkehrsentwicklung, Maria Gugging (Austria).

KOCH, H. (1991), *Parkraumbewirtschaftung Salzburg Phase I, Vorher-Nachher-Untersuchung*, by oder of City of Salzburg, Gmunden.

KOCH, H. (1994), *Parkraumbewirtschaftung Salzburg Phase II, Vorher-Nachher-Untersuchung*, by oder of City of Salzburg, Gmunden.

KÖRNTGEN, S. (1993), *Beispielsammlung Parkleitsysteme, Fachgebiet Verkehrswesen, Universität Kaiserslautern, Grüne Reihe 26*, Kaiserslautern.

KRAFFT, O. (1995), "Accessibility to the city centre: the value of parking", in *Parking Trend*, Vol. 7, No. 1, pp. 15-16.

KRUMM, V. *et al.* (1993a), *Parkraumbewirtschaftung durch private und öffentliche Unternehmen, Ergebnisse einer Befragung in Österreich, Deutschland und der Schweiz*, Salzburg.

KRUMM, V. *et al.* (1993b), *Verkehrsmittelwahl beim Einkauf. Eine verkehrspädagogische Untersuchung am Beispiel Salzburg.*

KUTTER, E. (1989), *Individualisierung des Stadtverkehrs und ihre Gefahr für urbane Lebensformen - dargestellt am Beispiel Berlin, in Mitteilungen der Deutschen Akademie für Städtebau und Landesplanung*, Vol. 33, No. 2, Hannover.

LANDESHAUPTSTADT HANNOVER (1991), *Verkehrskonzept für die Innenstadt Hannover, Beiträge zum Verkehrsentwicklungsplan 6*, Hannover.

LANDESHAUPTSTADT MUNICH, *Referat für Stadtplanung und Bauordnung* (ed.) (1987), *Planungsgrundlagen für die Münchener Innenstadt, Arbeitsberichte zur Stadtentwicklungsplanung*, Vol. 21, Munich.

LANDESHAUPTSTADT SALZBURG (ed.) (1995), *Räumliches Entwicklungskonzept, Entwurf vom 01.03.95*, Salzburg.

LAPPE, T. and R. MONHEIM (1995), *Verkehr in der Altstadt von Sulzbach, Analyse und Planungskonzepte, Arbeitsmaterialien zur Raumordnung und Raumplanung*, Vol. 98, Bayreuth.

LESSMANN, H. (1978), *Wechselwirkungen zwischen Parkangebot und Verkehrsaufkommen, Schriftenreihe 'Forschung Straßenbau und Straßenverkehrstechnik' des Bundesministeriums für Verkehr* No. 264, Bonn.

LOMBARDI, D. and M. MEINI (1995), *Per la salute nei centri storici: le "zone a traffico limitato" e le "aree pedonali urbane" in Italia*, in C. Palagiano, G. de Santis and M. C. Cardillo (eds.), *Atti del Quinto Seminario Internazionale di Geografia Medica 1994*, Roma.

MADSEN, J. (1992), "Parking in Copenhagen" (translation from a Danish article), in *Stads-og havneinge nifren* No. 8.

MEINI, M. (1995), *Traffico urbano e qualità della vita nei centri storici: un'indagine comparativa tra Firenze e Norimberga, Tesi di dottorato*, Pisa (not yet published).

MONHEIM, R. (1975), *Fußgängerbereiche. Bestand und Entwicklung. Eine Dokumentation. Reihe E, DST-Beiträge zur Stadtentwicklung 4*, Cologne.

MONHEIM, R. (1980), *Fußgängerbereiche und Fußgängerverkehr in Stadtzentren in der Bundesrepublik Deutschland. Bonner Geographische Abhandlungen 64*, Bonn.

MONHEIM, R. (1986), *Fußgängerbereiche: Das Beispiel Nürnberg*, in H. Hopfinger (ed.), *Franken, Planung für eine bessere Zukunft?* pp. 89-112, Nuremberg.

MONHEIM, R. (1987), *Entwicklungstendenzen von Fußgängerbereichen und verkehrsberuhigten Einkaufsstraßen, Arbeitsmaterialien zur Raumordnung und Raumplanung 41*, Bayreuth.

MONHEIM, R. (ed.) (1989), *Parkraummanagement und Parkraummarketing in Stadtzentren, Kolloquium an der Universität Bayreuth 1988, Arbeitsmaterialien zur Raumordnung und Raumplanung 75*, Bayreuth.

MONHEIM, R. (1992a), *Erschließung innerstädtischer Einzelhandels- und Dienstleistungsbereiche für Besucher, in Handbuch der kommunalen Verkehrsplanung* Chapter 2.4.3.1, Bonn.

MONHEIM, R. (1992b), "The importance of accessibility for downtown retail and its reception by retailers and customers", in G. Heinritz (ed.). "The attraction of retail locations." IGU-Symposium 1991, Vol. 1. *Münchener Geographische Hefte* 69, pp. 19-46, Munich.

MONHEIM, R. (1992c), "Town and transport planning and the development of retail trade in metropolitan areas of West Germany", in *Landscape and Urban Planning* 22, pp. 121-136.

MONHEIM, R. (1995a), *Verkehrskonzepte für historisch wertvolle Städte, in Bundesministerium für Raumordnung, Bauwesen und Städtebau und Institut für Regionalentwicklung und Strukturplanung IRS* (eds), Dokumentation 4. *Kongreß Städtebaulicher Denkmalschutz in den neuen Ländern 1994 in Quedlinburg*, pp. 45-61, Bonn, Berlin.

MONHEIM, R. (ed.) (1995b), *"Autofreie Innenstädte", eine Gefahr für den Handel? Arbeitsmaterialien zur Raumordnung und Raumplanung*, Bayreuth (under print).

MÖRNER, S. V. and H. H. TOPP (1984), *Parkgebühren und Parkverhalten in Kurzparkzonen, Forschungsarbeiten aus dem Straßenwesen, Forschungsgesellschaft für Straßen- und Verkehrswesen* No. 100, Cologne.

MOUDON, A. V. (ed.) (1987), *Public streets for public use*, New York.

MÜLLER, P., F. SCHLEICHER-JESTER, M.P. SCHMIDT and H. TOPP (1992), *Konzepte flächenhafter Verkehrsberuhigung in 16 Städten, Grüne Reihe des Fachgebietes Verkehrswesen der Universität Kaiserslautern* No. 24, Kaiserslautern.

MÜLLER-HAGEDORN, L. and L. M. SCHUCKEL (1992), *Die Umsatzentwicklung des Handels und des Handwerks in der Aachener Innenstadt vor und nach Beginn der Maßnahme "Fußgängerfreundliche Innenstadt". Universität Köln, Seminar für Allg. Betriebswirtschaftslehre, Handel und Distribution, Arbeitspapier* Nr. 9, Cologne.

NIELSEN, C. and K. MÜLLER (1992), *Teure Parkplätze, die zu billig sind, in Spurwechsel, Informations-Dienst des VCS* Zürich 2, pp. 1-13.

DER OBERSTADTDIREKTOR DER STADT MÜNSTER - Stadtplanungsamt (ed.) (1994), *Parkraumuntersuchung Altstadt/Hauptbahnhof Münster/Westfalen*, report by Gfk Marktforschung, Munster.

PARKRAUMBEWIRTSCHAFTUNG IN BERLIN / City-West, Erfolgreiches Modell für das Public-Private-Partnership (1995), in *Parkhaus aktuell*, Fasc. 18, pp. 8-9.

POLAK, J. W. and K. W. AXHAUSEN (1990), "Parking search behaviour: a review of current research and future prospects", Oxford University Transport Studies Unit (TSU) Ref. 540, Oxford.

POLACK, J. W., I. HILTON, K. W. AXHAUSEN, W. YOUNG (1990), "Parking guidance and information systems: performance and capability", *Traffic engineering + control.*

Project for Public Spaces (PPS) (ed.) (1984*), Managing downtown public spaces*, New York.

RIEDEL, U. (ed.) (1990), *Erlebnisraum Innenstadt, Beiträge zu einem Verkehrs-, Wirtschafts- und Kulturkonzept für Bremen*, Bremen.

RINSMA, I. J. (1995), "Social support for parking policy", in *Parking Trend* Vol. 7, Fasc. 1, pp. 21-23.

ROBERTS, J. (1981), "Pedestrian precincts in Britain*", Transport and Environment studies (TEST)*, London.

SAMMER, G. and F. WERNSPERGER (1993), *Parkraumpolitik in österreichischen Städten, Heutige Situation und zukünftige Anforderungen*, Graz.

SCHAAFF, R. W. (1995), *Kritisches Hinterfragen: Stehen unsere Städte vor dem Verkehrsinfarkt? in Internationales Verkehrswesen*, Vol. 47, pp. 250-254.

SCHLÜTER, T. and W. SCHWERDTFEGER (1993), *Ein Konzept mit blauen Augen, in Internationales Verkehrswesen*, Vol. 45, Fasc. 9, pp. 502-506.

SCHUSTER, A. (1995), *Widerstände bei der Umsetzung flächendeckender Parkraumbewirtschaftungskonzepte, Ursachen und Handlungserfordernisse, Kommunalpolitik in Stadt und Land*, Vol. 4, Erfurt / Vieselbach, Boonheim-Roisdorf.

DER SENAT DER HANSESTADT LÜBECK, Amt für Verkehrsanlagen (ed.) (1993), *Autofreie Altstadt Band I, Lübeck plant und baut*, Fasc. 38, Lubeck.

DER SENAT DER HANSESTADT LÜBECK, Amt für Verkehrsanlagen (ed.) (1993), *Park+Ride-Konzept für die Hansestadt Lübeck, Lübeck plant und baut*, Fasc. 47, Lubeck

DER SENAT DER HANSESTADT LÜBECK, Amt für Verkehrsanlagen (ed.) (1990), *Autofreie Innenstadt, Lübeck plant und baut*, Fasc. 23, Lubeck.

SONNTAG, R. (1991), *Vergleichende Parkhausuntersuchung II*, by order of *Landeshauptstadt München, Referat für Stadtplanung und Bauordnung*, Munich (unpublished).

SPD-Parteivorstand, Referat Umwelt/Energie/Verkehr (ed.) (1993), *Verkehrsberuhigung und Kommunalwahlverhalten*, Bonn.

SPD-Parteivorstand, Referat Umwelt/Energie/Verkehr (ed.) (1994), *Materialien: Verkehrsberuhigung und Kommunalwahlverhalten*.

STADT AACHEN, Baudezernat, Amt für Verkehrsanlagen (ed.) (1994), *Fußgängerfreundliche Innenstadt, Symposium 1993*, Aachen.

STADT FRANKFURT AM MAIN (ed.) (1990), *Parken in Frankfurt am Main - Einschränkungssatzung, Stellplatzablösung und Verwendung der Ablösebeträge*, 2 parts, Frankfurt.

STADT FRANKFURT AM MAIN, Amt für kommunale Gesamtentwicklung und Stadtplanung (ed.) (1988), *Parkraumkonzepte Frankfurt am Main*, Frankfurt.

STADT GÖTTINGEN (ed.) (1970), *Die Erneuerung der Göttinger Innenstadt. Entwurf eines Planungsleitbildes, Göttingen Planung und Aufbau Heft 8*, Gottingen.

STADT GÖTTINGEN (ed.) (1971), *Verkehrsstudie Innenstadt Göttingen, Göttingen Planung und Aufbau Heft 9*, Gottingen.

STADT GÖTTINGEN (ed.) (1974), *Die Entwicklung der Göttinger Innenstadt. Entwurf eines Planungsleitbildes, Stand Oktober 1974, Göttingen Planung und Aufbau Heft 20*, Gottingen.

STADT GÖTTINGEN (ed.) (1989), *Die Entwicklung der Göttinger Innenstadt. Planungsleitbild 1988*, Gottingen.

STADT NÜRNBERG (ed.) (1972), *Entwicklungskonzept Altstadt, Beiträge zum Nürnberg-Plan Reihe G*, Nr. 2, Nuremberg.

STADT NÜRNBERG (ed.) (1995), *Zukunft der Altstadt, Entwicklungskonzept und Strukturplanung - Zwischenbericht*, Nuremberg (unpublished).

STADTPLANUNGSAMT FREIBURG (ed.) (1971), *Zur Diskussion: Freiburg Innenstadt*, Freiburg im Breisgau.

STADTPLANUNGSAMT ZÜRICH (ed.) (1991), *Parkierung* 1991, Zurich.

STRASSER, R. (1990), *Die Grenzen der Mobilität, Gedanken zur Verkehrspolitik in der Stadt Salzburg, in Stadt im Umbruch, Salzburg 1980 bis 1990, Schriftenreihe des Archivs der Stadt Salzburg* Nr. 3, Salzburg, pp. 231-297.

SUCHY, J. (1992), *Die Bedeutung von Park- and Ride-Systemen für die innerstädtische Verkehrssituation unter besonderer Berücksichtigung von Verhaltensmechanismen und Restriktionen,* Dissertation University of Bonn, Bonn.

TEHNIK, K. (1995), "Munich's parking strategy - chances and problems", in *Parking Trend* Vol. 7, No. 1, pp. 17-20

TEST (ed.) (1981), "Park now, pay later? A study of offensive parking in the heart of London", *Report by Transport and Environment Studies*, London.

TEST (ed.) (1989), "Quality Streets: How traditional urban centres benefit from traffic-calming". *Report by Transport and Environment Studies*, London.

TOLLEY, R.S. (ed.) (1990), "The Greening of Urban Transport: Planning for Walking and Cycling in Western Cities", London.

TOPP, H. H. (1991), "Parking policies in large cities in Germany", in *Transportation* 18, No. 1, pp. 3-21.

TOPP, H. H. (1992), *Parkraum als Steuerungsinstrument, in Handbuch der Kommunalen Verkehrsplanung*, chapter 3.4.12.1., Bonn.

TOPP, H. H. (1993), "Parking policies to reduce car traffic in German cities", in *Transport reviews* 13, No. 1, pp. 83-95.

TOPP, H. H. (1994a), *Zur Rolle des Parkens in der Verkehrsberuhigung, in Straßenverkehrstechnik*, Fasc. 6, pp. 375-379.

TOPP, H. H. (1994b), *Ansatz zur Reduktion des Verkehrsaufwandes - Weniger Verkehr bei gleicher Mobilität?*, Vol. 44, pp. 486-493.

TOPP, H. H. (1995), "A critical review of current illusions in traffic management and control", in *Transport Policy* Vol. 2, No. 1, pp. 33-42.

TOPP, H. H. *et al.* (1994), *Parkleitsysteme - Wirksamkeitsuntersuchung und Konzeptentwicklung, Bundesanstalt für Straßenwesen, Reihe Verkehrstechnik*, Vol. 13, Cologne.

TOPP, H. and T. PHAROAH (1994), "Car-free city centres", in *Transportation* Vol. 21, pp. 231-247.

VEREINIGUNG DER STADT-, REGIONAL- UND LANDESPLANER E.V. (ed.) (1990), *Umweltorientiertes Verkehrsverhalten - Ansätze zur Förderung der ÖPNV-Nutzung*, Bochum.

VEREINIGUNG FÜR STADT-, REGIONAL- UND LANDESPLANUNG SRL (ed.) (1995), *P+R - ein Beitrag zum stadtverträglichen Verkehr? Bericht über die Tagung der Fachgruppe Forum Mensch und Verkehr, Hamburg-Harburg 1994*, Bochum.

VEREINIGUNG SCHWEIZERISCHER STRAßENFACHLEUTE VSS (ed.) (1980), *Fußgängerbereiche in der Schweiz, Beispielsammlung*, Zürich.

VOGGENHUBER, J. (1988), *Berichte an den Souverän, Salzburg: Der Bürger und seine Stadt*, Salzburg.

WILLEKE, R. (1995), *Weniger Verkehr bei gleicher Mobilität? - Zur Entwicklung und Beurteilung von Verkehr und Mobilität in der Stadt*, Vol. 1-2/95, pp. 13-19.

WINKLER, B. (1990), "Piano della mobilità per la città di Bologna", in *Parametro* 177, pp. 3-4.

WINKLER, B. (1994), *Die Renaissance der Innenstädte, in Bayerisches Staatsministerium für Wirtschaft und Verkehr* (ed.), *Die Erreichbarkeit der Innenstädte - Perspektiven für den Handel -*, Munich.

WIRSCHING, A., K.-A. BARTSCHMID, R. BREUKER e.a. (1993), *Konzeption, Planung und Betrieb von P+R, Verband Deutscher verkehrsunternehmen* (ed.), Cologne.

YOUNG, W. and M. A. P. TAYLOR (1991), "A parking model hirarchy", in *Transportation* 18, pp. 37-58.

YOUNG, W., P. G. THOMPSON and M. A. P. TAYLOR (1991), "A review of urban car parking models", *Transport Reviews* 11, No. 1, pp. 63-84.

Managing Traffic Growth in Polish Cities

Wojciech Suchorzewski
Warsaw University of Technology
Poland

TABLE OF CONTENTS

LIST OF TABLES

1. INTRODUCTION

The objective of this paper is to identify and examine the main policy issues concerning traffic growth and management in Polish cities as the country moves toward a market economy. The paper first examines the general picture of urban and transport development in Poland[1] and then focuses on four large cities (Warsaw, Krakow, Poznan and Wroclaw).

1.1 Background

More than 60 per cent of Poland's population of over 38 million live in cities. The capital city of Warsaw (approx. 1.7 million inhabitants), the Upper Silesian Agglomeration (GOP) centred in Katowice, (about 2.2 million people) and the Tri-City Agglomeration (TCA), consisting of Gdansk, Gdynia and Sopot, (about 1 million), are the largest concentrations of urban population. Lodz, Krakow, Wroclaw and Poznan each have between 500 000 and 1 million inhabitants. Average urban densities are 2 000-3 000 inhabitants per km^2. In most large cities there is a striking contrast between dense, multi-purpose historic centres and post-war developments on the periphery with single-purpose housing estates or industrial areas. City centres have remained the principal locations for jobs and services, mixed with some residential function.

1.2 Transport trends in Poland

In the post-war period, Polish cities developed relying on mass transport. Until the early 1970s, car ownership and use were at a low level. All cities above 500 000 population, and some smaller cities as well, developed extensive tramway networks. Frequent and low-priced tramway, bus and commuter railway services were offered by State-owned mass transport companies. Until a few years ago, mass transport companies carried 80-90 per cent of non-pedestrian trips in main cities and covered only about 20-30 per cent of their costs through ticket sales.

In the mid-1970s, the number of cars in some cities reached 100 per 1 000 population, and exceeded 150 in the mid-1980s. However, the economic crisis of the 1980s and rationing of fuels limited car use. Ambitious plans to build up the urban road and mass transport infrastructure also fell through in many cities, leaving a legacy of partially constructed road structures and/or new urban rail systems (Warsaw, Poznan, Katowice).

Economic, political and administrative reforms, which started at the end of the 1980s, have had both direct and indirect impacts on urban transport. A process of decentralisation gave the municipal governments a far greater degree of fiscal independence and decision-making power than they had before. Municipalities took over substantial current liabilities with limited current income. To improve cost recovery, municipalities were forced to raise fares, which had remained unchanged for decades.

As growth in motorisation accelerated (see Table 1) urban car ownership in large cities grew to 300 per 1 000 population in the early 1990s, close to that of Zurich and equal to 60 per cent of the highest western European rates.

Table 1. **Population and car ownership in Poland and four cities**

		1970	**1980**	**1985**	**1990**	**1992**
Poland	population (000)	32 660	35 730	37 300	38 183	38 400
	cars (000)	479	2 383	3 671	5 261	6 505
	cars/1 000	15	67	98	138	169
Warsaw	population (000)	1 316	1 585	1 610	1 651	1 656
	cars (000)	60	248	309	466	533
	cars/1 000	46	157	192	282	322
Krakow	population (000)	589	715	740	n.a.	744
	cars (000)	18	74	106	n.a.	157
	cars/1 000	32	104	143	n.a.	212
Wroclaw	population (000)	526	617	637	643	640
	cars (000)	18	73	85	120	145
	cars/1 000	34	118	133	187	227
Poznan	population (000)	469	552	575	590	590
	cars (000)	21	87	105	131	167
	cars/1 000	46	159	183	222	284

Various transition processes such as the growth of motorisation and public transport fares have led to substantive changes in modal split; share of public transport has decreased to 70 per cent and less. Total annual passengers carried by Polish urban transport operators fell from 9.1 billion in 1986 to 6.3 billion in 1991, a 7 per cent loss per annum; in 1993, it was just above 6 billion, roughly as many as in 1975.

Table 2. **Modal split for non-pedestrian journeys (%)**

		Bus	Tram	Rail	Total MT	Taxi	Car	Bike
Krakow	1975	-	-	-	85.7	-	12.6	1.7
	1985	-	-	-	3.6	-	14.8	1.6
Poznan	1968	23.0	58.8	5.1	86.9	2.6	7.6	1.6
	1986	29.4	37.4	5.3	72.1	6.4	20.4	1.1
	1990	28.4	36.0	4.6	69.0	2.6	27.0	1.4
	1993	23.9	32.2	4.1	60.2	2.9	35.1	1.8
Wroclaw	1986	26.7	49.5	-	76.2	8.8	14.0	1.0
	1990	30.5	46.0	-	76.5	8.5	14.4	0.6
	1992	29.6	44.8	-	74.4	7.5	17.1	1.0
Warsaw	1980	-	-	-	80.8	-	17.8	-
	1987	-	-	-	79.1	-	20.9	-
	1993	-	-	-	68.1	-	30.6	0.9

Notes:

-- MT stands for mass transport;
-- suburban railways are operated by the Polish State Railways (PKP);
-- 1993 data for Warsaw include trips by PKP in the mass transport category; trip definition includes travel with either origin or destination outside Warsaw borders.

The growth of motorisation and the shift of passengers from mass to private transport (see Table 2) have brought about a rapid increase in traffic volumes and demand for parking. Road networks in Polish cities are not ready for this growth. Consequently, traffic congestion and parking problems are rapidly increasing. Delays are higher than they should be, because traffic control systems are out of date. Mass transport vehicles suffer from traffic congestion on city streets more than do cars, because traffic control is designed with private vehicle traffic in mind. Road surfaces are deteriorating, because they were not designed for current traffic loads and vehicle weights, and resources allocated to road maintenance have been reduced. Through traffic is using city streets, because there are only a few urban expressways and by-passes. This situation is likely to continue and intensify.

Further, even more alarming are the external effects of motor vehicle use, particularly air pollution and noise, which are exceptionally high in Poland. Studies carried out in 1990 by The Motor Transport Institute and Warsaw University of Technology suggested that in cities, vehicles generated 45-75 per cent of air pollution and almost 100 per cent of lead [4]. About 25-45 per cent of the urban population was subject to noise level L_{Aeq}>60 dB, and in some urban districts of large cities, this reached over 60 per cent. The situation may have worsened since then. Rough estimates of the environmental costs of road transport indicate that in 1992, these costs were equal to at least 1.3 per cent of GNP; however, according to other calculations, they might be as much as five times higher.

Municipal governments in Poland face formidable challenges. On the one hand, they are under pressure to stop fare increases **and** improve mass transport services. At the same time, the dictates of the commercial approach to mass transport indicate that in a falling demand market, further reduction of service will be necessary. On the other hand, they are under even greater pressure to use scarce public funds for road and parking construction to reduce congestion and meet traffic growth. The two approaches are not in complete opposition, since mass transport can not operate well on poorly maintained and congested roads. Finally, if Poland is to join the European Union in the near future, it must try to meet much higher environmental standards than those currently in place.

Many large cities have taken active steps to meet these complex urban transport challenges within their current means, including reformulating their transport policies and updating urban transport development plans. On the traffic side, cities such as Krakow, Poznan and Wroclaw have taken the lead in introducing car restraint policies involving a combination of access prohibitions and charging for on-street parking aimed to discourage long-term occupancy. Most cities have advanced plans for correcting the most glaring deficiencies in their road systems and/or completing the works started long ago, but have come up against a lack of funds.

On the mass transport side, in addition to increasing mass transport fares, initiatives have been taken to restructure operating companies with a view to improving their performance and/or reducing costs. It is becoming common for municipalities to retain the regulatory function (service patterns, schedules, fares), often carried out by a specialised transport authority, leaving operations to company management. Relations between operators and the municipalities are increasingly regulated through service agreements, based on fixed rates for agreed vehicle km of service and stringent control of performance.

In the following sections, the cases of Warsaw, Krakow, Poznan and Wroclaw are examined.

2. WARSAW

2.1 Background

At present, Warsaw's population is 1.65 million inhabitants (metropolitan region -- about 2.5 million). In the immediate post-war period, the city followed a controlled development path. Ambitious urban and transport development plans provided for a transport-efficient urban system, in which single function zones (e.g. residential, industrial) were to be linked with rail transport. Main development axes were to be served by improved suburban railways and a planned metro system. Unfortunately, because of lack of resources, plans have been implemented only in small part. The development of large residential areas separate from employment centres has created excessive travel demand. With one exception, development corridors which were to be served by rail rapid transit (metro) are served by buses without any priority measures.

2.2 Characteristics of the Warsaw transport system

Despite the post-war development trends, Warsaw has an extensive, multi-modal mass transport system, comprised of suburban railways serving seven corridors, 119 km of tramway routes and an extensive bus system. For decades, capital investment, including purchases of vehicles, was financed from the central budget. Fares were kept low, and high subsidies were accepted. This policy, combined with a low car ownership ratio, meant that, for a long time, a very high proportion of mechanised trips (85-95 per cent) were made by public transport (see Table 2).

A tramway system (predominantly with right of way) holds great potential; however, because of the prevailing view that the city should be served by metro system, this option has been neglected. The poor technical condition of tracks and rolling stock, along with car-oriented traffic management, have been reducing the attractiveness of the tramway. Nevertheless, average operating speeds are still reasonáble: tramway, 17 km/h; buses, from 18 km/h for normal radial lines crossing the central area to 23 km/h for express buses.

Construction of a metro, planned since 1927, was not started until 1983. The pace of work was very slow, and the first leg of the first line (11.2 km in tunnel) only started operation in April 1995. The line serves the Mokotow-Ursynow-Natolin corridor (approximately 200 000 inhabitants) connecting it with the edge of the central area.

The road network -- although not complete -- is quite well developed, with wide arterial streets even in the central part of the city. However, the network is centre-oriented and not-hierarchical. The radial road system serves mixed traffic -- local, regional and long-distance -- and lacks by-passes and connections between outer zones. The average operating speed on the main network in the central area during peak periods is 17-23 km/h. Traffic congestion is especially problematic in the central area and on some radial roads connecting the high-density residential areas within the centre.

Among Polish cities, Warsaw has one of the highest rates of car ownership (see Table 1), reaching 351 personal cars per 1 000 inhabitants.

Modal split is rapidly changing. With the growth in motorisation and declining public transport, the share of public transport decreased from 93 per cent of non-pedestrian trips in 1970, to 80 per cent in 1980, 79 per cent in 1987, and 67 per cent in 1993. The combined effect of changes in public transport patronage is illustrated by the decreasing number of passengers carried by the Warsaw Urban Transport Company (from 1 600 million in 1984 to 1 232 million in 1992). The growth in traffic volumes is shown in Table 3.

Growing traffic congestion affects public transport operation. On some sections average speed of buses is in the order of 8 km/h. The situation has worsened because of outdated traffic management/control and lack of priority for public transport.

Table 3. **Daily road traffic volumes**

	1985	1987	1993
Bridges : 24 hours	214 450	243 542	335 671
peak hour	15 760	19 651	28 869
City centre: peak hour	36 250	37 350	40 890
Right bank, centre Prague: peak hour	20 860	21 960	21 270

There is an acute shortage of parking places, especially in the city centre, but lack of any parking policy (time limits and/or pricing are not used) encourages use of the private car for commuting. On-street parking is uncontrolled and while, in general, there is little kerbside parking on main roads, cars park on pavements and other places destined for pedestrian use. Attempts to introduce parking pricing have so far been unsuccessful.

The traffic safety problem is dramatic. And in a growing number of locations, the concentration of pollutants exceeds norms which are not very stringent. About 31 per cent of the Warsaw population is subject to noise level $L_{Aeq} > 60$ dB, and 5 per cent to $L_{Aeq} > 70$ dB.

Generally, things are moving in wrong direction. Warsaw has already entered the vicious circle of more cars, more roads, more traffic, worsening public transport. "With the present car ownership rate, the city is sitting on a traffic time-bomb, waiting for disposable income to grow and/or gasoline prices to go down" [2]. So far, it has been difficult to get public and political approval of proposals concerning car traffic constraint, parking charges and public transport priority measures.

In the last four years, several studies have been carried out to examine the urban transport situation and propose solutions to the emerging problems. Three of the most important were sponsored by The World Bank [2], EBRD and the European Communities [5].

The World Bank review of Warsaw urban transport proposed the following conclusions and recommendations:

-- Warsaw should look for various sources of revenue and modes of financing: parking charges, development taxes, commercial long-term borrowing, etc.;

-- attention should be diverted from large investments to expand the system to smaller-scale investments and policies meant to optimise the performance and utilisation of the existing system through better management of public transport, traffic management, etc.;

-- the Warsaw metro project should be reviewed and modified.

These recommendations were only partially adopted by the municipal authorities, who were opposed to reviewing the metro project. Only recently, the municipality has agreed to commission a study for the North-South corridor, in which options for the metro continuation project are to be analysed. This study is sponsored by the Phare Programme.

The ATKINS study [5] was commissioned by the EBRD based on a Partnership Agreement with the Warsaw City Council. The study identified main challenges facing public transport in Warsaw and proposed upgrading traffic signal controls and introducing an ATC system in the city centre to provide priority for buses and trams.

From all studies, it has became clear that there is an urgent need to reorient the transport policies of Warsaw and its agglomeration. Over the last decade, transport policy favoured investment in the metro and new roads at the expense of surface public transport, road maintenance and traffic management. This has resulted in a backlog of public transport infrastructure replacement and road maintenance needs. The most important consequence, however, has been the erosion of the level of public transport service as traffic congestion increased. Consequently, both programmes proposed by The World Bank and ATKINS target low-cost measures aimed at increasing the operational and financial efficiency of existing surface public transport serving the whole city area, and not investment in only one corridor, as has been the case over the last ten years.

These and other suggestions have led to a growing understanding on the part of city authorities and the regional administration that reorientation of urban transport policies is necessary.

In 1992, while in the process of approving the latest Master Plan for Warsaw, the City Council decided that the transport development plan should be reviewed over the next two years. A number of studies were commissioned, including a travel survey [6], which was completed in 1993, and proposals for a transportation policy for Warsaw and the *voivodship* [7]. These proposals, based on analysis of Polish and foreign experience and an extensive opinion survey of policy-makers, professionals, and the general public, are summarised below.

2.3 Transport policy proposals for Warsaw

Considering the latest motorisation forecasts for Warsaw, which predict that the car ownership ratio in the city will increase from 220-330 per 1 000 population^2 in 1993 to 320-460 in 2000 and 500-650 in 2020, along with the experiences of western European cities with motorisation growth, four basic policy strategies can be identified:

a)   Continuation of past policies.

b)   Car-oriented policy, aiming at creating conditions for unlimited use of private cars in all areas of Warsaw and the agglomeration.

c)   Car-free city.

d)   Sustainable-balanced development of the transport system. In this option, car traffic would be kept at a level not exceeding the environmental capacity of each zone.

In light of the experience of high-income countries and, more specifically, the results of most recent OECD/ECMT work on urban travel [9], it was recommended that strategy (d) be selected [7].

In the proposed strategy, objectives listed earlier could be met in the following ways [9]:

--   The effective functioning of the transport system in conditions of growing motorisation is to be assured, first of all, by the improvement of public transport. Needs of car traffic and road development are met to a different degree depending on the zone. In highest-density zone I (the Warsaw city centre), car use will have to be constrained (in some areas totally eliminated) and priority given to public transport and pedestrians. In the high- and medium- density zone II, public transport will have priority, but car traffic will have more freedom. In zone III (low density), the road network and parking capacity will be developed to fully meet the rising demands of car owners.

-- Improving parking conditions in the central area is considered a secondary objective, because car traffic in this area has to be controlled and car use discouraged. However, better organisation of parking is needed. In remaining areas, the supply of parking spaces should meet the demand arising from motorisation.

-- Urban freight traffic will be improved through the development of new forms of distribution and delivery based on transport logistics.

-- The negative impact of transport on the environment will be reduced by: promoting energy-efficient and less harmful means of transport (e.g. public transport of all types, bicycle traffic, pedestrian traffic), more-stringent emission and noise standards, traffic constrains in affected areas, environment-sensitive planning and transport infrastructure design.

-- Road safety will be improved as a result of policy measures promoting public transport and some car use constraints.

-- The financial efficiency of transport is to be improved by rationalising management and operation of the public transport and road systems; developing a system of stable financing for the transport sector from sources such as fuel taxes, parking charging, taxation of employers served by public transport and, in the more distant future, congestion and pollution pricing.

-- Demand for travel can be reduced by the co-ordination of urban and transport development, primarily, by mixing land-uses (housing, employment, services and recreation).

Policy and programmes have to take into consideration limited financial resources. It is not realistic to assume that in the next five to ten years, resources available for transport development and operations will be much higher than at present. Consequently, emphasis has to be placed on a more effective use of existing infrastructure and equipment, and on rehabilitation and modernisation. New, capital-intensive projects should be undertaken on an exceptional basis, and only when it can be assured that the project will be completed in a short time and lead to specific results.

Recommended measures involve the following areas: urban development, public transport and roads and traffic management.

- **Public transport**: *short-term measures* include:

    -- priority for tramway and bus traffic (e.g. exclusive bus lanes and actuated traffic control at intersections);
    -- rationalisation of routing and schedules;
    -- improvement of the fare system;
    -- introduction of time-tickets valid for all means of transport;
    -- wide use of marketing.

    Medium- and long-term measures include:

    -- continuation of programme to upgrade/modernise the tramway system;
    -- continuation of the metro construction (resources allowing);
    -- development of intermodal terminals;
    -- development of advanced operations control and information systems.

- **Roads, traffic management and parking:** *short-term measures* include:

    -- halting deterioration of pavements and bridges by allocating more resources to maintenance;
    -- modernisation of the traffic management system, including introduction of car-traffic constraints in some areas (e.g. car-free zones, traffic calming, 30 km/h zones);
    -- modernisation of traffic control system, including initiating the development of area traffic control system (ATC);
    -- introduction of bus and tramway priorities (bus lanes and streets, priority for trams and buses on traffic controlled intersections, etc.);
    -- reorientation of parking policy:

        i) in zone I (central area): rationalisation of use of existing space through parking fees, elimination of illegal parking, limited development of new parking facilities;

159

ii) in zone II: construction of park-and-ride facilities; enforcing rule that developers provide enough parking spaces at their sites; successive introduction of parking fees in concentrations of activities.

-- finalising capital investment road projects started in the past with focus on projects consistent with new transport policies;
-- initiating new road projects only in exceptional cases;
-- initiating development of bicycle routes;
-- selective upgrading of facilities for pedestrians with due consideration for needs of handicapped;
-- formulating a comprehensive traffic safety programme and its implementation;
-- enforcing traffic regulations.

Medium- and long-term measures include:

-- development of road network in order to: free the central area from through traffic, improve links between peripheral areas, improve access to outer stops of public transport, improve bus operations (bus lanes, busways), eliminate heavy traffic from residential areas;
-- further development of traffic control system, including ATC, expressways traffic control systems, information system on parking conditions, dynamic information system for travellers using telematics.;
-- development of the urban freight transport system based on transport logistics and telematics;
-- continuing the development of facilities for bicycles and pedestrians.

2.4 Implementation of policies

As mentioned above, these proposals, prepared on the request of the City Council, were submitted to the municipal authorities in mid-1994. After extensive evaluation by various bodies, including committees of the City Council, the policy proposals were approved by the City Board and prepared for final approval by the City Council. In the meantime, there was a local election and the composition of the Council and the Board changed. So far, the new City Board and City Council have not considered the proposals. Consequently, as of this writing, there is no formal document with declaration of transport policies for Warsaw.

Moreover, the latest declarations and decisions of the new president indicate that it is rather unlikely that the sustainable development policy will be adopted. These include declarations that: the costly metro project will be continued with no resources allocated to the renewal of aged bus and tram fleets; a new major road project (expressway crossing the Vistula river) is considered a priority investment; and a programme to build several underground parking-garages in the downtown area has been initiated. Only two messages can be interpreted as promising: (1) progress on preparations for introducing parking fees in the centre, and (2) plans to implement the first pilot projects of bus/tram priorities.

The hesitancy of city authorities to introduce car traffic constraint measures is, among others reasons, a result of a very active pro-car lobby, vigorously supported by mass media, which are very influential in a new political environment. Generally, media are extremely critical with regard to any restrictions in road traffic and the idea of parking fees was attacked on the grounds of both liberty and equity.

These developments are not necessarily consistent with public attitudes. Evidence of this comes from the results of the 1993 travel survey [6], in which 1 359 households were interviewed with the following results: (1) 64 per cent (58.7 per cent of car owners) in favour of bus/tram priorities in urban traffic, even if they worsen car traffic conditions with 16.1 per cent (22.3 per cent) against; (2) 45.4 per cent (37 per cent of car owners) in favour of parking charges in the centre in order to limit car travel and to increase parking opportunities for other users with 29.6 per cent (41.4 per cent of car owners) against.

Warsaw is at a critical point. The city still needs to decide whether to continue the present policy of responding to the growing needs of car traffic or to choose the more-difficult but promising option of reducing rather than catering to car demands, and efficiently promoting mass transport which -- as a whole -- is deteriorating.

3. KRAKOW

3.1 Background

Krakow, the capital of Polish kings from the eleventh to the sixteenth centuries is inhabited by nearly 750 000 people and covers an area of 326.8 km^2. The population density of Krakow is rather low -- 2 277 inhabitants per km^2. The highest density of population is found in Srodmiescie (the downtown area) -- 8 737 inhabitants per km^2.

3.2 Characteristics of the Krakow transport system

The car ownership ratio is lower in Krakow than in Warsaw: in 1992, there were 212 cars per 1 000 inhabitants.

Urban public transport serves the densely populated areas quite well. Of a network of 80 km, 62 km of tram tracks are separated from the road traffic. The length of bus routes is 378 km. Bus operations are influenced by growing road traffic; there are short sections of bus-only lanes.

Krakow is at the hub of the road network in south-east Poland. Three international and seven national roads meet there. The pattern of the primary road network is not well structured. Of three ring roads, only one in the central area exists; the second is not closed yet, and the third has only some sections. Most through traffic crosses the central built-up districts. Of 1 258 km of public roads, there are only about 5 km of controlled-access roads and 57 km of dual-carriageway roads. The most important constraints for the development of road transport connections are: the Vistula river, the hills in western part of the city, and the extensive railway infrastructure and facilities.

Localised and peak period traffic congestion exists on some sections of the road network, especially on the second ring road which serves intercity and through traffic. The lowest travel speeds reported are approximately 10 km/h.

Of all Polish cities, Krakow was the first to introduce car-constraint measures on a larger scale. The historic centre, a main business/service area, has been fully pedestrianised and parking zones with different rules have been in place since 1988.

The Old Town area is divided into three traffic restriction zones: Zone A, with an area of 50 000 m2, is for pedestrians only. Zone B is accessible to cars only for residents and some service/delivery cars during the period 20.00. to 8.00. In zone C, about 300 meters wide, surrounding the first ring road, there is parking charging with parking time limited to two hours. This zone is not accessible for heavy vehicles.

There is a very active environmental lobby in Krakow, including a pro-bicycle movement. At present, however, the bicycle route network is only a few kilometres long.

3.3 New transport policies and plans

The former Master Plan for the city, approved in 1988, has recently been amended with significant changes in the concept of spatial structure of the agglomeration. After decades of implementing the idea of a rapidly developing "socialist" city with large industrial complexes and single-function residential areas, a compact city concept with mixed land-uses has been adopted. The most important changes, however, have concerned urban transport.

In January 1993, the Krakow City Council adopted the principles of a transport policy for Krakow [10]. Taking into consideration undesirable trends (rapidly growing motorisation, declining public transport, increasing congestion) the following objectives were defined: *"reduction in transportation demand; reduction of road vehicle traffic flows; promotion of energy-efficient means of transport; reduction of emissions; increasing vehicle occupancy; improving traffic safety mainly for pedestrians and cyclists"*.

The policy document states that *"public transport is to be given priority in investment and traffic management (lanes, tracks and streets exclusively for buses and tramways, priority at signal controlled intersections). The traffic control system should enforce priority for public transport, assure and help to restore punctuality of operation, manage the park-and-ride system, reduce access of personal cars to the centre and other critical areas, etc."*.

The standards of urban public transport services should be improved so that public transport will be competitive with the car and efficiently serve areas with car-traffic constraints. The bicycle route network should be further developed to enable cycling in safe and environmentally attractive conditions.

The main goals of the future road network development are: elimination of through-traffic from densely populated areas; better road accessibility for development areas considering public transport; improved access to intercity transport terminals and park-and-ride facilities; by-passing the downtown area through inter-district road connections.

The short-term programme for improving transportation within Krakow includes: demonopolisation of urban public transport and priority for bus/tram transport; integrating suburban railway with the urban public transport system; completing the southern A4 motorway by-pass; modernisation of traffic control and public transport operation management; construction of park-and-ride parking lots.

Medium- and long-term programmes should lead to the following future modal split: no less than 38 per cent of journeys on foot (as it is now); significant increase in bicycle traffic, up to 5-10 per cent of total journeys; 75 per cent of motorised trips by mass transport; only 5-10 per cent of trips by car to the downtown area (40 per cent in inter-district trips bypassing the downtown area and 60 per cent within suburban areas).

It was estimated that to obtain such a modal split, the following investments will be necessary: 200 km of bicycle routes; 70 km of urban public transport routes; 84 km of arterial urban roads, 46 km of which motorways.

Options for road and public transport systems should be examined taking into consideration the economic and functional efficiency at each phase. The third ring road is the most important element of the future road system. The park-and-ride parking lots should be located close to the third ring road. The public transport modes should have priority in an area between the second and third ring roads. *"The development of parking lots in congested areas should be limited by defining the maximum number of places which can be built within development projects."* [10]

"As a starting point for all options of public transport development, the best use of the existing system should be accepted. Among several medium- and long-term options, the choice should be made, probably, between the system of express-bus lines (in part on separated bus-ways) and rapid tramway (collision-free). In addition, development options of trolleybuses, premetro, and metro should be considered (the last one is very little probable, even in the far perspective)".

Special attention should be paid to creating a financial system. Fuel and vehicle taxes, parking fees etc. should be devoted to financing the transport sector.

It is clear from the above that Krakow has chosen urban/transport policies which are close to the sustainable development strategy promoted by OECD/ECMT [9]. It can be expected that the implementation of these policies will help to solve the existing transportation problems in Krakow. In fact, this is the only case in Poland where the city authorities clearly stated their transport policies.

The promising developments in Krakow can be attributed to a very fortunate concurrence of factors such as: a stable local government assigning high importance to preservation of historical and environmental values and making use of a very strong group of professionals; public awareness of environmental problems, local mass media generally supporting the urban and transport policies of sustainable development. It does not mean that no problems have arisen with implementing the adopted policies; some developers, for example, are protesting against maximum parking norms limiting the capacity of parking facilities in the central area.

4. POZNAN

4.1 Background

Poznan, one of the oldest towns in Poland (over 1 000 years old), is inhabited by more than 580 000 people and covers an area of 261.3 km². The average population density of Poznan is rather low -- 2 231 inhabitants per km² -- about 30 per cent lower than in Warsaw (3 400 inhabitants/km²).

4.2 Characteristics of the Poznan transport system

Public transport coverage of the city is good. The tramway plays a major role in the mass transport system. The total length of the tram network is 57.3 km, about 67 per cent of which is segregated from road traffic. There are 253 km of bus routes.

As in other cities, modal split has changed over the last 25 years. Following rapid growth in motorisation (in 1992, 283 personal cars per 1 000 inhabitants) the percentage of car trips has increased from 7.6 per cent to 35.1 per cent.

The road system in Poznan has historically formed a radial pattern with seven inter-regional roads. The system of by-passes and roads connecting outer zones is underdeveloped. Through-traffic crosses the built-up areas of the city. Of 977 km of public roads, there are only 11 km with controlled access and only 52 km of dual-carriageway roads.

Traffic congestion is particularly serious in the central area and its access ways, causing problems for tramways, which in the city centre are often not separated from vehicular traffic. During major international fairs, congestion is more widespread; however, reported average travel speeds -- 24 km/h -- are still good.

There is an acute parking problem in Poznan, particularly during commercial events in the area surrounding the Fair Grounds which are located at the edge of the city centre. Most cars park along the streets at the kerbs and on the pavements. There are 54 100 parking lot spaces, of which 38 200 are located in the densely built-up residential estates.

Poznan is one of Poland's leading cities in the application of traffic engineering measures such as traffic signal control. Parkometers have been used for years in some locations. A section of Old Town was pedestrianised many years ago. In 1993, the Limited Parking Zone (SOP) with parking charging was created within the Old Town. Some areas are closed to heavy vehicles: the central business district to vehicles over 2.5 tons, other areas to vehicles over 10 tons. There are also areas with time-related (10.00-18.00) entry prohibitions.

The bicycle route network comprises a 4-km-long route in the Old Town and some other short sections with a total length of about 15 km.

Since 1980, all investment in transportation has been concentrated on the construction of the Poznan Rapid Tram (PST) system, upgrading and modernising radial roads and providing road connections to the residential areas. In 1992, construction of the first 7 km of the PST was 75 per cent complete. At that time, the municipality recognised that the idea of a separate new rail system was not feasible and decided to integrate the PST line with the existing tram system, which could be modernised.

4.3 Transport policy proposals for Poznan

In 1992, the directions of a new urban transport policy were formulated. The two main goals of a new policy were: priority for public transport and better organisation of road traffic.

A three-zone concept was proposed, dividing the city as follows: the first zone covers the downtown area inside the second ring road. In this zone, tramways and buses will have the highest priority and private traffic will be considerably constrained. The next zone, between the second and third ring roads, will be served by urban public transport as well as private cars with some priority given to public transport. The third zone outside the third ring road -- with a medium and low density of population -- will have no restrictions for personal cars; however, it will be also served by public transport network.

These three zones were further divided: zone I into a central business district and downtown area, and zone III into more and less densely populated/developed areas. The detailed planning rules for each of five sub-zones were formulated. Generally speaking, the plan would promote sustainable urban and transport development for the city; however, ways of implementing the concept have so far not been specified.

The general road development policy in Poznan is to complete the ring road system with priority given to the inner ring. An area traffic signal system is also a priority.

Among other principles of Poznan transport policy, two are particularly worthy of mentioning: (1) urban mass transport operation, investment and maintenance should be demonopolised and privatised: (2) some local roads (mainly roads and parking lots within residential areas) should be managed by land owners.

It is assumed that the financial resources for urban transport development will include local road taxes, revenues from parking fees and urban public transport, income from advertising along roads, traffic penalties, subsidies and loans.

5. WROCLAW

5.1 Background

The city of Wroclaw (population 640 000, area 293 km²) is the most important city of the Lower Silesia region. The city is located in the Odra valley and is cut by several branches of this river as well as by tributary streams and rivers. The transport system is severely affected by this; for example, all bridges across the Oder are concentrated along 3 km of the river in the Old Town area. The nearest bridges are located 30 km (east) and 50 km (west).

The spatial structure of Wroclaw is typical of monocentric cities. The average population density is only 2 188 persons per km^2 with the highest densities in the order of 8 000-9 600 persons in the central area. Employment is concentrated in the centre and in some industrial areas and housing in estates built after the war (usually, high-rise apartment buildings). Separation of activities and lack of services in housing areas encourages long trips.

5.2 Characteristics of the Wroclaw transport system

Wroclaw's car ownership ratio in 1992 reached 276 personal cars per 1 000 inhabitants. Specific features of Wroclaw travel patterns are: a very high share of tramway (44.8 per cent in 1992) and relatively stable share of private vehicle use (14 per cent in 1985, 17.1 per cent in 1992).

Sixty per cent of public transport passengers in Wroclaw use the tramway. At present, the tram network covers 88.3 km of route, of which 55.2 per cent is segregated from road traffic. The length of bus routes is 374.2 km.

The average tramway operating speed on weekdays is 14.59 km/h. For individual lines, it ranges from 14.2-20.2 km/h. Lines with low speeds are those crossing the centre and/or using tracks not segregated from road traffic. Average bus speed in daytime operation is 20.34 km/h. For individual lines it is 19.9-33.5 km/h.

The urban road system of Wroclaw developed as a typical radial system with all main roads going to the central area. Eight principal national and international roads meet in Wroclaw. At present all roads serving international, national and regional traffic go through the city centre. In many sections of the outer area, they run through densely built-up areas.

Generally, the urban road density in Wroclaw is adequate, however: (a) the configuration of the road system is not adjusted to direction of traffic flows (lack of circumferential connections between outer districts); (b) only a very low proportion of roads (47 out of 1 367 km) are wider then two lanes; 45 km of streets have tramway tracks built into the carriageway; (c) there are many at-grade railway crossings even on arterial streets with intense traffic; (d) the quality of pavements is generally poor and, in some cases very poor.

The average operating speed on the main network in the peak period is 24 km/h. Traffic congestion is noted mostly in the city centre.

A wide range of traffic engineering measures are used in Wroclaw such as one-way streets and traffic channelling. The traffic signal control system in Wroclaw is one of the most advanced in Poland with extensive use of co-ordination. Signal timing is regularly updated: every second year in the central zone and in three- to five-year intervals on remaining intersections.

5.3 New developments in urban transport

A great effort was made by the city to improve conditions in the congested central part of the city. In 1992, the following short-term policy was formulated:

1) preference for short-term parking in zones with concentrations of institution, services and commerce; elimination of long-term parking from these zones;

2)   returning pavements to pedestrians by removing parked vehicles;

3)   facilitating movement and parking for handicapped persons (e.g. lowering kerbs at crossings, ramps, wider parking spaces, acoustic traffic signals);

4)   initiating construction of multi-level parking facilities in the central area;

5)   giving priority to public transport.

In February 1992, the City Council approved the parking price system for the city centre [11] with two zones (A and B). In zone A , 1 700 parking spaces were priced.   In zone B pricing was introduced for 1 388 spaces out of a total 7 575 spaces. The system of prepaid tickets (cancelled when starting parking) was chosen. Residents of zone A can buy a seasonal ticket at reduced price.   After the first period of operation (May-October 1992), fee levels were corrected.   A well-prepared and on-going media campaign has helped users to understand the system, which was the second of its kind in Poland (after Krakow).

The project was very successful both financially and politically. In the first six months of 1993, 633 000 single tickets were sold (80 per cent for parking up to one hour). The total revenue was three times the cost of introducing the system.

As in other cities, parking on pavements (even where it is illegal) is common in Wroclaw.   To eliminate this practice, physical blocks are installed to protect pavements at selected places.

The city is experimenting with bus and tram/bus lanes and bus traffic-actuated signal controlled crossings.

In the past, some streets were built with bicycle facilities. At present, only a limited number of facilities is operational. The city has started promoting cycling: public stands were installed at eight sites. In 50 places, stands are provided by companies for employees.

5.4   Changes in organisation and new policy proposals

In July 1993, a process of fundamental changes in the management of the transport sector started in Wroclaw. Responsibilities of several agencies have been passed to a new agency in the city government: the Road and Transport Authority (*Zarzad Drog i Komunikacji* -- ZDiK). ZDiK's responsibilities include: the management of the whole road system within the city border (national, *voivod* and local)[3], public transport management (including contracting operators), traffic management, transport policy formulation and transport system planning.

One of the first tasks of ZDiK was to prepare proposals for "Principles of the transport policy for the City of Wroclaw" to be presented to the City Council for approval. The following four objectives for short- and medium-term programmes were formulated: (1) improvement of traffic management and control; (2) increasing the attractiveness of public transport; (3) stopping the deterioration of roads; (4) modernisation and gradual development of the road system.

The following tentative programme was developed for a 10-15-year period:

1)   Modernisation of the traffic control system by introducing an area control system with the following functions: (a) co-ordination of arteries and networks; (b) limiting the volume of vehicles trying to access the city centre; (c) priority for public transport; (d) dynamic information on parking conditions;

2)   Upgrading conventional public transport through: limited development of the tramway network; introducing exclusive bus-tramway lanes on sections where tramway tracks are built into the normal carriageway; introducing priority for buses and tramways in traffic control; creating six to seven multimodal terminals; increasing punctuality and improving economic efficiency of public transport;

3)   Continuing the development of the urban road system with emphasis on: completing the central ring road; constructing three new Odra bridges;

4)   Development of a cycle-track system, including provision of parking facilities in multimodal transport nodes;

5)   Introducing traffic calming in low-density residential areas and "30 km/h" zones in higher-density residential areas.

A two-year programme called for: installation of traffic-actuated control on 30 intersections; creation of centralised traffic control (Area Traffic Control) for 21 intersections; modernisation of controllers on 40 intersections; introduction of traffic-actuated control at 12 pedestrian crossings and five tramway crossings; elimination of heavy traffic from the centre from 9.00-18.00 and from 21.00-8.00; introducing preferential treatment of public transport in traffic control at 30 intersections; introducing bus-lanes and tramway-bus lanes on selected streets; completing selected on-going road construction projects.

In summary, Wroclaw is one of only a few cities in Poland which made significant progress in upgrading its transport system through low-cost measures before the transition period. During transition, with a more favourable political environment, further progress has been made in redirecting transport policy.

6. SUMMARY AND CONCLUSIONS

Transportation problems in large Polish cities are similar and are related to the following factors:

--   The urban structures inherited from the old urban planning system impose long trips and excessive transport demand.

--   Underdeveloped, non-hierarchical, centre-oriented, radial road systems have to serve local, regional and long-distance traffic; growing motorisation is causing congestion and parking problems.

--   The financial capacity of municipalities is very limited, and it is not expected that the situation will change in the near future.

--   The operational efficiency and quality of the extensive system of conventional public transport (tramway and bus) is hampered by the growing impact of road traffic using the same road space; changes in travel behaviour have led to significant reduction in public transport patronage.

--   Past transport policies underestimated the potential of existing tramway and bus systems, which have been considered as an inferior solution; for a long time, plans to build new metro/light rapid rail systems diverted attention from the potential of existing systems and low-cost measures such as traffic management, parking pricing, and priority for public transport. For many decision-makers and professionals, it is still difficult to modify their way of thinking.

--   It is difficult to get public and political approval of proposals concerning car traffic constraint, parking charges and introduce public transport priority measures; personal cars are considered a symbol of freedom, and it is difficult to enforce restrictions and regulations, starting with speed limits and obeying essential traffic rules; unfortunately, many policy-makers and journalists are car enthusiasts.

--   Cities which are late in reorienting their transport policies, have already entered the vicious circle of more cars, more roads, more traffic, worsening public transport.

--   The situation has been made worse by a lack of co-operation and conflicts of interest among many participants in the decision-making process: elected officials, officers, car and construction industry professionals, labour unions and mass media representatives.

In the transition period, with its more favourable political environment, considerable changes have been made in transport policies:

--   Many large cities have taken practical steps to react to the new urban transport challenges stemming from the growth of motorisation and market-related changes in economic environment; significant progress has been made in reducing mass transport deficit and solving emerging traffic problems through low-cost measures.

--   Cities such as Krakow, Poznan and Wroclaw have taken the lead in introducing car restraint policies through a combination of access restrictions and parking management, including charging; these measures have not been used in isolation but were elements of innovative transport policy packages adopted by the city governments.

--   In many cities, including those mentioned above, old "wishful thinking" type of transport development plans have been reviewed and revised; in particular, plans to build completely new urban rail systems have been replaced with much more pragmatic and feasible programmes of tramway system upgrading, modernisation and development; Krakow is the first to have a comprehensive transport policy adopted by the city council.

Institutional structures have been changing:

--   Cities are setting up special agencies for roads; in Warsaw, Poznan and other cities, these agencies have taken over the care of roads of all categories (national, regional, local urban).

--   In the area of mass transport, it is becoming usual for cities to separate regulatory functions from the management of operations; new, specialised agencies -- Urban Mass Transport Authorities -- have been set up in several cities, including Warsaw.

-- The most progress has been made in Wroclaw, where the municipality has set up an Urban Road and Transport Authority with jurisdiction over all aspects of transport in the city: roads, traffic and mass transport.

From the lessons learned from the foreign and Polish experience it is clear that the practical, feasible solutions to emerging urban transport problems should be based on the following principles:

-- The existing road and public transport systems have great potential, which can be used to radically improve public transport operation and traffic management; limited resources will not allow investment in new, expensive systems, and attention should be turned to making better use of already existing means of public transport through modernisation and better operation.

-- Priority should be given to conventional mass urban transport (tram/bus) using traffic management measures.

-- Walking and cycling should be promoted and facilitated.

-- Parking management (including pricing) and car traffic constraints and calming in the highest density areas should be used as tools to reduce the use of car in congested areas.

-- In the long-run, road pricing seems to be the most promising measure as a financial instrument based on the Polluter and User Pays principle.

Final remarks

As it was stated in [1] *"Poland has the advantage of starting afresh, before its urban mass transport systems have been nearly destroyed. Its major cities have a priceless asset of reserved lanes for tramways in the most important corridors, which can be extended to benefit street buses as well. The key to success, however, is use of the price mechanism to tighten the screws on motor vehicle use, while at the same time progressively increasing cost recovery in mass transport services. This approach should be based on progressively recovering congestion and environmental costs from motor vehicle users. There is a whole array of approaches that can be used for this, from a relatively simple one based on parking, access and pollution fees to using smart cards for a full, time- and location-based charging method"*.

173

These recommendations are consistent with the final results of work done by the OECD/ECMT Project Group on Urban Travel and Sustainable Development. A recommended policy plan should take cities *"towards the goals of less congestion, reduced energy consumption, improved access for those without cars, higher environmental standards and reduced overall costs."* [9, p. 23]. The right definition of problems/issues and of ideas to solve these problems is not sufficient, however, to assure success in directing cities toward sustainable development. Political will is essential to implementation of these new ideas. Such will is still rare in cities of Central and Eastern Europe.

NOTES

This section is based on paper [1] in Bibliography.

Depending on the zone.

Previously, as in most Polish cities, national and *voivod* roads were managed by agencies not subordinated to the city government.

BIBLIOGRAPHY

1. MITRIC, S., SUCHORZEWSKI, W., "Urban transport in Poland: the challenge of the ascending private car", Paper presented at the OECD/ECMT/IEA/UNECE/UNEP Conference "Reconciling Transportation, Energy and Environmental Issues: The Role of Public Transport", Budapest, 30 May-1 June 1994.

2. THE WORLD BANK, Poland: Warsaw Urban Transport Review, June 1992.

3. THE WORLD BANK, Poland: Urban Transport Review, October 1994.

4. WALSH M., "Motor Vehicle Pollution in Poland: The Problem at Present and a Strategy for Progress". Report prepared for The World Bank, October 1990.

5. *Warsaw Public Transport Review*. WS/ATKINS Planning Consultants, 1992/1993.

6. *Warszawskie Badanie Ruchu 1993 (Warsaw Travel Survey, 1993)*. Warsaw Development Planning Bureau, November 1993.

7. *Wariantowe polityki komunikacyjne dla Warszawy i wojewodztwa stolecznego* (Transport policies for Warsaw and the *voivodship*). SUCHORZEWSKI, W., Transportation Engineering Consulting, March 1994.

8. SUCHORZEWSKI, W., "The effects of rising car travel in Warsaw", International Conference: Travel in the City: making it sustainable. 7-9 June 1993, Düsseldorf.

9. *Urban Travel and Sustainable Development*, ECMT, OECD 1995.

10. *Uchwala Nr. LXX/468/93 Rady Miasta Krakowa z dnia 8 stycznia 1993* (City Council Resolution on New Transport Policy in Krakow), January 1993.

11. *Obsluga komunikacyjna w obszarach zurbanizowanych w Polsce* (Transport services in urban areas in Poland), Polish Academy of Science, Transport Committee, December 1992. Team leader: A. RUDNICKI.

12. BAUER, R., *et alt. Zagrozenie srodowiska w Polsce przez rozwoj motoryzacji* ("Impact of the growth of motorisation on the environment in Poland"), Polish Academy of Science, Transport Committee, Warsaw 1993.

III. ORGANISING AND FINANCING URBAN PUBLIC TRANSPORT SERVICES

Integrating Urban Transport and Land Use Planning Policies

Susan Owens
University of Cambridge
United Kingdom

TABLE OF CONTENTS

LIST OF TABLES

1. INTRODUCTION

It is ironic that as urban policy makers and planners in western Europe are beginning to recognise that land use and transport trends are environmentally unsustainable, many large cities in Central and Eastern Europe (CEE) face unprecedented growth in the use of motor vehicles and rapid change in established transport networks and patterns of development. It is certain that changes in travel behaviour will interact with urban development in complex ways and, if cities are to be sustainable socially, economically and environmentally, land use and transport must be recognised, and treated, as an integrated system.

This paper sets out the main policy issues which arise in this context. Chapter 2 provides a framework for the relationship between land use, transport and the environment. Chapter 3 considers experience in western European cities and regions, looking both at problems associated with existing trends and policies which are being adopted in an attempt to modify them. Chapter 4 draws together conclusions and policy recommendations and raises a number of issues for consideration in a CEE context.

An important theme of the paper is that of choice. In travel and location decisions, the immediate benefits of exercising "consumer choice" may pre-empt our own future choices for access and environmental quality in urban areas and beyond, as well as the choices of others and those of future generations.

One important point should be stressed at the outset: it is not possible at this stage to isolate the effects of urban land-use policies on travel and its associated environmental impacts. This is partly because land-use planning has only recently been acknowledged as a means of managing the demand for travel and has not yet been much employed as a policy instrument (ECMT and OECD 1995; Owens 1994a). Even when policies are in place, effects are mainly long term, because the physical fabric of urban areas changes relatively slowly. Most importantly, perhaps, experience suggests that it is extremely difficult, if not impossible, to isolate the effects of land-use policies from the many other forces influencing travel behaviour.

2. LAND USE, TRANSPORT AND THE ENVIRONMENT

2.1 The need for a systematic approach

Interactions between land use and transport and their implications for the environment, are complex. Transport systems have direct land requirements and significant effects on urban landscapes (as well as impacts outside urban areas). They also interact with land use in more subtle ways and in the long term. Transport is an important factor in the evolution of city regions: transport infrastructure and, in a more general sense, the cost of travel, influence activities, development pressures and land-use patterns. In turn, patterns of urban development influence both the need for movement and choices between different modes of transport.

Though it has long been recognised that land use and transport systems influence each other (there is ample historical evidence of this interaction), renewed interest in this relationship and its policy implications has been stimulated by mounting concern about the environmental impacts of transport. These impacts are wide ranging and manifest at all geographical scales: they include direct and indirect landscape and habitat loss, pollution at the local, regional and global scales and the dominance of otherwise attractive physical environments by traffic. They have been analysed in considerable detail elsewhere, most recently, in an important report by the UK Royal Commission on Environmental Pollution (1994). Many of the effects are particularly acute in urban areas because of high traffic concentrations and congestion. Transport infrastructure occupies a high proportion of urban land (some 20 per cent of urban land in the UK, for example [RCEP 1994]); air pollution, often exceeding legal limits or guidelines, damages health and buildings; and community and social life is disrupted in cities dominated by -- indeed sometimes designed for -- motor vehicles.

There is growing recognition of the need to consider land use and the transport system, together with their environmental implications, as a whole. As well as improving the performance of individual vehicles and managing traffic, we need to understand what is generating the demand for movement of people and goods. This approach accords with a general shift of emphasis towards a more systematic view of polluting processes. But in any case, emissions reductions which might be achieved through pollution controls, improvements in energy efficiency and the use of alternative fuels are likely to be outweighed by the growth of traffic and by factors such as a preference for larger and more powerful cars. The latter is evidenced, for example, by the fact that travel in most OECD countries is becoming more energy intensive, in spite of technical improvements (Schipper, Steiner and Duerr, forthcoming; see also Martin and Shock, 1989; RCEP, 1994; Transnet, 1990).

Technical fixes are unlikely to be sufficient, even in dealing with the problem of vehicle emissions. When it comes to congestion, social impacts, landscape degradation and other non-pollution effects of transport, the necessity to manage the demand for travel, rather than simply improving the performance of individual vehicles, becomes inescapable. It is in this context of demand management that the relationship between land use and transport is highly significant. Transport is largely a derived demand. There is broad consensus that location and land-use patterns are among the determinants of that demand.

In mature economies, land-use policies are, for the most part, relatively long-term instruments of demand management (though the impact of specific locational decisions should not be underestimated). But city regions such as those of Central and Eastern Europe, where development is likely to be rapid and transport systems are in transition, offer significant opportunities for integrating land use and transport policies. It is important that these opportunities are grasped before unsustainable patterns of urban development become, almost literally, set in concrete. Before considering some of the lessons which might be offered by experience in western Europe, it is necessary to outline the nature of the relationship between land use and transport.

2.2 How land use and transport interact

Interactions between land use and transport have been recognised, analysed and modelled for many decades and there is extensive literature on the subject. Most of what we know about the influence of transport systems on land-use patterns and vice versa comes from empirical observation or from modelling. In neither case is it possible to provide definitive answers which might enable us to make clear predictions or design "ideal" urban forms: empirical work has to deal with the real world in all its complexity, while many question the utility, or even the fundamental validity, of models used in this context. Irreducible uncertainties in this field must be acknowledged. Nevertheless, there is now a considerable body of knowledge about land use and transport and it is possible to identify a broad consensus on certain principles.

Although in practice we are dealing with an iterative process, for ease of presentation, this section considers first the effects of transport on land use (including the potential impacts of restraint on travel) and then the influence of development patterns on travel behaviour. Key policy implications of these interactions are then identified.

2.2.1   Effects of transport on land use

The cost of travel -- measured in terms of both money and time ("generalised cost") -- affects the mobility of individuals, the accessibility of locations and, potentially, the development of land: there is ample historical evidence of the power of transport infrastructure to shape patterns of land use. Developments in urban transport systems alter the way in which activity is distributed within the urban environment and lead to new development pressures and changes in land values and use. The availability of cars and lorries has generally spread accessibility rather than concentrating it in fixed transport corridors, and together with decreasing travel costs, has permitted much greater dispersal of activities.

Because of the long time scales and other factors influencing development pressures, the effects of transport infrastructure on land use are not easy to measure or predict. Nevertheless, there is growing evidence that the effects are significant. A report for the UK Government (ECOTEC, 1993) concluded that road, and in some cases commuter rail, schemes can significantly affect development pressures when they substantially change the relative accessibility of parts of an urban area or where they facilitate movement between an area with a buoyant land market, but development constraints, to another with lower land prices but more development opportunities. A more recent report has confirmed that new roads both redistribute and generate trips as people and businesses adjust to different patterns of accessibility (SACTRA, 1994). Evidence suggests that new roads around urban areas create particularly strong development pressures, encourage decentralisation of service and retail facilities, and can have significant impacts on land uses at the boundaries of urban areas (Headicar and Bixby, 1992; RCEP, 1994; Webster et al, 1988). Districts adjacent to the M25, the London orbital motorway, for example, attracted 2.4 million m² of office space between 1989 and 1991.

There is an emerging consensus that, at least in certain circumstances, provision of new transport infrastructure, especially major roads, can have a dynamic effect on land uses and hence on further demand for travel. The implications for appraisal of road schemes, for urban planning policies and for the environment are considerable.

There is one other area in which the effects of transport on land use are potentially important. Just as increasing mobility has had a profound influence on patterns of urban development, restraints on travel might also lead to changes in land-use patterns. In the 1970s, there was considerable interest in the possible effects of scarcity-induced fuel price rises on urban form. Since that time, concern about resource depletion has receded, but there is growing interest in the use of the price mechanism -- additional fuel taxes or road pricing, for example -- as an instrument of deliberate restraint, to alleviate congestion and pollution. The effects of such measures on land use are difficult to predict because we do not understand very well how people and firms would respond. Such evidence as there is suggests that in the short term, travel demand is relatively inelastic. In the medium term, it seems that people find ways of saving fuel without loss of mobility (by buying more efficient cars, for example), suggesting that any impact on land-use patterns would be small.

In the longer term, individuals and firms might respond to increasing travel costs by relocation (Dix and Goodwin, 1982; Goodwin, 1992; Oum, 1992). The effect could be to modify recent trends towards dispersal of activities, and some models suggest that the outcome might be a pattern of "decentralised concentration", with existing urban and suburban centres becoming increasingly attractive. Locations accessible only by road, such as the periphery of the larger cities and green field sites in rural areas, might become less attractive for many activities. Other forms of restraint might have different effects on land use. For example, urban road pricing or other measures such as stringent central area parking controls, in the absence of complementary policy measures, might lead directly to new development pressures by increasing the attraction of out-of-town locations for employment and services (Martin and Shock, 1989).

2.2.2 Influence of land use on transport

It is widely accepted that land-use patterns influence travel demand. This has led many to argue that planning policies could lead to a reduction in the need for movement and pollution. Potential reductions in travel demand from modification of land-use patterns would be long term and the effects cannot easily be isolated from those of other policies. However, a number of estimates have been made which suggest that travel demand could vary, in theory, by a factor of two or three between the most- and least-efficient land-use patterns.

Many of the studies from which these results are derived were conducted in the US where densities are low. In Europe, where patterns of urban development are more compact, the differences between existing and "ideal" are likely to be smaller. Furthermore, change in the urban fabric will in most cases be incremental. Nevertheless, recent modelling work in the UK suggested that land-use planning measures could achieve a 10-15 per cent reduction in carbon dioxide emissions over 20 years in a large urban sub-region (ECOTEC, 1993).[1] If modification of land-use patterns were part of a more comprehensive policy package, different measures may reinforce each other to achieve even greater reductions.

Variables usually considered significant in the land use/transport relationship are shown in Table 1.

Table 1. **Land-use variables and travel demand**

Land use	Travel
Physical separation of activities	
Density	Trip length
Mixing of land uses	Trip frequency
Degree of centralisation	Mode of travel
Size of urban area	Speed
Shape of urban area	
Relation of land uses to transport network	

Many of these variables are related. For example, density and the mixing of land uses both influence the physical separation of activities, and trip length is related to mode of travel. Furthermore, it is difficult to separate questions of density and mixing of land uses from those of urban shape and size. As mobility increases, so does the area over which land use and transport interact. Scale is important. Concentration of activities in a small town, for example, may represent decentralisation at the larger, regional scale

Most research has focused on the urban area or city-region. Often the existence of a relationship between land use and transport is not in doubt, but the strength, significance and policy implications of specific interactions are disputed (for reviews see ECOTEC, 1993; Owens 1986, 1989, 1990). Many studies link the amount and mode of travel to the physical separation of activities, which in turn is related to density and the degree to which different land uses are centralised, decentralised, clustered or dispersed. In theory, if facilities are close together, trips can be shorter, journeys can be combined and more trips can be made on foot. This might be achieved by higher densities, which permit greater choice for less travel with some sacrifice of space. Alternatively, decentralisation of facilities (so they are better mixed with residential areas) provides accessibility with less travel, with some loss of choice and economies of scale or agglomeration.

These considerations have led to the frequent assumption that higher densities and mixing of land uses will lead to less travel. But the picture is more complex than this. When the evidence is considered in more detail, it suggests that the physical separation of activities, the "need" to travel and the demand for travel are too easily confused.

Densities

Higher densities can reduce the physical separation of activities and provide a concentration of potential travellers in public transport catchment areas. In theory, higher densities could lead to shorter and fewer trips by car. This aspect of the land use/transport relationship has attracted considerable attention because of an implied conflict with established trends towards lower densities in western cities.

Both empirical and theoretical research broadly support the proposition that higher densities are associated with lower travel demand (e.g. Clark, 1974; Edwards and Schofer, 1975; Naess, 1995; Roberts, 1975; Keyes, 1982; Keyes and Peterson, 1977). Newman and Kenworthy's, (1989) much-quoted empirical work, for instance, found a strong inverse correlation between fuel consumption per capita and urban density, both within the US and in different world cities. Their results suggest that fuel consumption for transport rises sharply below densities of about 30 persons per hectare. In the UK, National Travel Survey data show that distance travelled by all modes, and by car, falls with increasing density; travel demand rises quickly as densities fall below 15 persons per hectare and falls sharply as density increases above 50 persons per hectare (ECOTEC, 1993). Results of research within metropolitan areas point in the same direction, suggesting that people living in low density outer suburbs travel further and more frequently by car than people living in the centre of the city (Gilbert, 1991; Mogridge, 1985; Naess, 1995).

Causality remains more difficult to demonstrate, because other variables, including income, car ownership and the extent of the public transport network are co-determinants of travel behaviour. When such factors are taken into account, the strength of the density/travel relationship is weakened. There is disagreement about the independent significance of density as an explanatory factor, with some authors maintaining that it is significant (ECOTEC, 1993; Keyes, 1982; Naess, 1995; Newman and Kenworthy) and others arguing that it is not a key variable (Gordon and Richardson, 1990; Mogridge, 1985; Rickaby, 1992).

Even if density is not a significant independent determinant of travel patterns, it is not irrelevant from a policy perspective. Reducing the physical separation of activities is a necessary if not a sufficient condition for reducing travel demand, and it is widely accepted that certain threshold densities are required for viable public transport systems. If other measures are adopted to reduce the amount of travel by private car, higher densities would be a way of maintaining accessibility and choice, and congestion should be reduced by other means. It is also important to note that quite moderate densities could (potentially) achieve many transport-related objectives. Integrated land use and transport planning is by no means incompatible with a high quality urban environment.

Mixing land uses

Physical separation of activities can also be reduced by mixing of residential and other land uses. Land uses may be centralised, decentralised, clustered or dispersed, not only within an urban area, but also on a sub-regional or regional scale. The question of urban size and its relation to travel demand (discussed below) is essentially about the distribution of activities on a larger scale.

"Clustering" of land uses makes multi-purpose trips more feasible (Markovitz, 1971), while some studies have suggested that dispersal of employment and services in large urban areas could lead to lower travel demand (Hemmens, 1967; Schneider and Beck, 1973). However, when factors like the propensity to travel, the premium placed on choice, and alternative modes are introduced, the picture becomes more complex. In particular, the ordering of alternative development patterns in terms of travel demand depends on assumptions made about mobility. Physical proximity does not have such a marked influence on travel requirements when mobility is high (Owens, 1981; Stone, 1973). It is not difficult to find examples of urban areas which have the potential or which were intended (as in British new towns) to be relatively self-contained, but which experience considerable in- and out-commuting and other travel (Breheny, 1990; Keyes, 1976). The autonomy of settlements tends to increase with size, but it is also a function of relative isolation (Breheny, 1990).

Assumptions about mobility (typically that it is the same as at present) explain why some researchers report little difference between land-use patterns which aim to bring facilities into close proximity and those which do not (ECOTEC, 1993; Rickaby et al., 1992; Webster et al., 1988). If people are not deterred by distance, travel requirements may be minimised by land-use patterns which do not minimise the physical separation of activities. Naess (1995) suggests that centralisation may be the best pattern for urban areas (see also Rickaby, 1987), but "decentralised concentration" is preferred on the regional scale.

Two considerations follow from this brief discussion of density and mixing of land uses. First, we cannot define the most travel-efficient forms of urban development without qualification, though there is broad consensus that peripheral or ex-urban residential development unrelated to jobs and services is a travel-intensive pattern, as is the siting of traffic-generating facilities in locations only accessible by car. Second, land-use planning in isolation is not an effective way of reducing travel demand. This presents interesting dilemmas. To opt for land-use patterns which minimise travel under conditions of high mobility (the centralised city) sets planning policies in opposition to other trends, risks congestion and in any case, seems curiously contradictory. But alternatives -- for example, decentralised concentration -- will only succeed if other policies (or forces majeures) come into play.

The fact that planners do not know future levels of mobility apparently introduces a major element of uncertainty into land-use planning to reduce travel demand. One response is to identify robust options. Although the best cannot be defined unambiguously, there is consensus about what is transport-inefficient, and some urban development patterns perform relatively well under a range of possible future conditions.

An alternative way to look at this problem is that if no other steps are taken to restrain traffic growth, planning to reduce the physical separation of activities is reduced to a "contingency safeguard" (Webster et al., 1988, p. 377)[2]. It would also be extraordinarily inconsistent to use a relatively blunt long-term instrument to influence travel behaviour without applying more direct measures, such as pricing. However, if planners could assume that their policies would not be working in isolation, they could aim more confidently for patterns which reduce the physical separation of activities. Avoidance of obviously transport-intensive development, and concentration of growth in moderately sized centres, especially along public transport routes, would then be a logical complement to other policy measures.

Land-use planning and public transport

Land-use variables are often claimed to affect the mode as well as the amount of travel. Reducing the physical separation of activities could encourage people to walk or cycle. In fact, most trips are short, but our understanding of travel behaviour at this level is hampered by the lack of data.[3] Policies directed towards safety, amenity and priority for cyclists and pedestrians are of crucial importance.

Other factors, such as density, may influence the viability of public transport.[4] For obvious operational reasons, certain urban patterns are better suited to the efficient and economic operation of public transport than others. Relative concentration of homes and facilities maximises accessibility to transport routes and encourages high-load factors, whereas dispersed patterns of development are difficult to serve by conventional public transport facilities.

Many modelling exercises suggest, however, that location policies are likely to have only a minor impact on modal split. Webster *et al.*, (1988, p. 394) conclude that *"the only way to achieve appreciable shifts in the modal shares is to attack the problem directly using measures which change the relative costs and/or speeds of travel by competing modes"*. However, these results are predictable given the assumptions (lack of traffic restraint or management) and reinforce the conclusion that land-use planning policies will not be effective in isolation (Rickaby *et al.*, 1992). This is not the same as denying a role for planning measures to facilitate the implementation of other policies.

Models tend to deal with broad distributions of population and employment, rather than the location of specific developments, but a growing body of empirical evidence suggests that the latter is an important influence on mode of travel. Examples are shown in Table 2. These findings are worrying when so many facilities have been sited to be accessible by car and lorry and are virtually inaccessible by any other means. These trends are considered in more detail in Chapter 3.

Table 2. **Examples of effects of location on travel behaviour**

Location/land use	Effect	Source
Major office centre, UK; adjacent to railway station or 0.25 miles away	Proportion of train journeys falls from 11 per cent to 0.4 per cent	ECOTEC, 1993
Out-of-town business parks, UK	93 per cent use cars to travel to work	RCEP, 1994
UK Gateshead MetroCentre cf. Newcastle City Centre, UK	80 per cent travel by car cf. 27 per cent	TEST, 1989
Copenhagen insurance company moving from site near central station to suburbs	Car commuting increase from 26 to 54 per cent	ECMT and OECD, 1995
Supermarkets, inner London and freestanding site, outer London	Car journeys 33 per cent and 95 per cent respectively	RCEP, 1994

Telecommunications

Access to some facilities can be provided with no need for movement at all through telecommunications, and it is often suggested that advances in this field will reduce the need for personal travel. Evidence for this substitution is currently slim. (Indeed, in some circumstances telecommunications may stimulate rather than replace travel, by establishing contacts who then need to meet). It is plausible that more people may be able to work from home for at least part of the time, and some organisations are already encouraging their employees to do this. However, the option is restricted, at least initially, to a relatively small group of people.

In the short term, developments in telecommunications seem unlikely to have a major impact on travel. In the longer term, telecommuting and teleshopping, and perhaps telecommunications with doctors and various advisory services, may become significant, even if the effect is mainly to spread the travel peak. One estimate suggests that if a third of journeys were replaced by telecommuting for 4 million UK residents per year, about 2 per cent of present car energy use could be saved (Transnet, 1990). The effects of substituting telecommunications for travel could have significant implications for land-use planning and are certainly too important to be ignored. As yet, however, the magnitude of any effect is unclear, and the relevant time scales are probably quite long.

Conclusions on land use and transport

The following conclusions about the impact of land use on transport emerge from a large body of research:

-- Reducing the physical separation of activities is often a necessary but rarely a sufficient condition for reducing the amount of travel.

-- Density is inversely related to travel demand and energy consumption, but its significance as an independent variable is disputed. Higher densities may provide a necessary but not sufficient condition for less travel, and need not conflict with amenity.

-- The strength of the land use/transport relationship depends on assumptions about mobility and other policies. In some models, land use has very little impact on travel behaviour; in others, variations in the amount of travel of up to 150 per cent are reported between land-use patterns.

-- The relative efficiency of different land-use patterns depends on assumptions made about people's mobility.

-- If mobility is high, travel behaviour is not very sensitive to land-use patterns; compact urban development and centralisation would probably minimise travel demand; but congestion could be a problem. However, it is illogical to consider the impacts of planning policies in isolation.

-- If mobility is restrained, decentralised concentration performs well. Large urban areas perform better as "clusters". However, transport efficiency in settlements of different sizes depends on the context.

-- Small- to moderate-sized urban areas with a good mix of employment and services would offer efficiency, accessibility and choice. Towns with populations from 10 000 to 100 000 or even more are variously reported to be efficient, with some emphasis on the 20 000 to 30 000 range (as independent towns or forming sub-units of a larger settlement).

--   Mode of journey to work seems to be influenced by the proximity of employment to public transport and by the availability of parking spaces.

--   Peripheral or ex-urban development unrelated to jobs and services is inefficient in transport terms, as is the location of traffic-generating activities in places which can only be reached by car.

--   Telecommunications have some potential to substitute for movement, but effects are unclear and are not likely to be substantial in the short- to medium-term.

The evidence reviewed above suggests that, within an appropriate policy framework, land-use planning in cities and urban regions could be employed to bring about changes in travel patterns. Forward planning and development control should seek to encourage land-use patterns that achieve a high level of accessibility whilst minimising the need for movement or the use of environmentally harmful modes of transport. This points to integrated development within existing towns and cities, closely related to public transport links. Where transport networks do not already exist, they should be planned in conjunction with the development of land. Appropriate policies need to be adopted in urban development plans, and enforced through development control.

Research can indicate what "ought to be". Actual trends, in most OECD countries, have been moving in the opposite direction. These trends, together with their social and environmental implications, are considered first in the following chapter.

3. PROBLEMS AND POLICIES: LEARNING FROM EXPERIENCE?

Many city regions in OECD countries face a seemingly intractable dilemma over trends in patterns of development and transport. On the one hand, there is a widely held view that current trends are not environmentally sustainable, even in the short- to medium-term. On the other hand, many people feel that trends are deep-seated and if not exactly immutable, then at least politically impossible to change.

197

This section has three objectives: first, to explore the forces underlying trends in urban land use and transport and their effects in city regions; second, to consider examples of policies, both well-established and more novel, designed to control, modify or reverse these trends; and third, to draw some lessons about the principles underlying effective integration of land use and transport planning. The illustration of problems and policies is drawn mainly from western European cities since these have more in common with CEE counterparts than cities in other OECD countries, though the latter too might provide some valuable lessons. Caution must always be exercised in applying experience in one social and cultural context to another and in assuming the logic of learning from others' mistakes. Nevertheless, there is a great deal of experience which might be shared to mutual benefit.

3.1 What has gone wrong?

Current patterns of traffic growth and congestion in western European cities are largely the result of mutually reinforcing land use and transport trends over half a century or more. While cities have adopted widely differing policies with varying degrees of success, the spiral of increasing mobility and dispersal of land uses is remarkably consistent. It is leading to "excessive travel by car in cities and their immediate surroundings" (ECMT and OECD, 1995) and the social and environmental impacts are widely acknowledged to be severe.

Typically, in western European city regions, the trends may be summarised as follows. Rapidly increasing personal mobility has led to decentralisation of population and employment to the suburbs and, since the 1950s, to smaller freestanding settlements in non-metropolitan areas. Growing mobility has also encouraged increasing physical separation of homes, jobs and services; this has been reinforced by the concentration of shops, schools, hospitals and other facilities into fewer, larger units. Increasingly, retail and commercial facilities are located outside city centres so that they are easily reached by car and lorry but may be virtually inaccessible by any other means (while reducing the viability of facilities which can be reached on foot). At the same time, within some cities, transport options have been pre-empted by insensitive development decisions: residential and office development along the banks of the river Thames in London, for example, have resulted in the cumulative loss of riverside sites to non-river related uses.

These trends have been associated with a significant increase in the amount and complexity of travel, especially by car. In the UK, for example, the total amount of personal travel grew by 61 per cent between 1965 and 1985, with people making both more and longer journeys; the distance travelled by car doubled over the same period (May, 1992). The picture is similar elsewhere (ECMT and OECD, 1995). As well as reinforcing the outward spread of cities initiated by more linear forms of transport, the car has permitted more diffuse and geographically spread patterns of activity. The changed pattern of demand is then confirmed by new roads, which in turn generate more traffic and stimulate further development (possibly running counter to existing planning policies). Even when urban areas have been planned with the intention of being self-contained, high mobility has led to complex travel patterns which have become increasingly difficult to serve by public or non-motorised transport.

The environmental impacts of these trends are the subject of mounting alarm. They threaten the sustainability of cities both internally -- because traffic undermines the quality of life and environment within urban areas, in spite of technical fixes -- and in its external dimension, because cities have to be supported by wider resources and environmental capacities (Owens, 1994b). Economic and social impacts are an important part of this general picture. It is well known that congestion imposes high economic costs. Social effects include the severance of communities and increasing difficulty of social interaction in urban spaces, as well as the polarisation of society into those with and without access to cars. The latter group remains substantial, in spite of a tendency for it to be overlooked by planners, and suffers from a new dimension of social deprivation arising not so much from lack of access to a car *per se*, but from deterioration in local services which can no longer compete with car-oriented facilities.

Trends in travel, car ownership and use, urban decentralisation and associated economic and lifestyle changes have been thoroughly documented elsewhere, and it is not the intention to provide further details here (for recent analysis and illustration, see ECMT and OECD, 1995; RCEP, 1994). It is important to recognise that the changes are complex and interrelated, and that it would be too simplistic to say that mobility "causes" land-use change or vice versa. Land use and travel patterns are themselves manifestations of demographic, economic and social developments. It is worth exploring, however, the most fundamental question for those concerned with urban land use and transport policy: whether trends towards greater mobility and dispersal are so deeply rooted that it would be extremely difficult, and perhaps even wrong, to attempt to change them.

Those who argue this point of view tend to make two important assumptions: that trends are the inevitable outcome of the expressed preferences of people and firms for mobility and decentralised locations; and that the resulting development patterns meet such aspirations. These assumptions are questionable on several grounds. First, in many OECD countries, so called "deep-rooted trends" have been stimulated by actions of the state which in turn may reflect powerful corporate interests. Investment criteria favouring roads, tax relief on company cars (e.g. in the UK) or on commuting (e.g. in the Netherlands) and permissive planning policies all stand accused of promoting decentralisation. The important recent confirmation by a UK Advisory Committee that new roads generate traffic -- sometimes in very substantial amounts -- (SACTRA, 1994) reinforces the point.

It might be argued that even if policies encourage decentralisation they nevertheless reflect "consumer choice" (see Breheny, 1995). This is a questionable assertion in itself, but even if it is true, it is not axiomatic that the development patterns which reflect consumer choice ultimately meet the aspirations of individuals or represent what the community would consciously choose if the consequences were anticipated. Location and transport choices have many of the characteristics of prisoners' dilemmas, where rational self-interest does not produce the best outcome, even for each individual, and planning is needed in the interests of efficiency. More importantly, perhaps, there are circumstances in which our preferences as citizens for social and environmental outcomes can be satisfied only by policies that counter our immediate preferences as consumers (Owens, 1995; Sagoff, 1988). Indeed if consumer choice were sovereign, we would not have urban planning policies at all.

Another crucial factor about the choices which are manifest in current trends is that they have been made in a context in which many of the costs, including environmental costs, are externalised. Thus market failure, as well as the influence of particular policies, contributes to the blunting of real costs and influences the evolution of land use and travel patterns.

3.2 Putting things right

If transport systems are to serve patterns of urban development, instead of dominating them, it will be necessary to change the trends outlined above. The need for management of traffic demand is now widely acknowledged, as is the role of integrated land use and transport planning in demand management. We do not always need to think afresh: certain long-established policies -- urban containment through green belts in the UK (Hall, 1973) and through a "compact city" policy in the Netherlands (ECMT and OECD, 1995), integrated land use and transport planning in the radial suburban development of the Copenhagen

"Fingerplan" (City of Copenhagen, 1995) and in cities like Stockholm and Vienna (ECMT and OECD, 1995), control imposed on out-of-centre retailing in France and the Netherlands (TEST, 1989) -- all work in the right direction. However, the primary rationale of these policies was not related to transport and the environment, and (while the effects might otherwise have been worse) they have been unable to stem the growth of travel demand as mobility has increased.

Recently, however, a more purposeful set of policies has begun to emerge with the clear objectives of reducing the demand for travel and encouraging the use of environmentally-friendly transport modes. These range from broad-brush strategies at the national or regional scale to specific measures which can be implemented at the micro-level in urban areas. Furthermore, it is generally recognised that these policies must be part of a more comprehensive package if they are to achieve their objectives. Here some examples of new policies at different scales are considered. While it is normally too soon to judge how effective such policies might be, some sense of how policies are working in practice is given wherever possible.

3.2.1 Strategic integration of transport and land-use planning

In a number of countries, attempts are now being made to use the land-use planning system as an instrument of transport and environmental policy. The Netherlands National Environmental Policy Plan, for example, aims to reduce car use through policies involving the concentration of housing, work, services and leisure facilities (Netherlands Second Chamber of the States General, 1989; Netherlands Ministry of Housing, Physical Planning and the Environment, 1990b, 1994b). These policies have been adopted in the context of emissions targets which necessitate a reduction in the rate of growth of traffic.

The Netherlands ABC Policy

More specifically, but still at the strategic level, the Dutch government has adopted the now well-known "ABC location policy" (Netherlands Ministry of Housing, Physical Planning and the Environment, 1990a), which relates mobility profiles of businesses and amenities, in terms of labour and visitor intensities and vehicle dependence, to accessibility profiles of locations by different forms of transport. The rationale for the policy is that spatial planning can be used to influence the amount and mode of travel: it is not an end in itself, but a contribution towards policy goals relating to urbanisation, mobility and environmental protection. Its objectives are both environmental and economic, since it is recognised that good accessibility and a high quality environment and living space are vital for the economic and social functioning of the Netherlands' (Netherlands Ministry of Housing, Physical Planning and the Environment, 1994a, para 1.3). Traffic growth threatens both accessibility and environmental quality.

Development of the policy, which has been in force since the late 1980s, involves drawing up procedural plans for each region by representatives of central government, the provinces and municipalities, in consultation with representatives from business, industry, public transport operators and other interested groups. These classify locations (A being the most and C the least accessible by public transport), consider infrastructure requirements, indicate the types of development which will be permitted in particular locations and set priorities for development. Implementation involves the use of different instruments by different levels of government, with the emphasis on co-ordination.

Progress with the policy is being carefully monitored. The response of the provinces to the requirement to implement ABC policy has been mainly positive, though it has been necessary to permit some degree of regional differentiation of policy, based on extent of urbanisation, the (improved) quality of public transport and the opportunities for using bicycles and other transport modes. For example, in areas where public transport is still inadequate, a phased introduction of parking standards -- among the most controversial provisions of the ABC policy -- will be allowed, and criteria for B locations are quite variable. A recent assessment suggests that nearly all provinces are paying due regard to location policy (de Jong, 1993, discussed in Netherlands Ministry of Housing, Spatial Planning and the Environment 1994a). At municipal level, it has taken longer than anticipated to draw up procedural plans for urban districts, due to "over-optimistic expectations of administrative co-operation between different municipalities" (Netherlands Ministry of Housing, Spatial Planning and the Environment, 1994a, section 2.3).

The policy is inevitably taking time to have an impact. Though it has been in operation for some six years, "labour intensive industry is still being established in locations which are poorly served by public transport" (Netherlands Ministry of Housing, Spatial Planning and the Environment, 1994a, Section 2.4) due to time lags in the planning system. While the underlying philosophy is now widely accepted, support remains stronger in the Randstad and the Stedenring, where congestion and environmental problems are more apparent, than in less urbanised parts of the Netherlands (Amundson, 1993; Netherlands Ministry of Housing, Spatial

Planning and the Environment 1994a). Perhaps not surprisingly, businesses display a somewhat ambivalent attitude towards the policy, with parking limits, in particular, becoming a bone of contention.

As the Dutch government acknowledges, *"the effects of location policy on traffic can only be measured in the longer term"* and in any case, are difficult to isolate (Netherlands Ministry of Housing, Spatial Planning and the Environment 1994a). Growth in motor traffic has been less than expected since the policy was introduced, but this might be attributed to a variety of causes. One specific example relates to the Environment Ministry itself. When it moved to its present location adjacent to the Central Station in the Hague, the percentage of employees travelling to work by car fell from 41 per cent to 4 per cent and the percentage using public transport increased from 34 per cent to 77 per cent.[5] The change is attributed to the A location combined with parking policy.

The Dutch Environment Ministry has concluded that the ABC policy is successful and should be maintained. It is only to be expected that the Ministry will be positive about its own policy, while recognising the more obvious problems of implementation. The official view does not necessarily reflect a consensus, however. Others have suggested that the government may have implemented the ABC policy too soon and have failed to resolve certain inconsistencies, in particular the lack of integration of walking and cycling (which may be more important substitutes than public transport outside the Randstad) and the failure to distinguish modal share from the number of kilometres driven (Amundson, 1993). B locations are criticised as providing a "get-out" clause for municipalities while in reality not achieving anything significant.

UK Planning Policy Guidance on Transport

In the UK, new Planning Policy Guidance (PPG) on Transport is similar in spirit to the ABC policy but less specific in its provisions. Local planning authorities must take this guidance into account in preparing their development plans. It aims to encourage planning and transport policies to:

-- reduce growth in the length and number of motorised journeys;
-- encourage alternative means of travel which have less environmental impact; and hence
-- reduce reliance on the private car.

The means by which the guidance suggests these objectives should be achieved are shown in Table 3.

Table 3. **Policies in UK planning policy guidance on transport**

Development plans should aim to reduce the need to travel, especially by car, by:

-- influencing the location of different types of development relative to transport provision (and vice versa); and

-- fostering forms of development which encourage walking, cycling and public transport use.

To meet these aims, local authorities should adopt planning and land-use policies to:

-- promote development within urban areas, at locations highly accessible by means other than the private car;

-- locate major generators of travel demand in existing centres which are highly accessible by means other than the private car;

-- strengthen existing local centres, which offer a range of everyday community, shopping and employment opportunities, and aim to protect and enhance their viability and vitality;

-- maintain and improve choice for people to walk, cycle or catch public transport rather than drive between homes and facilities which they need to visit regularly; and

-- limit parking provision for developments and other on- or off-street parking provision to discourage reliance on the car for work and other journeys where there are effective alternatives.

It is too early to evaluate the operation of the new planning policy guidance. It is likely that British planning authorities will face similar problems to those encountered by the Dutch in implementing the ABC policy. These include problems with development in accessible locations (e.g. contaminated land); conflicts of interest between municipalities wanting to attract commercial development; conflicts between the need to provide efficient and frequent public transport and increasing emphasis on cost-effectiveness; and conflicts over parking standards.

3.2.2   The city scale

The Dutch ABC policy, the UK's PPG 13 and similar developments in other countries represent a broad strategic approach to urban development and transport planning. More specific policies at the urban region or city level also provide interesting examples of integration, though as yet relatively few cities have explicitly adopted land-use planning measures as instruments of transport and environmental policy. Even when they have, the development is so recent that it is usually too soon to judge the effectiveness of the policies. Nevertheless, it is worth commenting on several characteristics.

First, it is useful to have a framework. Policies in some cities are related to broad objectives or even to more specific targets. In York, an historic city in the UK with a population of 104 000, there is a quantified aim of holding the number of cars coming into the city in the morning rush hour constant (against projected increases in local traffic of 25-29 per cent by 2006). This in turn is related to two broad objectives in the plan for the City:

-- to implement land-use transportation strategies which facilitate the implementation of land-use objectives of the plan, whilst minimising traffic and travel generation; and

-- to achieve development patterns which give people the choice of using more environmentally-friendly means of transport than the car (City of York, 1993).

Second, there are attempts to plan land uses so as to facilitate and promote the use of public transport. Development of the Copenhagen "Fingerplan" in the 1980s, for example, placed greater emphasis on public transport and sustainability, advocating more compact urban patterns, with points of high accessibility where bus and train routes intersect as primary locations for employment: in addition, the 1993 Plan encourages construction on former industrial sites, vacant railway land or along the inner harbour, resulting in a change of land use, but a retention of a compact urban structure. It is significant that the level of car traffic in Copenhagen is no higher than it was 20 years ago.

In York, developments are to be concentrated in locations well-served by public transport and within 400m of a bus stop or regular public transport service, and development control policies will employ maximum standards for parking. It is also crucial that where public transport does not already exist, its provision is integrated with the development of land. In Schiedam in the Netherlands, expansion of the tram service connecting a large-scale urban expansion project (Spaland, with 3 500 dwellings) with the centres of Schiedam and Rotterdam was built into the development plans for the neighbourhood. It was considered very important that public transport infrastructure should be in place before rather than after the development of housing (Municipality of Schiedam, 1991).

A third important characteristic of integrated land use and transport planning at the city scale is the discrimination in favour of environmentally-friendly modes of transport: this extends, of course, to the local scale where specific measures may make walking and cycling safe, attractive and normal. Interestingly, the City of York has adopted a clear hierarchy of users for consideration in land use and transport policy:

i)   pedestrians;
ii)   people with mobility problems;
iii) cyclists;
iv)   public transport users;
v)   commercial/business users;
vi)   car-borne shoppers;
vii) coach-borne visitors;
viii) car-borne commuters and visitors.

This is an example of privileging the use of green modes. The City of Groningen (the world's third ranking city for bicycle use) refers to a similar policy as "selective accessibility". There is an important land-use dimension, not only in the provision of dense network of cycle and footways, but in the location of facilities close to this network, in the emphasis on compact and mixed urban development (City of Groningen, 1994) and in integrating environmentally-friendly modes, for example by providing cycle parking facilities at public transport stops, as in some Norwegian cities (ECMT and OECD, 1995). In Schiedam too, the policy is to make cycle routes direct, whereas routes by car may be more circuitous. The network of foot and cycle paths includes recreational routes through green areas running from the city centre to the open countryside. It is also recognised that cycle paths used for access to everyday activities must be perceived to be safe and secure, so they are designed to be wide and free of shrubs (Municipality of Schiedam, 1991).

Not only the movement of people, but also freight deliveries constitute a significant traffic problem and environmental impact in urban areas. Some cities are now putting emphasis on transhipment facilities, where freight can be transferred from large vehicles to smaller ones. York makes provision for such facilities in its local plan. In Leiden (Netherlands), goods bound for the city centre will be taken to a distribution centre on the outskirts of the city from which they will be transferred into ecologically sound vehicles (Shankland Cox, 1994).

3.2.3 The local scale

Many of the measures discussed above have land-use implications at the local as well as at the city scale and require co-ordination between land use and transport planning for their successful implementation. In York, as in many cities in Europe, environmental conditions for pedestrians and shoppers have been greatly enhanced by pedestrianisation. The objective must be for urban spaces to be for people, rather than cars, whether moving or stationary. In some cities, for example Copenhagen, not only are many streets dedicated to pedestrians and cyclists but also car parking spaces are being removed, so that attractive squares and other spaces become areas for social interaction rather than car parks. Increasingly it is recognised that planning and traffic management in residential areas beyond the city centre also need to make walking and cycling safe and attractive, with the car the mode of last resort.

3.3 Emerging principles

From theory and practice to date, principles for integration of land use and transport planning rather than blueprints for "ideal" cities emerge. Though there are many uncertainties, enough is known about the transport implications of alternative development patterns for basic principles to be incorporated into urban planning practice. It is possible to identify urban forms that are robust and flexible and to avoid forms of development which are clearly travel intensive. People cannot be forced to travel less, but they can be given the choice to do so: planning can help to avoid car dependency. Here a number of broad principles are outlined. It will be necessary for these to be adapted to local contexts. With this in mind, questions to be explored in relation to CEE cities are highlighted.

Planning is necessary but not sufficient

Land-use planning is a necessary but not a sufficient condition for reducing travel demand and encouraging environmentally-friendly modes; urban planning is only likely to be effective in reducing the environmental impacts of transport if it forms an integral part of a comprehensive package of policy measures. Within this framework, planning becomes a key instrument for shifting the focus from mobility to accessibility. In the context of CEE cities, the strength of the land-use planning system and the opportunities to combine it with other policy instruments will need to be considered.

Targets are needed

Land-use planning is most likely to be successful within an environmental policy framework which sets clear targets, for example, for reduction in emissions of pollutants by specified dates, for levels of traffic or for modal split. Planning then becomes one of a range of policy instruments, including information, regulation and use of the price mechanism, applied consistently in order to achieve these goals. Realistic but challenging targets for CEE cities need to be explored.

Vertical and horizontal integration are essential

Co-ordination between the local, strategic and regional scales and between transport and land-use planning is essential. This has been an important feature of the Netherlands ABC policy, for example, though it has not always been easy to achieve. From the outset, the co-operation of authorities at different levels was considered essential and a "common working procedure" was agreed by relevant Central Government Departments, the Interprovincial Consultative Committee and the Association of Dutch Municipalities.

In addition to such vertical co-ordination, the need for horizontal integration between different government functions was explicitly recognised. In Groningen, the travel management policy developed initially for the city *"has shown its limits in terms of action on a territorial scale"* (City of Groningen, 1994), and since 1991, has been extended to the Groningen region. The Regional Mobility Plan has involved national, provincial and local decision makers. Unless there is a strategic level of application, competitive pressures will defeat attempts to restrain traffic and to plan for more sustainable land-use patterns. Relevant questions for CEE cities include their relationship with the wider city region and the extent to which different aspects of municipal policies can successfully be co-ordinated.

Integrated development should be encouraged

Planning policies should encourage development in centres large enough to provide access to a good range of jobs and services without the need for long journeys, and with good public transport links to employment and other facilities to offer a viable alternative to the private car. An important question is to what extent such centres already exist within CEE cities: are suburban centres well served by local services and jobs, for example, and how well connected are they to larger centres?

Avoid car dependence

There should be a presumption against dispersed, low density residential areas and developments heavily dependent on car use (such as out-of-town retail centres). Some degree of concentration, though not necessarily centralisation, of facilities is desirable: this will depend on the scale. To what extent are pressures for dispersal and lower density development building up in CEE cities?

Promote selective accessibility

Development -- especially that which generates a large amount of traffic -- should be integrated with public transport, cycle and pedestrian routes; moderately high densities along transport routes should be encouraged. Policies of "selective accessibility" should discriminate in favour of environmentally-friendly modes. It will be very useful to explore the potential for selective accessibility in CEE: does the potential already exist or must it be created?

Integrate land use and transport planning

Land use and transport planning need to be integrated at all scales. Broadly, this means the full consideration of the land-use implications of transport infrastructure provision, as well as of the travel and consequent environmental implications of land-use policies. When there are intensive development pressures -- as is now likely to be the case in CEE cities -- it is both difficult and important to ensure that these conditions are met.

Resist "car culture"

The operational and institutional implications of integrated land-use and transport planning need to be carefully considered. They include not only the horizontal and vertical integration noted above, but a change of culture which associates car use with freedom. This has proved a major political challenge in the West and may constitute an even greater one in CEE cities. Political courage is essential.

4. CONCLUSION

Transport, land-use and environment are fundamentally interrelated. As a result of complex social and economic changes, land-use and travel patterns have become less sustainable, environmental costs have been externalised, and extrapolation of these trends implies unacceptable environmental consequences. Furthermore, it is now widely accepted that the environmental impacts of transport cannot be mitigated by a technical fix alone.

Land-use planning is an important means of maintaining accessibility and choice whilst controlling mobility. It is not a panacea, and in order to be effective must be set within a wider framework. In this context, however, it becomes a key element of sustainable urban transport policies.

Many commentators in the West now talk of a "new realism" in transport policy (e.g. Goodwin *et al.*, 1991). But the intellectual recognition of the need for demand management, for a cohesive transport policy framework, and for the integration of land use and transport planning still has to be translated into social behaviour. This will be a major political challenge.

Perhaps the most important lesson to be learned from the recent reconsideration of transport policy is that the urban future can be planned as well as predicted: sustainable land use and transport systems are a matter of choice. In relatively compact cities, with extensive public transport networks and relatively low car dependency, the choice is to build upon this to improve urban quality and accessibility and to encourage environmentally-friendly modes of transport or to enter the spiral of mobility, dispersal and environmental degradation from which so many cities in western Europe now realise that they must escape.

NOTES

1. This includes effects on mode as well as travel demand.

2. It is often argued that even if policies have little impact on travel patterns under current conditions, they are still useful because they keep options open for the future.

3. In the UK, for example, information on journeys of less than one mile is not routinely collected or included in official transport statistics.

4. Rail and bus systems are generally more energy-efficient than cars, though actual efficiencies are affected by a number of variables, including load factors. On the basis of average passenger loads, most estimates suggest that cars (and taxis) in urban areas use the most energy per passenger-kilometre, and buses (or minibuses) travelling in uncongested road conditions use the least; rail systems occupy a position somewhere in between. The higher the load factor for public transport, the more significant its energy advantages become.

5. M. Post, Ministry of Housing, Spatial Planning and Environment, personal communication 1994.

BIBLIOGRAPHY

AMUNDSON, C. (1993), Public Policy and Public Transport: An Associated Research Project Report: Research Visit to the Netherlands 20-27th March 1993 (available from Chris Amundson, DipTP, MRTPI, MCIT).

BREHENY, M. (1995), "The compact city and transport energy consumption", *Transactions of the Institute of British Geographers NS*, 20, 1, 81-101.

CITY OF COPENHAGEN, Lord Mayor's Department (1995) "A tale of two cities: II", presented at Conference on The European City, Copenhagen, April.

CITY OF GRONINGEN (1994), *Groningen General Travel Management Policy*, City of Groningen, The Netherlands (contact Mr. Bloemkolk).

CITY OF YORK (1993), *York Local Plan*, City of York.

CLARK, James W. (1974), "Defining an Urban Growth Strategy which will Achieve Maximum Travel Demand Reduction and Access Opportunity Enhancement", *Research Report 73* (7 UMTA WA 0003 74) Seattle, Department of Civil Engineering, Washington University.

DE JONG, B. (1994), "Area based approach: vision and action", presented at The European Conference on Sustainable Cities and Towns, Aalborg, May (The Hague, Province of South Holland, Integrated Environmental Management Section).

DIX, M. C. and GOODWIN, P. B. (1982), "Petrol prices and car use: a synthesis of conflicting evidence", *Transport Policy Decision Making*, 2, 179-195.

ECMT and OECD (1995), "Urban Travel and Sustainable Development", Paris, OECD.

ECOTEC (1993), "Reducing Transport Emissions Through Planning", London, HMSO.

EDWARDS, J. L. and SCHOFER, J. L. (1975), "Relationships between Transportation Energy Consumption and Urban Structure" Results of Simulation Studies, Minneapolis, MN: Department of Civil and Mineral Engineering.

GILBERT, R. (1991), "Cities and Global Warming", Toronto, Canadian Urban Institute.

GOODWIN, P (1992), "A review of new demonstrations of elasticity with special reference to short and long run effects of price change", *Transport Economics and Policy*, May.

GOODWIN, P., HALLETT, S., KENNY, F. and STOKES, G. (1991), "Transport: The New Realism", Report to the Rees Jeffreys Road Fund, Oxford, University of Oxford Transport Studies Unit.

GORDON, P. and RICHARDSON, H. (1989), "Gasoline consumption and cities - a reply", *Journal of the American Planning Association*, 55, 342-345.

HALL, P. (1973), "The Containment of Urban England: Vols I and II", London, Allen and Unwin.

HEADICAR, P. and BIXBY, B. (1992), "Concrete and Tyres", London, CPRE.

HEMMENS, G. (1967), "Experiments in urban form and structure", *Highway Research Record 207*, 32-41.

KEYES, D.L., "Reducing travel and fuel use through urban planning", in R. W. Burchell and D. Listoken (eds) *Energy and Land use*, Centre for Urban Policy Research, New Brunswick, 1982.

KEYES, D.L. and PETERSON, G. (1977), "Urban Development and Energy Consumption", Working Paper No. 5049, Washington DC, Urban Land Institute.

MARKOVITZ, J. (1971), "Transportation implications of economic cluster development", *Interim Technical Report* 4245-4424, New York, Tri-State Regional Transportation Commission.

MARTIN, D. and SHOCK, R. A. W. (1989), "Energy Use and Energy Efficiency in the UK Transport Sector up to the Year 2010", London, HMSO.

MAY, A. D. (1992), "Future lifestyles: transport", paper to RTPI National Planning Conference.

MOGRIDGE, M. (1985), "Transport, land-use and energy interaction", *Urban Studies* 22, 481-492.

MUNICIPALITY OF SCHIEDAM (1991), "Physical Planning and Ecology: the Spaland-area", Entry for ICLEI Competition, Schiedam, Municipality of Schiedam.

NAESS, P. (1995), "Urban Form and Energy Use for Transport: A Nordic Experience", Dr. Ing Thesis, University of Trondheim.

NETHERLANDS MINISTRY OF HOUSING, PHYSICAL PLANNING AND ENVIRONMENT, Ministry of Transport and Public Works and Ministry of Economic Affairs (1990a), Working Document "Guiding Mobility by a Location Policy for Businesses and Amenities", The Hague, May.

NETHERLANDS MINISTRY OF HOUSING, PHYSICAL PLANNING AND THE ENVIRONMENT (1990b), "National Environmental Policy Plan Plus", English Version, The Hague, Ministry of Housing, etc., Department for Information and International Relations, p.53.

NETHERLANDS MINISTRY OF HOUSING, PHYSICAL PLANNING AND ENVIRONMENT, Ministry of Transport and Public Works, Ministry of Economic Affairs (1994a), "Location Policy in Progress: The Story So Far", Ref. 31220, The Hague, Ministry of Housing, Spatial Planning and Environment.

NETHERLANDS MINISTRY OF HOUSING, PHYSICAL PLANNING AND ENVIRONMENT (1994b), "National Environmental Policy Plan 2: The Environment: Today's Touchstone Summary", The Hague, Ministry of Housing, Spatial Planning and Environment.

NETHERLANDS SECOND CHAMBER OF THE STATES GENERAL (1989), "National Environmental Policy Plan" The Hague, The Netherlands, Ministry of Housing, Physical Planning and Environment.

NEWMAN, P.W.G. and KENWORTHY, J.R. (1989), "Gasoline consumption and cities", *APA Journal*, Winter.

OUM, T.H. *et al.* (1992), "Concepts of price elasticity of transport demand and recent empirical estimates", *Transport Economics and Policy*, May.

OWENS, S. (1981), "The Energy Implications of Alternative Rural Development Patterns", PhD Thesis, University of East Anglia, Norwich.

OWENS, S. (1986), "Energy, Planning and Urban Form", London, Pion.

OWENS, S. (1989), "Models and urban energy analysis: a review and critique", in L. Lundqvist *et al* (eds) Spatial Energy Analysis: Models for Strategic Energy Decisions in an Urban and Regional Context, London, Gower, pp. 227-44.

OWENS, S. (1990), "Land-use planning for energy efficiency", in J.B. Cullingworth (ed) *Energy, Land and Public Policy*, Center for Energy and Urban Policy Research, University of Delaware, USA, Transaction Publishers, pp. 53-98.

OWENS, S. (1994a), "From predict and provide to predict and prevent: pricing and planning in transport policy", *Transport Policy* 2, 1, pp. 43-49.

OWENS, S. (1994b), "Can land use planning produce the ecological city?", *Town and Country Planning*, 63,6, pp. 170-173.

OWENS, S. (1995), "The compact city and transport energy consumption: a response to Michael Breheny", *Transactions of the Institute of British Geographers NS*, 20, 3, in press.

RICKABY, P., STEADMAN, P. and BARRETT, M. (1992), "Patterns of land use in English towns: implications for energy use and carbon dioxide emissions", in M. Breheny (ed) *Sustainable Development and Urban Form*, London, Pion, pp. 182-196.

RICKABY, P. (1987), "Six settlement patterns compared", *Environment and Planning B, Planning and Design*, 14, pp. 193-223.

ROBERTS, J.S. (1975), "Energy and land use: analysis of alternative development patterns", *Environmental Comment*, September, 2-11.

ROYAL COMMISSION ON ENVIRONMENTAL POLLUTION (1994), "Transport and the Environment", Eighteenth Report, Cm 2674, London, HMSO.

SACTRA (Standing Advisory Committee on Trunk Road Assessment) (1994), "Trunk Roads and the Generation of Traffic", London, HMSO.

SAGOFF, M. (1988), "The Economy of the Earth", Cambridge, Cambridge University Press.

SCHIPPER, L., STEINER, R. and DUERR, P., "Energy use in passenger transport in OECD countries", forthcoming in *Transportation, an International Journal*

SCHNEIDER, J. and BECK, J. (1973), "Reducing the Travel Requirements of the American City: An Investigation of Alternative Urban Spatial Structures", Research Report 73, US Department of Transportation, Washington DC

SHANKLAND COX (1994), "Good Practice Guide for PPG 13", First Draft of a Report to the Department of the Environment, London, Shankland Cox.

STONE, P.A. (1973), "The Structure, Size and Costs of Urban Settlements", Cambridge, Cambridge University Press; Romanos, M.C. (1978), *op. cit.*

TEST (1989), "Trouble in Store: Retail Location Policies in Britain and West Germany", London, TEST.

TRANSNET (1990), "Energy, Transport and the Environment", London, Transnet.

WEBSTER, F.V., BLY, P.H. and PAULLEY, N.J. (1988), "Urban Land use and Transport Interaction: Policies and Models", Report of the International Study Group on Land use/Transport Interaction, Aldershot, Avebury.

Financing Urban Public Transport in OECD Countries

Alain Méyère
Syndicat des Transports Parisiens
France

TABLE OF CONTENTS

SUMMARY

The aim of this paper is to take stock of the methods used in the different OECD countries to deal with the problem of financing urban public transport.

Curbing the financing requirements for public transport systems calls for tighter management of income and expenditure. The control of operating expenditure generally involves delegating more responsibility to the individual production unit, which is the level best able to identify potential sources of internal productivity improvements and to take the necessary steps. Another method of controlling production costs, which does not exclude the first, is to use private enterprises to provide services defined by a public authority. Their methods of working, often different from those of the public sector, together with their experience, constitute assets from which advantage can be derived.

Another cause of the financial difficulties is the indebtedness of transport undertakings. Investing wisely; avoiding over-indebtedness through the attribution of public funds; seeking additional financing, notably through associated property development operations are methods to be used here. Lastly, financial techniques related to leasing, which enable part of the tax relief of the lessor to be passed on to the final investment cost, may be useful solutions.

As regards income, the first rule is that tariffs should increase at a rate at least equal to that of operating costs. It is possible to increase the tariff share of total income, in particular when the overall inflation rate is low, provided that attention is paid to the social exclusion effects which could result. The diversification of tariff products, with the introduction of better-targeted products and subscription cards makes it possible to establish a loyal clientele and increase occupancy rates, thus demonstrating their social utility. This income can in some cases be complemented by that from the management of other local public services, which may or may not be connected with transport.

Whatever the effort made, there is no OECD country's urban public transport system which operates without public financial support. The question of the level of government to be called upon therefore arises. The growing trend is to bring this level as close as possible to the final user, i.e. the local level. This is possible only if the local government has sufficient financial independence and adequate resources, however. The existence of earmarked resources raised from the indirect beneficiaries of public transport is one solution which ensures stable funding for the sector. The attribution of public funds is increasingly being subordinated to prior commitment on criteria and objectives, sometimes in the form of contracts.

Collaboration with the private sector in the implementation of transport projects is developing in several countries. It concerns two main fields: urban development operations and new infrastructures. The first field is that of voluntary participation of external economic partners in the financing of an operation. The second is that of setting up projects where the private sector can accept the risks of construction and operation and, when the market is suitable, the complete financing of the operation.

1. INTRODUCTION

In recent decades, OECD countries have had to deal with two successive crises affecting urban public transport:

The first appeared during the 1960s, as the result of urban growth and increasing car ownership. Urban transport networks meeting growing competition from the private car saw their quality of service decline and lost many customers. This first crisis was overcome thanks to policies introduced in the early 1970s aimed at upgrading and developing the sector.

Implemented in various regulatory contexts, these policies were all based on a common organisational model: that of a public monopoly within the urban area concerned. The policies followed different paths, but all had another common feature: they were costly to the public purse. The Webster report on "Changing Patterns of Urban Travel", produced for ECMT in 1985, showed that as a percentage of total operating costs, subsidies generally remained below 20 per cent throughout the 1960s, then rose significantly during the 1970s to range between 20 and 80 per cent depending on the country and the town at the beginning of the 1980s.

Thus OECD countries found themselves faced with a second crisis, that of financing their urban public transport systems. This crisis, linked to factors outside the transport sector such as the slowdown in economic growth and the question of the respective roles of the state and the private sector, led to a re-examination of the organisational model in place. As a result, reforms and in some cases, radical rethinking of the model followed. The successes and failures of the initiatives undertaken during this time may provide potential lessons for the cities of Central and Eastern Europe (CEE) today.

Chapter 2 of this paper examines the methods used to contain the expenditure and increase the income of transport enterprises: management measures and financial techniques, tariff measures and the quest for profitable activities.

Since public budgets have to be called upon, Chapter 3 deals with public contributions: what level of government should this concern? What resources should be available to it? According to what criteria should public aid be attributed?

Lastly, Chapter 4 considers the subject of recourse to the private sector for financing transport operations. Are there situations which favour voluntary contributions by the indirect private beneficiaries of public transport? What lessons can be drawn from the so far limited and still recent experiences of private funding?

2. EXPENDITURE AND INCOME OF URBAN TRANSPORT ENTERPRISES

The need for public financing for transport activities depends on many factors, first among which is the performance of the managing enterprise, whatever its nature: public or private. The growing deficits which characterised the 1970s often gave rise to the introduction of measures intended to increase productivity. Producing more efficiently, and contracting to outside sources rather than providing services directly were the main factors. In addition to these initiatives on the expenditure side, action on the income side was no less important: better tariff yields and the identification of profitable activities proved helpful in resolving the financing problems.

2.1 Reducing operating expenditure

2.1.1 Labour productivity

In recent years, many networks have been paying particular attention to their productivity. One of the first methods used was the decentralisation of responsibilities, particularly in the networks of the large conurbations. In France, for example, the Marseille system and the Paris RATP now leave the basic production units (bus depot, metro line) to organise the work themselves, within the general rules laid down and the resources allocated to them. This trend has gone even further in London, where the only large transport enterprise in operation at the beginning of the 1980s has been replaced by a number of smaller operations.

a.   London Buses Ltd.: a spectacular improvement in performance

In 1984, the London Transport Executive was replaced by London Underground Limited (LUL) and London Buses Limited (LBL). In four years, between 1984 and 1988, the cost per kilometre of LBL (at constant prices) fell by 20 per cent. At the same time the number of kilometres per employee increased by almost 30 per cent. This result was largely due to the extension of one-man operation, which now accounts for 88 per cent of the annual kilometrage, as compared to 55 per cent in 1984. However, these savings in production costs achieved by exploiting the existing productivity reserves had a social cost: London Buses Limited shed almost a quarter of its workforce between 1984 and 1988.

In parallel with these measures LBL introduced a thorough decentralisation programme. Since 1 April 1989, its activities have been divided between 12 subsidiaries -- 11 bus depots and a tourist coach activity. These subsidiaries have autonomy of management.

2.1.2   Contracting, delegated management and privatisation

The public enterprise remains the dominant form of organisation for the provision of urban public transport services. The big ideological debate over the deregulation of the urban transport sector has really only taken place in one country, the United Kingdom. Elsewhere, any recourse to private enterprises has come about only within an organisational model in which the public authorities remain in charge of the general orientations and the major transport policy choices. It is a matter of having the private sector produce services for which the public authorities retain the initiative.

a.   France: Role of private sector is largest in towns outside the Paris region

Although the organisation of urban public transport is exclusively a public responsibility exercised at the local level by the municipalities, the provision of services may be entrusted to an outside enterprise, either public or private. This case of delegated management concerns almost 90 per cent of the market outside the Paris region. In most cases the enterprise concerned is a subsidiary of a private (54 per cent) or public (22 per cent) group rather than an independent local company. Fixed-term contracts for the management of the entire network are concluded between the local authority and the enterprise after a tendering procedure.

The case of Copenhagen is comparable with the French case, with two differences: in order to avoid the constitution of a private monopoly, involvement of a private enterprise is limited to one line or set of lines, not the whole of the network. Furthermore, the public enterprise still operates a large part of the network.

b. Copenhagen: public organisation; private provision of services

The Greater Copenhagen transport company, Hovedstadsområdets Trafikselskab (HT), is a public body. It is in charge of all expenditure and receives all the income connected with the public transport network, except for the services provided by the Danish State Railways (DSB). To provide its services HT uses several private companies whose share of total bus services was over 20 per cent in 1990, 30 per cent in 1992 and 45 per cent in 1994. The contract between HT and these enterprises covers the provision of services in return for a pre-established price. HT retains responsibility for setting tariffs and deciding routes and timetables.

The provision of transport services in accordance with a specification is common practice for many North American networks: recent figures indicate that some 20 per cent of vehicle-kilometres are contracted out in this way in the United States, mainly in small towns for road transport. In Europe, this system is found, for example, in Belgium and Spain in addition to Denmark.

c. London: participation of private enterprises in non-deregulated system

London Regional Transport (LRT), the public transport authority for the conurbation, has a department specially in charge of subcontracted bus lines, the Tendered Bus Unit. Some 20 per cent of vehicle-kilometres have been contracted out under the tendering procedure (contracts of a fixed-price nature). London Buses Limited (LBL), a public enterprise, accounts for 60 per cent of the total. The lines contracted out were selected according to several criteria: existence of potential subcontractors, one-man operation, possibility for LBL to compensate the costs associated with the subcontracted lines, distribution according to the different operating subsidiaries. LRT management considers that this contracting out policy has had the effect of reducing production costs and dynamising the public enterprise by exposing it to competition.

The reform of the public passenger transport sector in the United Kingdom in 1986 brought about radical change. Targeting public road transport, its main objective was to improve efficiency and develop services by stimulating competition among operators. Its main features were as follows:

--   The system of authorisations was abolished, leaving operators free to provide, on a commercial basis, any service they considered appropriate.

--   Public transport enterprises were either privatised or converted into commercial companies under private law, not entitled to any direct or automatic subsidies.

--   Local authorities may subsidise services running at a loss provided that they are "socially necessary" services and after a tendering procedure, but cross-subsidies are no longer permitted. Local authorities may impose tariff reductions on commercial services, in which case they must make compensation payments.

d.   Financial impact of deregulation of public road transport in metropolitan counties of the UK

Deregulation had an undeniably positive impact on the finances of the transport authorities of the metropolitan counties, because there was a reduction of the funding requirement of between 11 and 22 per cent at constant prices, depending on the estimate. Constrained to balance their budget by commercial means, the new private operators sharply increased tariffs by 30 per cent on average at constant prices (twice this in Sheffield), while reducing their unit production costs by 30 per cent.

However, while the volume of supply was virtually maintained thanks to the public authorities supplementing the basic commercial services, there was a sharp fall in ridership, approximately 16 per cent in the metropolitan counties in the first year. Productivity in terms of expenditure per trip thus increased only very slightly. The result today is all the more mediocre, as the fall in ridership has continued in subsequent years. The economic pressure exerted on the enterprises appears to have resulted in the ageing of the vehicle stock, as well. In the longer term, this could result in increased maintenance costs.

2.2   The cost of capital

2.2.1   To borrow or not to borrow?

In many transport enterprises, self-financing is limited to the depreciation of assets and does not permit any extension investment. The lack of any possibility to finance expansion out of profits may lead them to borrow, if they do not receive any capital injection from the public authorities. As a result, the final cost of any investment will increase. It is important to note, however, that this problem does not arise everywhere, and it is frequently the public authorities who are responsible for financing investment.

a. Copenhagen and London: no recourse to borrowing

In Copenhagen, investments are paid for in cash. The Greater Copenhagen Council, responsible for financing the transport system, accepts the cost of the difference between operating income and expenditure, and investment gives rise to no depreciation or financial charge on the transport budget.

In London, the investment financing requirement, after deduction of the product of any real estate promotion and voluntary contributions by indirect beneficiaries, is covered by the Ministry of Transport in the form of a subsidy, without any recourse to borrowing.

When enterprises borrow, it is common practice for the public authorities to guarantee the loan, as is access to soft loans and sometimes the acceptance of part of the debt service.

b. Public transport investment financing in the Ile de France region

Investment expenditure on the creation or extension of public transport infrastructures is covered to the extent of 80 per cent by the public authorities. The remaining 20 per cent and the cost of the vehicles are the responsibility of the transport enterprises, which resort to loans to cover this. The Ile de France region makes soft loans available for the funding of new infrastructure.

2.2.2   Investment resources

When a transport enterprise cedes certain types of assets, it obtains resources which can be devoted to investment. This kind of situation is frequently found, but is often a matter of chance. Thus in New York, the sale of the Coliseum belonging to the Metropolitan Transport Authority brought in US$384 million, representing 2.4 per cent of its ten-year investment programme.

In order to increase its level of self-financing, London Regional Transport decided to systematically develop its real estate activities.

a.   London Regional Transport: property promoter

Property business from the development and sale of assets has been a growing source of funding for LRT in recent years. This activity represented only a few million pounds a year at the beginning of the 1980s, but rose from £10 million in 1985-86 to £72 million in 1988-89. This resulted on the one hand from the sale of land belonging to LRT (old repair shops and depots) and on the other from property development operations (shopping centres, offices) on the premises of certain underground stations. In addition, there is the exploitation (development and then rental) of shopping facilities at the most heavily frequented stations. The revenue from these activities is used for self-financed upgrading or extension investments.

b.   Ferrovie Nord Milano: mixed enterprise for mixed activity

The Lombardy region in Italy created a mixed enterprise for the purpose of taking advantage of certain external benefits of transport operations. The Ferrovie Nord Milano company (FNM) is a mixed holding company in which the Lombardy region holds 55 per cent of the capital, the other shareholders being in the private sector. Its activities cover regional passenger and goods transport by rail, road and waterway, as well as cable television.

In order to internalise as much as possible the external benefits resulting from the creation of infrastructure, FNM decided not to limit the development of intermodal interchange nodes in densely populated periurban areas to the transport aspects alone, but to systematically proceed to property development operations. Twelve sites were selected according to their situation on the network, their interest from the standpoint of urban development and the commercialisation potential. The resources thus obtained help finance the investment.

It should be pointed out, however, that this type of funding resource is extremely dependent on the state of the property market. This market is subject to fluctuations, as shown by the crisis of the early 1980s in the western world. It is therefore prudent for such financing to be relied on for only a minor proportion of the total resources mobilised for a project.

2.2.3   *Financial techniques*

In addition to conventional funding through borrowing, certain transport enterprises have had recourse to various financial techniques intended to reduce the cost of capital. These techniques are connected with leasing. They were used in the 1980s by North American networks to finance the purchase of rolling stock, and also by national railway undertakings such as the SNCF in France in 1993. The principle of this type of financing package is as follows: an external partner acquires the legal (or merely fiscal) ownership of a good which it then makes available to the enterprise through a leasing contract. If it derives a tax advantage from this ownership the lessor can pass part of it on to the user of the good.

a. *The New York Metropolitan Transport Authority's Safe Harbor Lease and Cross-Border Lease*

Until September 1987, the law authorised public enterprises not paying taxes to sell the fiscal ownership of certain goods to beneficiary enterprises which could thus benefit from the tax relief associated with the depreciation of these goods.

From 1981 to 1987, the Metropolitan Transport Authority (MTA) was the US network which made most use of leasing to take advantage of the tax allowances on new and reconditioned rolling stock. These operations, known as Safe Harbor Leasing, procured a total of US$500 million of income for investment, amounting to 3.1 per cent of the funding of the 1982-91 investment programme. It was the federal government which was the final payer, since it lost tax revenue.

This possibility now having been abolished, MTA has turned to foreign investors who do not pay US taxes, by creating what is known as the Cross Border Lease. The first of these operations was set up in 1988 with a group of Japanese investors and concerned 190 Kawasaki metro cars. The principle is identical to that of Safe Harbor Leasing. The Japanese investors receive the tax relief associated with the ownership of the rolling stock and pass it on to the MTA through a lease-back contract. The net benefit from this operation has been estimated at about 5.5 per cent of the cost of the rolling stock.

2.3 Increasing the user share

The continuing decline in the user share of total financing has naturally led to consideration of whether it is possible to stop this trend by taking action on tariff income, i.e. have the direct beneficiaries of the service make a bigger contribution. It must be admitted however that not enough is known about how to best use the tariff instrument, and it is true that the objectives assigned to tariffs are sometimes contradictory. It may be considered that their purpose is first of all financial: to procure income; it may be considered that they should permit the optimal allocation of resources, and should thus be closely related to marginal cost; they may be assigned more of a social and redistributive role; it may be desired that they should reflect all the costs associated with the transport function and thus include externalities; lastly, in the case of public tariffs, they may be frozen in periods of inflation. The fact that the public authorities have not made a clear choice among these different functions may partly explain the general lack of knowledge and of experimentation in this field.

2.3.1 Raising tariffs: market limits and social constraints

A relatively low rate of coverage of expenditure by traffic income may lead to the introduction of a policy of systematically adjusting tariffs. Belgium and the Netherlands tried this in the early 80s, but the results where such that they abandoned these programmes. In Paris, the average fare increase to users in constant francs was 36 per cent between 1975 and 1992, and this policy has continued to be pursued prudently, because user reactions (reduced ridership, higher risk of fraud) remain little understood. In the United Kingdom, the road transport service deregulation policy, by forcing both public and private transport enterprises to balance their accounts by commercial means, has led to results in terms of ridership which are now well-known. Two general conclusions can be drawn from these experiences:

The **first conclusion** is that tariff adjustment, if very strictly applied, rapidly reaches market limits: the resulting reduction in ridership may be very substantial. An example of this follows.

a. Belgium and the Netherlands: tariff increases

Until 1989, the central governments of Belgium and the Netherlands funded all urban public transport and set tariffs in Belgium and the Netherlands. A programme of systematic tariff readjustment was introduced in these two countries because of the relatively low rate of cost coverage by income (20 to 40 per cent, depending on the city).

In Belgium, the urban transport enterprises were obliged to adjust their tariffs every year as from 1983 at a rate which was determined half by the consumer price index and half by a composite index of the cost of transport production. The resulting tariff increases were higher than that of the consumer price index.

Application of this formula caused no problems in 1984 and 1985, but in 1986 there was a fall-off in traffic and income, probably due in part to strikes in the transport sector, but also due, according to the Belgian authorities, to the level reached by tariffs. The procedure was therefore dropped as from 1987 and subsequent fare increases have been closer to the consumer price trend.

In the Netherlands, the government in power in 1982 decided, in line with its general objective of reducing public spending, to introduce a general tariff adjustment plan in order to curb the increase in subsidies. This plan, covering the period 1984-87, provided for tariff increases equal to inflation plus 10 per cent, a formula which was applied as from 1983.

Drops in ridership were expected, of course, but these were greater than foreseen, leading the Netherlands government to abandon its plan in 1985. One of the conclusions drawn from this experience by the Ministry of Transport was that in seeking to achieve a more favourable ratio of income to expenditure, action on the expenditure side is more effective than tariff policy.

A **second conclusion** is that upward tariff adjustment also has social limits: if the public authorities wish to avoid social exclusion effects they have to make a financial commitment through paying compensation for social tariffs. This is what happened in the United Kingdom after deregulation.

b.   United Kingdom: tariff increases and compensation payments

The constitution of private law companies on the basis of the municipal transport companies of the former metropolitan counties and the fact that they cannot receive automatic subsidies led to sharp increases in tariffs: 25 to 30 per cent in two years, depending on the case. Ridership fell by 16 per cent over this period, more than was expected from such fare increases.   This phenomenon was partly due to uncertainty about the services.

In order to maintain access to public transport for the most disadvantaged social categories, the new transport authorities were authorised to request enterprises to introduce concession fares.   In return, they pay compensation which amounts to one-third of their expenditure.

2.3.2   Tariff innovations

The tariff innovations seen in the 1980s reflect two principal, seemingly contradictory trends. The first goes in the direction of greater tariff modulation and leads to an increase in the number of types of tickets and passes, while the second is aimed at increasing the attractiveness of the tariff scale by creating subscription fares which are as simple and universal as possible.

Tariff modulation finds its justification in the economic theory argument that modulations based on differences in the marginal cost of production increase the collective surplus as compared to unmodulated pricing. It is also justified by marketing considerations, according to which the diversification of services wanted by the public should also include the diversification of tariff products. It is above all in North America that modulation according to time of travel is most often practised, though many European networks also offer reduced fares for travel outside peak periods.

The use of personalised travel passes is long-established in certain countries. In France, the *carte orange* for the Paris region first went on sale on 1 July 1976, and it has been successful ever since. Elsewhere in France, roughly half of all passenger trips are made using travel passes. They have a shorter history in other countries. The London Travelcard was introduced only in May 1983. In 1984, Basel introduced an "ecological" subscription fare which became a trend-setter in Switzerland, with similar schemes being introduced subsequently in Geneva and Lausanne. A similar phenomenon is to be seen in Germany. It should be pointed out that there is a trend in Switzerland and Germany to use non-personalised travel passes, the main concern being to have an intermodal ticket and to foster among the public a perception of the unity of the conurbation's transport network, regardless of the modes used.

There is a widespread idea that because of their preferential tariffs this kind of travel pass leads to bigger deficits. However, many networks which have tried them find that this is not the case at all. They base their opinion on the fact that in making their choice, the users do not consider only the number of trips they make, but also the convenience a travel pass gives them: they may not derive any economic benefit at all, but they are willing to pay for the greater convenience. Thus in Paris, 40 to 50 per cent of *carte orange* users could in theory use other, cheaper tickets. If they did so, tariff income would fall by 5 per cent. London and Bremen (which introduced a non-personalised travel pass in 1988) conclude from their experience that it is possible, thanks to innovative tariff strategies, to stabilise markets which had been declining and to stimulate the most dynamic segments.

a.   Travelcard and Capitalcard in London

In London, the reform of the tariff structure carried out in 1983 was very close to the choice made in Paris and its region in 1976; to replace the old season tickets for given trips on the underground and those for bus zones, users were offered a multi-modal Travelcard, whose introduction was associated with the adoption of a zonal system for the entire network (5 zones were defined), and a modulated reduction in tariffs. The Capitalcard introduced in 1985 made it possible to extend the system to the railways and in 1989 these two cards were combined. Though it is difficult to separate the effects of the tariff reduction from those of the restructuring of the system, the results of the London tariff reform were as follows:

-- the number of subscriptions increased by 150 000 units and the traffic lost in earlier years due to tariff increases was won back;
-- there was an increase in underground traffic at the expense of bus traffic during peak periods and a general increase in traffic outside peak periods;
-- there was a significant switch back to public transport from private cars;
-- in a single year, the share of total trips made using the various passes increased from 51 to 65 per cent.

2.4 Managing profitable activities

Being able to procure income additional to tariff income obviously helps a transport company's financial position. Such income may come from activities directly complementary to traditional passenger transport activities: advertising, maintenance services for third parties, rental or management of shop premises. They may also stem from activities complementary to those of urban transport, both in the fields of travel and local public services.

2.4.1   Other transport services

Even though it is still rare today for motorists to have to pay for the right to drive in town centres, they generally have to pay to park and also to use certain infrastructures such as bridges or tunnels. The management of the service concerned may be very profitable once the cost of the infrastructure is amortised or when demand is very heavy. For the transport enterprise, participation in this type of operation also has the advantage of involving it to some extent in the management of car travel.

a.   New York transport authorities manage related services

In the United States, the transport authorities, public bodies responsible for urban public transport, are often in charge of the management of other services connected with travel or transport.   Buffalo and New York City offer two examples of this: The Niagara Falls Transport Authority (NFTA), responsible for the Buffalo (metro) transport network, is also in charge of the bus stations, the port of Buffalo and the two airports in its area.   Part of the profits from the other units of the NFTA thus help fund the deficit of the metro (3.5 per cent).   In New York, the toll income from the Triborough Bridge and Tunnel Authority (TBTA) are even more important, amounting to over 10 per cent of the total resources of the MTA, or 17 per cent of the operating expenditure funding requirement.

b.   Milan transport authority (ATM) also manages parking stations

Since 1984, Milan has entrusted the municipal transport authority, ATM, with the management of the park-and-ride facilities in the proximity of metro stations and the parking stations at the modal interchange nodes, as well as street meter parking.   The meters and barriers are supplied and installed by the ATM, which is also responsible for policing and for collecting the receipts. Users with an ATM subscription pass can also obtain a half-price weekly parking card for the interchange parking stations.   Any profits from these activities are shared fifty-fifty between the ATM and the municipality of Milan. The municipality has to bear the cost of any deficits.

2.4.2   Other local public services

The stage of development of the municipal or paramunicipal sector varies considerably from one country to another, and covers very diverse activities.

a.   The local public sector: diverse activities

The municipality of Milan is the biggest shareholder in the MM company, specialising in metro studies, and SEA which serves the airport.   It also has a number of "municipal enterprises", which are a kind of public establishment with no specific legal status.   Among these enterprises are ATM for public transport;   AEM which produces and distributes the town's electricity and gas; and AMSA for garbage collection.   In addition to these activities, which traditionally belong to the public sector but whose management may be delegated in a number of countries (such as in France) or may come under a national public monopoly, other unusual activities include the collection and distribution of milk by CL and the management of chemists by AMF.

Certain management methods may authorise transfers of income from profit-making to loss-making services. These transfers, which actually take place in the municipal budget or within the municipal enterprise responsible for industrial and commercial public services, scarcely constitute an example of economic orthodoxy, but are fairly widespread in Austria and Germany. In the western *Länder* of Germany, almost 60 per cent of the municipal transport enterprises were integrated with other local public services (water, gas, electricity, district heating) and thus benefited from funding from the surplus earnings of these other services. Among the criticisms commonly levelled at such practices are those concerning the lack of transparency in the procedure (these transfers are not the subject of any public policy debate) and the arbitrary nature of this charge on a form of consumption very different from that of public transport.

3. PUBLIC CONTRIBUTIONS

3.1 Who finances what?

The distinction between central and local level gives rise to no real difficulties in a unitary state, but it is more complex to establish when analysing countries with a federal or confederate structure, where the intermediate level -- or "regional" level -- has considerable power. Thus the Italian regions, like the German *Länder*, the Canadian Provinces or the States in the United States, have more or less extensive legislative and regulatory powers, which the French regions and the counties in the United Kingdom do not have.

Generally speaking, in the majority of developed countries, the central government limits its financial contribution to investment, and most often to extension investment, while the local level is responsible for operation. The regional level, where it exists, may be associated with one or other of these fields. There are nevertheless a number of exceptions to this rule.

a. Capital cities

The capital cities of London and Paris are comparable in many respects. They are the biggest conurbations in western Europe, both of them capital cities. In both cases the transport system comprises several modes, and in particular suburban train services. The state is very much involved in the organisation and in the financing system, very different from that found in the rest of the country. It owns the main transport enterprises (British Rail and the SNCF, London Regional Transport and the RATP). It is responsible, directly or indirectly, for transport policy. It thus contributes not only to the financing of investment, but also to that of operation, for it is the state which has the power of decision.

b. National pricing

Urban pubic transport in the Netherlands is dominated by the public sector and centralised on a national basis. It is as if, or at least was until the reform of 1988, there were a national urban travel market for which the state is the supplier through local or regional production units, for which it has financial responsibility. Sources of financing include subsidies and an integrated national tariff system which permits access to all public transport lines with the exception of interurban train services. As the attribution of subsidies to a given network by the Ministry of Transport and Public Works is subject to its prior approval of the operating budget, the central government level has thus found itself increasingly involved in decisions affecting the day-to-day management of the local networks.

Therefore, if we disregard the examples of certain capitals or countries that have particularly centralised organisations, the state only contributes to the funding of operating expenditures where experiments or demonstration operations are concerned, or when obligations are imposed on the state, such as in Switzerland, for those services considered to be of interest to the country.

3.2 Local authority resources

3.2.1 Traditional public resources

Public authorities have four categories of income: the product of rates and taxes, the product of tariffs and charges received in exchange for services, income from loans, and lastly transfers (grants or subsidies) from other public authorities.

The capacity of local authorities to be financially responsible for public transport results from their degree of financial independence. From this standpoint the positions of local authorities in different countries vary enormously. Some have a substantial local direct tax system or block grants from authorities at a higher level, while others on the contrary are very dependent on subsidies from the central or regional government, awarded on a case-by-case basis.

a. *Financial independence of local authorities in Europe: contrast and diversity*

In this respect the situation is very different in France and Germany, Italy and the Netherlands, and in the United Kingdom.

In France, local taxes provide 45 per cent of municipal income, while 26 per cent comes from subsidies, a good part of which is in the form of block grants. In Germany, some 40 per cent of urban municipality income comes from taxes. Charges and receipts from the operation of local public services represent something in the order of 30 per cent of this income.

In Italy, local taxes make up only 7 per cent of municipal income. The proportion is even lower in the Netherlands: 2 per cent. It is therefore the state, which, directly or through the regions as in the case of Italy, funds the greater part of the municipal budget. In the case of transport, grants are provided specifically for this sector, which thus limits local choices in both countries.

Some 60 per cent of the income of local authorities in the United Kingdom consists of subsidies. The central government, considering that local authority expenditure was increasing faster than other public expenditure, introduced in the 1980s a mechanism intended to curb this expenditure. Local authorities, which spend more than what the central government considers necessary, receive a reduced subsidy. In order to avoid the resulting additional local burden being passed on to local residents, a ceiling is placed on local taxes ("rate capping").

It is striking to see that the countries where the contribution of public authorities to covering urban public transport operating expenditure is the highest are those where the towns have little financial autonomy: Italy and the Netherlands. This could result from the fact that the responsibilities for funding and for local transport policy lie with different levels of government.

3.2.2　The search for stable resources

A major responsibility of elected political authorities each year is to decide what resources will be available and how they should be used according to the perceived needs of the population. In Europe, there is particular reticence with regard to earmarked tax revenues, which result in the targeted area escaping from the budget trade-off mechanism. For similar reasons, The World Bank advises against the use of this technique; the Bank considers that a guaranteed resource leads to a poor overall allocation of resources. A systematic examination of the origin of public funds allocated to transport nevertheless shows that this option is by no means exceptional, and that it permits at central, regional and local levels a guaranteed minimum level of public funding. An earmarked income, the level of which is foreseeable, has the advantage of taking expenditure "off budget" and avoids the risk of unfavourable trade-offs in periods of budgetary restriction.

An inventory of different taxes and charges shows a wide variety of solutions; however, few European countries make use of them; for example, Germany, Austria (for the Vienna metro) and France. In the United States, on the other hand, this practice is very common.

Although there is often a desire to make the indirect beneficiaries pay, it would appear that when the area covered is extensive, other considerations determine the choice of the tax base.

a.　An earmarked local tax in Atlanta

The greater part of the public funding of MARTA, the body responsible for public transport in Atlanta (USA), comes from additional cents on retail sales within its area of competence. The rate has been fixed at one cent to the dollar up to 2012 and 1/2 cent thereafter. In principle, half of the tax revenue is for funding operations, and the other half for funding investment. If the proportion used for operations exceeds 50 per cent in any tax year, MARTA has to re-establish the balance over the next two years. If the operating share is less than 50 per cent, the surplus can be carried over to the next year.

In particular, the main criteria put forward appear to be the level and stability of the income, together with the legal and political feasibility of the system. Other factors such as the link between the tax base and the service to be funded have in some cases been given much less importance. Thus in the United States, taxes on alcoholic drinks or lotteries have been introduced through public pressure after local referendums.

It should be noted that there is a strong link between the earmarked revenue system and the public funding of public transport. In particular, the share of resources allocated by the local authority will be greater or smaller according to whether or not it benefits from the earmarked resource.

b.   France and Germany: state aid and earmarked resources

France and Germany both have a resource earmarked for local public transport. A comparison of the two systems sheds light on the sharing of roles between the different public actors in the funding of public transport.

In Germany, an additional fuel tax of DM 0.54/litre is collected by the state throughout the country. This goes into a fund intended to finance local transport investment (municipal roads and public transport). In France, local transport authorities (municipalities or associations of municipalities with over 20 000 inhabitants) have the possibility of taxing the payroll of enterprises with over ten employees. They are free to set the rate of taxation within limits set by the law.

The total tax take is of the same order of magnitude in the two countries. It is devoted entirely to urban public transport in France, while in Germany it benefits either the car or public transport, but only through funding investment projects of local interest.

In Germany, the tax revenue is attributed to the local level through a project approval procedure which involves the federal and *Länder* levels. In France, the income is collected directly by the local level, which remains totally in control of its use within the regulatory framework. For this reason, the amount of subsidies paid by the state in France is significantly less than in Germany, because in the latter, it is the federal government which collects the earmarked tax.

3.2.3   Sharing the costs and benefits

Theoretically, the contributions from certain economic agents can be regarded as financial payment for advantages derived by indirect beneficiaries of the service. This is the case with the techniques described below, which are more directly connected with externalities. These are methods of collecting funds which represent payment either for benefits stemming from the existence of a transport service or costs engendered by an economic agent. Here, it is a case of establishing a clearer link between a compulsory charge and the use of the resulting revenue. This type of technique is most developed in the United States, using *ad hoc* fiscal instruments.

The Special Benefit Assessment is used when a public facility is created or extended in order to recover part of the resulting land or property value-added. Generally, an authority empowered to raise a local tax defines a geographical area within which a tax will be collected to fund the investment in the facility concerned. In the case of transport, the area is defined so as to include all the properties which will benefit from the infrastructure. This technique was used in Miami for the Miami-Metromover, and in Los Angeles to finance the first phase of the metro there.

a.   Benefits assessment for funding Miami's Metromover

The first phase of the Miami metro, a 3-km overhead circular line running through the city centre, came into operation in 1986. In 1983, Dade County approved the creation of a Special Benefit Assessment district to permit the raising of a tax on those benefiting from the line. The aim was to collect US$20 million towards a total investment cost of US$148 million. US$20 million in bonds backed by the county's tax revenue were therefore issued for a 15-year period. The district, created for this period, sets the tax rate each year to apply to all rentals of commercial premises located within its territory. Projected tax revenue of US$27 million over 15 years will be earmarked for repaying these bonds.

Given the success of the operation, the County decided in 1986 to extend the first phase of the Metromover using the same financing technique.

A similar technique is "tax increment financing". This involves earmarking the additional property tax revenue from higher property prices for funding the investment in public facilities responsible for the tax increase. This causes tricky problems as to the choice of reference date, of course, but the technique is even less painful than the above system, because neither the tax base nor the tax rate have to be modified.

Making an agent who benefits from public transport pay a proportion of the costs he generates can be complicated. When a promoter or shopping centre requests direct access to the metro, it is possible to make this agent pay the resulting costs, but it is more difficult to take into account increases in the service and in operating costs. The San Francisco authorities have developed a form of taxation which seeks to resolve this problem.

b.   A cost-sharing tax in San Francisco

The San Francisco municipal network, MUNI, receives the revenue of a tax designed to partly cover the additional costs resulting from the extension of office space in the Central Business District (CBD).

The "Transit Impact Development Fee" (TIDF) is set at US$5 per square foot. It is imposed on all new buildings or office space conversions in the CBD.

The tax take each year depends on the economic situation and the state of the office space market, which means that long-term forecasts are not very reliable. The tax revenue is therefore used solely for short-term rolling stock investment. The total tax take for the 1980s is estimated at some US$50 million.

3.3   From automatic to conditional attribution of public funds

The automatic attribution of public funds is a procedure which may have been widespread when the funding requirement was modest, but which is now becoming more rare. It is primarily found where there has been a transfer of powers and responsibilities from a higher level to the local level. This was the case in France when the state transferred the responsibility for school transport to local authorities.

As regards operating costs, subsidies are generally conditional upon the achievement of objectives set in advance. This is the case in Italy for state funds passing via the regions: since the framework law of 1981, operating subsidies are granted to enterprises on the basis of a standardized economic cost, and the difference between the standard cost and the actual cost has to be borne by the enterprise. Canada is a good example of this trend. Originally, the subsidies paid by the Provinces were considered to be temporary, to permit operations to continue while a solution was found. The more recent trend has been for the granting of subsidies to be dependent upon fare income covering a certain proportion of operating expenditure, as illustrated by the example of Montreal.

a.   Montreal: operating subsidy subject to constraints

The Province of Quebec grants an operating subsidy to urban public transport under the following conditions:

--   An operating subsidy equal to 40 per cent of the income generated by regular public transport services is granted. This income consists of tariff receipts and compensation payments.

--   A specific subsidy for the annual travel pass is also granted under particular conditions.

--   The sum of these two subsidies cannot exceed 75 per cent of the deficit to be covered by the municipalities before the payment of these subsidies.

The case of France is interesting because of the systematic recourse to an outside operation in the great majority of towns outside the Paris region. The contracts concluded between the local transport authorities and the operators are generally no longer simple management contracts where the carrier bears no risk, but are increasingly contracts in which the carrier has to accept part of the risk.

b.   *France: making carriers accept partial risk through use of operating contracts*

The contracts concluded between transport authorities and enterprises can be classified according to the sharing of the commercial and industrial risk between the two partners:

--   In the **management** contract, the carrier assumes no risk. It collects fares and manages expenditure in the name of the organising authority. Its remuneration may be a function of the operating results.

--   In the **fixed-price** contract, the carrier agrees in advance on the amount of operating expenditure, but not on the receipts. It therefore accepts only the industrial risk. In this type of contract the operator's remuneration may partly depend on receipts.

--   In the **fixed-subsidy** contract, the operator agrees in advance on the total subsidy. It accepts responsibility for any overshooting on the operating expenditure side and any shortfall on the income side. It thus bears both types of risk.

In the field of investment, the use of standard or maximum rates is very usual when the state grants subsidies. These rates vary greatly according to the country or to the region in the case of federal structures. In Germany, for example, the rate of subsidy for eligible projects (criteria of size and conformity with certain objectives) is 60 per cent. In France, since 1994, in order to encourage the least costly solutions, the rate has varied according to the type of project: higher for separate lane bus systems than for tramways; and higher for tramways than for metros.

In the United Kingdom, the procedure for granting subsidies for major investments such as metros or tramways does not set rates, but determines the subsidy on the basis of a financial evaluation and a cost-benefit analysis. It implicitly recognises the existence of indirect beneficiaries and imposes the recovery through tariffs of service quality improvements which benefit users.

c.   Financing of major urban transport projects in the United Kingdom

The Ministry of Transport of the United Kingdom subsidises only extension operations costing over £5 million which are of an exceptional nature. Eligible projects include, in particular, light metros which help revitalise town centres, innovative projects and those which concern more than one municipality.

The application for a subsidy must be accompanied by a complete economic and financial evaluation demonstrating that the project is the most cost-effective way of achieving the stated objectives. It must also demonstrate that the possibility of increasing tariffs has been fully studied with a view to minimising recourse to public funds, it being understood that the benefits derived by passengers should preferably be paid for through fares rather than through taxes or charges. Furthermore, the public contribution (local, national or European Community) should be less than or equal to the indirect benefits of the project.

The normal rate of state subsidy is 50 per cent of the net investment cost after deducting the net forecast income (which normally involves savings as compared with subsidies to bus services), other public subsidies (such as from the European Regional Development Fund) and private sector contributions. The remaining 50 per cent has to be found by local transport authorities.

3.4 Global management of urban travel

The idea of the global management of travel by a single authority comes up against the problem in most countries of the fragmentation of technical tasks and political responsibilities.   Certain attempts have nevertheless been made in countries such as France.

a.   Regional transport accounts in Ile de France

In the Paris region, the Syndicat des Transport Parisiens (STP), the regional transport organising authority, has for some years, in association with all the partners concerned, been compiling consolidated regional accounts covering all public and private expenditure connected with travel.   This monetary cost account is completed by a section concerned with social costs (congestion, environmental impact, accidents).   It is thus possible to follow total regional expenditure each year and over time;   breakdown of expenditure according to the different activities and the different financing sources;   and the estimated cost of the externalities associated with passenger transport.

The fact that different administrations with different locations are responsible for road traffic and roads on the one hand and the organisation of public transport on the other, whose geographical areas do not necessarily coincide probably explains why this kind of approach is not often adopted.

Nevertheless, the desire for better knowledge of the different costs of transport modes and their distribution among the different economic agents will grow in the future, as interest increases in urban road pricing and in public transport's impact on the environment and on congestion costs.

The debate on the place of the private car in towns is being revived in the majority of European cities in the mid-1990s.   The feeling is that the economic crisis is coming to an end, that car ownership rates are again rising rapidly, and that public opinion concerning environmental protection and the quality of life is becoming more forceful.   Public space in urban areas is a scarce resource whose use can be regulated only by rationing or pricing.   When over 40 Italian towns decided in 1989 to restrict car access to their historic centres, they chose the first option, while Hong Kong and Singapore opted for pricing.

However, it was not this problem, but questions of financing, which were at the origin of certain urban toll systems or projects which appeared in northern Europe.   In Bergen, Norway, it was in the first place the need to fund the road infrastructure programme without resorting to tax measures, and there was no co-ordination between this operation and public transport. In the Netherlands, the government had considered raising revenue by a zonal toll system not linked to any particular infrastructure project, but to be used to fund a number of road tunnels for which concessions would be awarded to private operators. The government was to play the role of intermediary between the users and the concessionaires; however, the project never came to fruition. In Sweden, a number of urban toll projects have been studied for the city of Stockholm, several of which provide for partial allocation of the toll income to public transport; the idea is that if traffic is to be switched to public transport, the latter will need additional resources. In Oslo, 20 per cent of the toll income is allocated to public transport.

b.   *Urban tolls in Oslo*

Since February 1990, vehicles entering the town of Oslo have been subject to toll charges. A toll cordon is designed to help fund a main road programme in the conurbation. There is no direct physical connection between the location of the toll points and the roads to be funded by the receipts. In order to prevent the formation of queues, the use of subscriptions has been encouraged.

In 1991, the system brought in NKr 600 million, 20 per cent of which was allocated to Oslo public transport. The rest was used to cover the annual cost of the system, which is in the order of NKr 100 million (operating costs and depreciation), and to fund road improvements.

The introduction of tolls had only a very slight impact on the volume of car traffic, probably because of the charging system adopted.

It should be pointed out at this stage that in OECD countries, infinitely more theoretical writings, technical studies and doctrinal stances for or against generalised road pricing exist than there are actual applications. Public opinion is in general very hostile to this idea, and the long-term effects on traffic, urban development and land use are very poorly understood. It is understandable that policy-makers should hesitate to introduce measures which are not only unpopular, but also have very uncertain effects. It is striking to note that the only time a government was defeated on a transport measure in the Netherlands was over a toll project for the Randstad urban area.

4. EXTERNAL PARTNERS

Collaboration between the public and private sectors in operations of general interest is developing in several countries. This collaboration concerns two main fields:

-- joint urban development operations;
 infrastructure financing packages.

4.1 Calling on the indirect beneficiaries

Targeting the indirect beneficiaries for contributions to funding of operations may be achieved by imposing a compulsory tax measure, or by negotiating a contribution in the case of a precise operation. These two approaches are not mutually exclusive, but in general, one of the two is dominant in a given country or region. We examine voluntary contributions here.

a. Extension of the Docklands Light Railway to the City

After the construction of the first section of the Docklands Light Railway, the main promoter of the area served by the Canary Wharf station, the Anglo-Canadian group Olympia and York, which wanted to make the site a pole of development for London's higher tertiary and financial activities, offered to pay a substantial part of the cost of extending the line to the City.

The promoter was to pay about 40 per cent of the total extension cost estimated at £170 million. In return, London Regional Transport accepted the remaining cost and made a commitment as to the opening date of the new service to be introduced.

Although it was not the aim at the outset, this experience in the United Kingdom illustrates the risk involved in relying too heavily on private sector funding. The same promoter was supposed to accept part of the cost of constructing another metro line to serve the area, but it went bankrupt in the 1993 property crisis, upsetting the whole proposed financing package and forcing the public authorities to step in to make good the broken private sector commitment.

The lesson is therefore that when the construction of a transport link is vital for an urban development operation, the promoters should be made to pay, but not to the extent that the realisation of the transport project becomes totally dependent on the private sector. The funding of the Paris RER (Regional Express Network) stations serving the Eurodisney theme park is a good example of the use of voluntary contributions: the extra cost of these stations due to the particular facilities required was paid for by the Disney company. Examples of this type are also found in the United States.

b.   Tampa: public transport system funded by the private sector

The Harbour Island sector near downtown Tampa was the site of a major development operation involving the construction of several thousand dwellings as well as offices and a luxury hotel. The promoter installed a downtown people mover system at a cost of US$7.3 million, obtaining a concession for its operation and maintenance for a period of 15 years. At the end of this period, the transport authority will take over the system for the symbolic price of one dollar.

It should be noted that such operations remain exceptional. A simulation study carried out for metro Line D in Lyon, a French conurbation with over 1.2 million inhabitants, concluded that in the case of a major project likely to benefit a large number of small operations, it was very difficult to construct financial packages of this type. Experience in the United Kingdom outside London is similar; there is only one private initiative project, in Bristol, out of approximately 30 being studied. Among the public projects, the first to have come into service was that of Manchester, where the logic was exactly the opposite: it was not economic activity which was to support public transport, but public transport which was to contribute to the economic revival of the region, directly during the construction phase and indirectly thereafter.

Projects which obtain voluntary contributions from outside economic partners thus have certain features in common, which seem to be necessary conditions for success:

-- localised impacts in connection with a well-defined development operation;
-- small number of actors;
-- small size of the transport project as compared with the total size of the development operation.

4.2 Concessions and project financing

The granting of concessions corresponds in theory to a logic radically different from that just discussed: it is only the direct beneficiaries, i.e. the users, who are to finance the project. Tariff income is intended not only to cover operating costs but also to repay the loans and pay a return on the own funds put into the project by the investors. This funding technique is by no means new in urban transport, for this is how the majority of the tramway networks were introduced in many countries between the late nineteenth century and the outbreak of the First World War. It is still relevant to the financing of interurban road infrastructures and other services connected with urban travel, such as, for example, off-street parking facilities and certain underground roadworks in Lyon and Marseille in France.

The use of this financing technique for new public transport infrastructures is infrequent, apparently because of the difficulty of finding projects likely to be sufficiently profitable. The case of Orlyval in France has shown that this caution appears justified.

a. Orlyval: the problem of exclusively private funding

Following consultation of the design, funding, construction and operation of a dedicated infrastructure public transport line between the RER and Orly Airport, on 21 April 1988, STP granted a concession to the Orlyval company effective through 31 December 2021.

The project was to be funded as follows:

-- FF 150 million own funds;
-- FF 150 million convertible loan stock;
-- FF 1 460 million in loans.

No public subsidy was requested. The target public was essentially passengers on domestic flights, primarily business passengers travelling at company expense, and therefore considered to be well able to pay. The link began service in October 1991, on time and within the planned cost envelope. However, receipts rapidly proved much lower than forecast, rendering operation uneconomic. The problem can partly be explained by the generalised air transport crisis and the difficulty of using traffic forecast models in contexts very different from those of their normal use.

The public authorities were therefore obliged to terminate the concession as early as the beginning of 1993. The concessionaire company was dissolved and operation of the line was handed over to the RATP, the public enterprise which runs the Paris metro. A financial restructuring plan was introduced, under the terms of which the financial partners accepted to renounce more than FF 1 billion francs of capital and debt. Repayment of the residual debt depends on a certain minimum ridership being achieved.

The results just described lead to the conclusion that this type of financing package is likely to remain an exception in urban areas for a long time to come. The case of the light metro in Manchester, where infrastructure funding is public, but where the private sector handles operation and maintenance, has a quite different logic.

b.   Metrolink in Manchester: public investment and private operation

At the beginning of January 1988 the UK Ministry of Transport agreed in principle to the first phase construction of the Manchester light metro, provided that a contract would be concluded with a single outside partner. The GMA consortium of GEC-Alsthom, Mowlem, AMEC and Greater Manchester Buses Ltd., won the contract.

The forecast study had shown that the annual surplus of income over operating expenditure, estimated at £1 million, would be insufficient to finance a project costing over £100 million. The private sector was therefore called upon to accept two risks:

-- design and construction of the line in accordance with specifications and at a fixed price;
-- operation of the system when built, without pricing constraints.

The public sector, for its part, funds the infrastructure and the rolling stock, ownership of which it retains. These resources are made available to the operator for 15 years, for a payment. This is what is known as a DBOM (design, build, operate and maintain) contract.

It is true that project financing gives rise to certain difficulties, despite its undeniable advantages: potential cost savings, renewal of technological approaches and time savings as compared with public financing packages. However, an urban transport infrastructure is rarely isolated and its impacts go beyond the transport sphere. Therefore, unless they are to renounce any possibility of implementing an overall urban policy, the authorities have to be involved in both the definition of projects and their funding. Like it or not, we therefore find ourselves in a mixed economy logic, where the legitimate quest for profitability on the part of private investors has to serve the overall economic and social interest for which the public authorities are responsible.

5. CONCLUSION

There is no OECD country in which urban public transport systems operate without the support, notably financial, of public authorities. This means that it is accepted everywhere, implicitly or explicitly, that public transport cannot be considered an ordinary traded good. The economic, social and political impacts of public transport are such that they imply public intervention, the type and extent of which varies according to the country considered. Despite the institutional differences, the financing of public transport gives rise to a common set of problems for public authorities.

The first concerns the choice of who should be the final payer, or rather the distribution of the burden among the different categories of payer. In most cases, it is accepted that users are not the only beneficiaries, and therefore, should not be the only ones to contribute. The main non-tariff resource is still of a fiscal nature however. This is true, of course, where the public sector is very much involved, but it is also true in highly market-oriented economies such as the United Kingdom today.

Where the public purse is involved a second question arises, that of the geographic area concerned or level of government funding. Here again, there is a distinct trend, in this case towards the decentralisation of decision-making and financial responsibility. This trend is much more marked in some countries than others, but this point is linked essentially with the degree of financial autonomy of the territorial authorities. It is only to the extent that local authorities have control over significant resources of their own that they are able to assume the financial consequences of their transport choices.

The existence at local level of general resources earmarked for urban public transport remains exceptional in Europe: it is found only in France and in Austria for Vienna. This practice is widespread in the United States and appears to be connected with the local taxation systems in that country.

Another trend is clearly apparent, at least in certain countries, that of linking non-tariff contributions to well-identified projects. As regards public contributions to operating expenditure, this means that they have to be associated, for example, either with public service obligations (tariff compensation, social services) or operating constraints (impact of traffic congestion). As regards indirect beneficiaries, we see in the English-speaking countries the development of initiatives associated with precise projects, whether in the form of voluntary contributions (United Kingdom) or compulsory taxes (United States). Experience in this field demonstrates not only their feasibility, provided that certain conditions are fulfilled, but also the limits of this financing technique which can rarely provide more than 10 per cent of the total cost.

In addition to these aspects, public transport financing raises the question of production and management methods. In view of the size of the market for private enterprises -- represented by services and infrastructure building -- the question arises of the possible relation which can be established between the public and private sectors. These relations should result in the clear division of responsibilities, detailed in contracts between public authorities and private operators.

6. RECOMMENDATIONS FOR CITIES IN CENTRAL AND EASTERN EUROPE

In light of the case histories discussed in this paper, the following recommendations may be made.

6.1 Income and expenditure

(i) Public transport enterprises should systematically seek out potential productivity gains both internally (e.g. work organisation, maintenance) and externally (e.g. bus operating conditions). In this respect, co-operation with western European enterprises that are members of the UITP would be very beneficial.

(ii) Although contracting out certain jobs to private sector companies may sometimes lead to savings, a regulated system is more likely to combine the objectives of better management with the general aims of public service.

(iii) As far as tariffs are concerned, the introduction of more up-to-date ticketing systems should lead to greater flexibility. Tariff income should move in line with costs, and tariff ranges should be extended in order to reflect the diversity of users' travelling behaviour.

(iv) With regard to the latter, transport companies should develop new market-oriented approaches. This means creating new services relating to passenger information, reception and service-quality expectations (e.g. convenience, cleanliness, safety).

6.2 The role of government

(i) The delegation of responsibility to the local level, which has already taken place, only makes sense if accompanied by a set of measures establishing a coherent institutional and financial framework. In the largest conurbations this would involve setting up bodies to co-ordinate planning, tariff structures and market relations.

(ii) Financial responsibility can only be delegated to the local level if local authorities possess the necessary resources. In other words, the rules of the game need to be established: What proportion of funding is to come from transport revenues? What share of income must revert to the various levels of government (local, regional and central)? How will the various types of government funding be allocated and for what purposes?

(iii) It is also necessary to indicate the origin of public funding: general budget or earmarked taxes?

(iv) Whatever the case, the rules and level of funding must remain the same to ensure that transport policies can be implemented over the long term. This question goes beyond the sphere of transport, since it primarily concerns local authority funding and taxation. For this reason, it should be examined separately.

(v) A financial contribution from economic agents benefiting from public transport might be considered, based on the principle of cost- and profit-sharing. A systematic inventory should be made of these potential sources of revenue, which will vary according to the local situation, bearing in mind that taxation is not necessarily the easiest method of collecting such contributions.

Regional Railway Transport in Germany: Changing Conditions; New Services

Jutta Völker
Deutsche Eisenbahn-Consulting GmbH
Germany

TABLE OF CONTENTS

257

1. INTRODUCTION

One of the many challenges facing public transport decision-makers in Central and Eastern Europe (CEE) is how to render urban public transport networks more accessible to suburban communities. This is particularly true in Bucharest, where Metro officials are seeking to establish a link between regional railway and urban metro transport, thus improving the accessibility of these areas to the city.

Among regional transport experiences in countries outside of CEE, that of Germany provides a pertinent example. This paper presents a brief overview of the current situation and trends in regional railway transport in Germany and makes some recommendations to cities in CEE seeking regional transport solutions.

2. PUBLIC TRANSPORT IN GERMANY

Public transport is considered to be important in Germany for environmental, social and economic reasons. It is a precondition for the effective mobility of people in all regions of the country. In recent years, however, the share of public transport in overall transport has been decreasing and private car transport increasing. This evolution can particularly be observed in eastern Germany (former area of the GDR), where car ownership has experienced high growth over the last five years.

Figure 1. **Transport developments in Germany 1991-93**

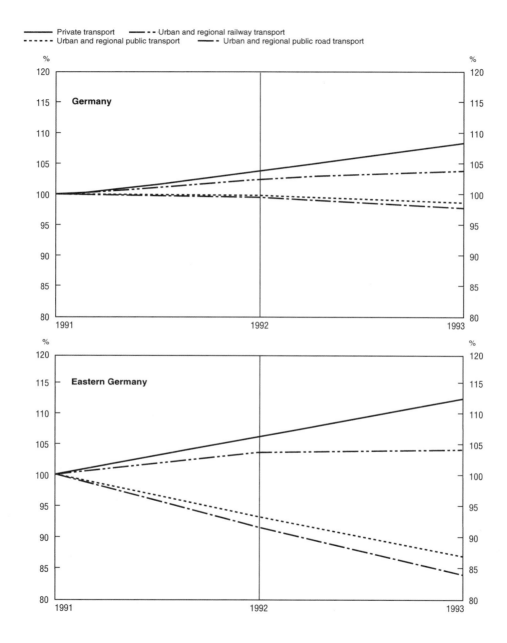

───── Private transport   ───── Urban and regional railway transport
- - - - - Urban and regional public transport   ───── Urban and regional public road transport

260

In view of this development, the German public transport sector is undergoing change, especially as concerns planning, organisation and financing. Numerous measures are under preparation to improve public transport services, with the objective of increasing the share of public transport in total passenger transport in both cities and regions (modal split between public and private transport). Regional railway transport has an important role to play in these changes, and initiatives are now being taken to increase the share of railway transport use in cities and regions.

3. REGIONAL RAILWAY TRANSPORT AND *"REGIONALISIERUNG"*

3.1 Background

In 1993, 1 436 million passengers used regional railway transport (including *S-Bahn*) in Germany, about 90 per cent provided by Deutsche Bahn AG and 10 per cent by other railways owned by *länder*, regional authorities or private companies. The regional railway system operates 31 000 trains per day, 12 000 of which serve large cities and urban agglomerations.

The share of regional railway in total public transport was on average 15 per cent. In eastern Germany, this share was higher, about 17-19 per cent.

The number of regional railway passengers has been rising in recent years. Road transport users, in comparison, have decreased considerably.

Table 1. Development of transport in eastern Germany relative to Germany as a whole 1991-93

(1991 = 100%)

		1992	1993
Germany	Private transport	103.9	108.6
	Public urban and regional transport	100.3	99.0
	of which:		
	Urban and regional railway transport	102.8	104.0
	Public urban and regional road transport	99.8	98.1
Eastern Germany	Private transport	106.9	113.4
	Public urban and regional transport	92.7	86.0
	of which:		
	Urban and regional railway transport	103.7	104.4
	Public urban and regional road transport	90.9	82.8

3.2 *"Regionalisierung"*

The conditions and requirements under which regional railways operate in Germany are evolving. The framework for this development, known as *"Regionalisierung"*, includes the following elements:

- in 1994, structural and organisational reforms of the railway began;
- the former state-owned railway (Deutsche Bahn) has become a private enterprise;
- the railway infrastructure, which can be used by other public railway companies, remains under state ownership.

New responsibilities and conditions for regional railway transport will be defined in the future, and all railways will eventually operate within this framework.

Under *"Regionalisierung"*, the responsibility for planning, organisation and financing regional railway transport will be shifted from the federal government to the regional *länder* authorities (*Bundesländer*). *Länder* officials will then be able to transfer these tasks in a number of ways to other regional entities. (There are several ways the *länder* can distribute responsibility; therefore, laws addressing this initiative should be formulated on a *länder* level.)

The *länder* governments will receive financial support from the state budget for financing regional railway transport. The reason for this has to do with the social function that regional transport carries out and the difference between fare revenues and actual costs resulting from this activity. The level of financial support is established in the *"Regionalisierung"* law for 1996 and 1997. After that time, subsidy levels will be adjusted.

Länder authorities and railway companies will work together in new ways: the *länders* will order a fixed volume and quality of railway traffic from the railway company (Deutsche Bahn or non-State-owned railway companies) and will have to pay for the ordered traffic volume.

The *länder* or regional authorities have been in charge up to now for the planning, organisation and financing of public road transport (tramway, subway, bus). With their new responsibility for regional railway transport, the *länder* will be in effect responsible for all public transport in cities, peripheral zones, urban agglomerations, and rural areas. Urban and regional transport services will therefore be delivered "from one hand" to the people.

In addition, the railways will have to compete with other regional traffic companies, especially bus companies. Under the new regional transport structure, the regional railway will handle the following services:

--   traffic by suburban railways (*S-Bahn*) in large cities;

--   traffic between towns and suburban areas/peripheral zones, and in agglomerations;

--   connection of the rural regions with the nearest medium-sized and large towns or economic centres;

--   connection of small- and medium-sized rural centres.

Expected impacts of this new organisation include:

--   greater efficiency in the planning and use of transport mode capacities;

--   improved consideration of particular regional aspects of traffic demand;

--   more attractive supply of public transport services for clients;

--   further evolution of public and private modal split, especially as concerns reduction of car-use in cities and urban agglomerations.

3.3   Initiatives of the railway operators

Deutsche Bahn AG is the largest regional railway transport company in Germany. It is responsible for all suburban railway systems (*S-Bahn*), which account for 40 per cent of Deutsche Bahn AG's turnover.

The railway companies, in particular Deutsche Bahn AG, and the *länder* authorities have developed common new measures and services for the regional railway system. By working together on these initiatives, they hope to increase the volume of passengers using regional rail, thus improving the modal split in favour of public transport.

Key initiatives underway include:

--   development of new products in the regional railway transport of Deutsche Bahn AG:

- suburban railway (*S-Bahn*);
- city express train (*Stadtexpreß*);
- regional train (*Regionalbahn*);
- regional express train (*Regionalexpreß*);

--   improvements to networks and lines in regional transport;

--   introduction of a system of "integrated timetables" for the regional railway system with direct connections and short changing times between lines;

--   development of an "integrated system for using different transport means", especially for direct connections (concerning space and time) and transfers between railway and bus;

--   participation in tariff co-operation in regional transport (common tariffs and tickets);

--   development of new technologies for common use of the railway infrastructure by railway and light rail or tramway vehicles (Karlsruhe model);

--   use of modern and innovative vehicles for regional railway transport.

The realisation of this programme is underway, and partial introduction of these new services has already led to a considerable increase in passenger volume. It is expected that the railway will play an important role in the future as an ecologically beneficial and efficient mode of transport and in the evolution of modal split.

Table 2. **Products of Deutsche Bahn AG**

Product	Operations Area	Characteristics
Suburban Railway (*S-Bahn*)	• large cities and agglomerations with more than 500 000 inhabitants • transport connections within cities • travel distance on average 15 km	• short distances between stops • high number of passenger places (including standing places) • high frequency
City Express Train (*Stadtexpreß*)	• agglomerations with more than 500 000 inhabitants or cities with less than 500 000 inhabitants • connection between peripheral areas and towns or other large centres (economic, cultural, leisure), especially for commuter traffic • travel distance on average 22 km	• stops in all railway stations in peripheral areas • high number of passenger places • minimum frequency of 60 minutes
Regional Express Train (*Regionalexpreß*)	• connections within rural regions and to the nearest agglomerations and towns • fast regional connections • travel distance on average 45 km	• stops in important railway stations only • size of vehicles and number of places varies depending on regional traffic demand • minimum frequency of 60 minutes
Regional Train (*Regionalbahn*)	• connections within rural areas and to the nearest medium-sized cities • connections among all railway stations • travel distance on average 22 km	• stops in all railway stations • vehicle size adapted to demand, therefore small-capacity vehicles used • minimum frequency of 120 minutes

Source: Deutsche Bahn AG, *Geschäftsbereich Nahverkehr.*

4. RECOMMENDATIONS FOR CENTRAL AND EASTERN EUROPEAN COUNTRIES

Adapting the German experience in regional railway transport to the CEE context is only possible within limits, given the different transport needs and conditions. Economic growth and improvements in living conditions in CEEC, however, will create new problems for transport in the region, due to the rising rate of private car ownership. It will therefore be necessary to develop ecologically beneficial, more attractive and low-cost solutions for public transport in these countries as well.

A few recommendations for development of regional railway transport in CEEC are as follows:

--   A regional railway system should be developed as an integral part of the public transport system in cities and suburban areas. It could form the "backbone" for transportation between cities and peripheral zones. To achieve this, common plans for all transport modes -- including regional railway -- should be developed. Municipal and regional authorities should combine urban and regional public transport companies to provide integrated services for clients -- an important precursor for effective development of integrated transport solutions.

--   A special organisation to co-ordinate urban and regional traffic co-operation should be created to assure:

- joint responsibility for urban and regional transport;
- co-ordinated planning of transport services for cities and their peripheral areas;
- common marketing initiatives for urban and regional transport;
- preparation of common tickets and tariffs for all transport means in the area;
- introduction of a transport management system integrating urban transport companies and the railway for regional transport.

--   Railway transport can complement an urban transport system if direct transfer points between regional railway and other urban and regional transport means are provided. A system of direct transfer points should therefore be established between regional railway and other public transport means (subway, tramway, bus) with minimum transfer times and distances. This system should be developed hierarchically (i.e. "high-level" transfer points between different regional transport systems -- railway, light rail, bus -- and "lower-level" transfer points between regional public modes and private means).

It is essential to maintain the social function of the regional railway system, as well. It follows that state support may be necessary to compensate for the financial discrepancy between high operating costs and low fare revenues. Demand for this compensation is expected to increase in the coming years in CEE cities and regions.

One way to handle this expected increase in demand is to decrease regional railway operating costs. Possible approaches include:

-- Better adapting transport supply to demand by introducing and developing hierarchical systems for regional railway trains with:

- fast-, medium-, and low-speed transport;
- different systems for stops;
- different frequencies of service;
- connection with other urban and regional transport systems through direct transfer points.

-- Using cost-saving technologies for railway operation, e.g. common use of the railway infrastructure by regional rail and other rail systems (light rail, tramway).

-- Minimising personnel needs (one-man service for driving and ticket sales and control in trains during low-demand times).

-- Using modern and innovative vehicles: adapting vehicle size and place availability to real demand; applying energy-saving techniques; low-maintenance demand; using vehicles of light construction and high technical capacity (speed, acceleration, braking force).

-- Contracting regional railway services to outside sources, facilitating more efficient management and lower overhead costs.

Organising and Financing Urban Public Transport in Krakow

Andrzej Rudnicki
Krakow University of Technology
Poland

TABLE OF CONTENTS

LIST OF TABLES

LIST OF FIGURES

SUMMARY

This paper examines the organisational and financial issues of urban public transport in Krakow, Poland. Presented in the context of other Polish cities of comparable size to Krakow, these issues include: the existing and future public transport system in Krakow; transportation policy and behaviour; organisational changes (e.g. management, employment) and financial aspects (e.g. fares, revenues and costs) in urban public transport.

The number of cities served by urban public transport in Poland will probably remain unchanged; small cities will be primarily served by private operators. Stopping unfavourable transport trends and taking action to encourage more sustainable transport behaviour will help to maintain the high share of mass transport in urban travel (50 to 75 per cent of non-pedestrian travels). In several large cities, the decrease in public transport ridership has been stopped. There is, however, an urgent need to create a system for monitoring changes in travel behaviour, especially as concerns modal split and hourly variation of demand. In general, public transport companies adapt their services too slowly to changing passenger behaviour.

The transportation policy approved by the City Council of Krakow is designed to ensure protective treatment of mass public transport. A public transport-friendly policy with restrictions for private car usage could stop car ownership in Polish cities at the level of 350 cars/1 000 population.

The public transport company has been divided into smaller parts based on transportation function and auxiliary activities (e.g. repair of vehicles and tracks). Separation of the transport administrator from the operator should become standard as well. Such solutions promote market relations in urban mass transport and are beneficial to the improvement of efficiency. The much-desired co-ordination of transportation in urban and suburban areas has been introduced with much difficulty.

Public transport companies in Poland possess more fleet than necessary for ordered transportation tasks. However, the fleet comprises primarily old and technically worn-out vehicles. Insufficient funds for new vehicles and repair of tracks have caused a rapid depreciation of fleet and infrastructure, diminishing the reliability of transportation services and generating higher operating costs.

Operating cost savings have enabled city authorities to reduce subsidies gradually and to soften the scale of ticket mark-up. The lack of adequate funds and stability in their allocation for repair purposes is the reason for the depreciation of infrastructure (mainly rolling stock and tramway tracks).

To improve the financial management of the public transport company, a system of cost control should be introduced; this is especially important under conditions of monopolistic operation. There has been an increasing trend in cost recovery in Poland; currently, the average rate is about 75 per cent. Further increases in cost recovery through higher ticket prices (in real prices) should not yet be considered.

Fare discounts and trips free-of-charge overload the budget of public transport companies (and therefore, that of the city), causing losses of 25 to 35 per cent of income. There are no special fares for individuals with modest means. Public transport ridership can be increased by lowering the price of the network pass.

1. INTRODUCTION

Urban public transport systems in Poland (population 38.5 million) serve about 270 cities and 19 million people in addition to three million persons living in suburbs. In urban areas, public transport accounts for 50 to 75 per cent of non-pedestrian trips with a total annual ridership of about six billion trips. The transition to new political systems, however, has created not only opportunities, but also difficult challenges.

In one of its first legal decisions of this transition period, expressed in the Local Government Law (1990), the State transferred ownership of mass transport companies from the central government to municipal governments. Therefore, there is no national agency or ministry whose scope of work includes urban mass transport. Cities work with the State by placing representatives on various national commissions and interest groups, e.g. the Commission for Administrative Reform or the Association of Polish Cities and the Chamber of Urban Transport. The Chamber, which is the association of mass transport operators, is very active in collecting industry statistics (see Chamber of Urban Transport in Poland, 1994), developing sectoral policy, and lobbying the parliament in connection with transport-related laws. In addition, the Polish Academy of Science, in particular the Committee of Transport, supports the merits of mass urban transport (see Rudnicki, A. *et al.*). The mission of the World Bank in Poland has also played a very important role in creating a rational policy for improvement of the operation and development of mass urban transport (see The World Bank, 1994). Their analytical data and results have been very useful, and many of their recommendations -- accurate and generally compatible with the author's opinions -- will be frequently quoted in this paper.

The change in the legal and organisational status of publicly owned mass transport companies in Poland is described in the 1994 World Bank report and updated by Suchorzewski (see Suchorzewski, 1995), based in part on the works of the Institute for Physical and Municipal Economy (see Rozkwitalska, C. *et al.*, 1993).

This paper describes the urban public transport system in Krakow, including issues such as: policy, management, transportation behaviour, financing, and current operations and development. Most issues described in this paper are presented using Krakow as an example, but frequently a broader context is provided using cities with comparable populations.

2. BACKGROUND ON KRAKOW PUBLIC TRANSPORT SYSTEM

2.1 Present situation

Krakow, the former royal seat of Poland, today is the capital of the extensive south-east region of the country and the third city in Poland in terms of population (approximately 750 000 inhabitants). It is one of the largest cultural and educational centres in the country with many historical monuments.

The history of the city's public transport system dates to the nineteenth century: in 1875, a horse-drawn omnibus system was created, which became a horse-drawn tramway in 1882. In 1901, an electric tramway system was built, which progressed into a standard-gauge tramway in 1913. The first bus line opened for operations in 1927, and in 1952, a tramway line was extended to Nowa Huta (formerly a separate city, now a big industrial district of Krakow).

Krakow is the cross-roads for three international and seven national roads. The total length of the urban road network in Krakow is 1 270 km, 6.5 per cent of which is dual-lane.

The southern by-pass of motorway A-4 is under construction. Average density of the road network is 8.5 km per 1 km^2 of urbanised area. There are approximately 10 000 parking spaces in the downtown area, primarily kerbside and on the pavements (only about 800 in parking lots). Seventeen per cent of all vehicles crossing the city limits consists of through traffic. The recent bicycle route network has three sections and totals 12 kilometres in length.

The existing urban public transport system in Krakow includes:

-- 80 km of streets with tramway; 520 tramways serving 28 lines; 62 km of tram lines separated from road traffic.

-- 652 km of streets with bus traffic (384 km inside the city and 268 km outside); 627 buses serving 112 lines (including 40 running outside).

-- Network density is: tramway 0.57 km/km^2; bus 2.74 km/km^2; total density: 3.31 km/km^2. This density corresponds to values recommended for areas with high population density.

Since 1991, the tramway network and number of lines has remained constant. The total length of lines has increased by 3 per cent. In the same period, the number of bus lines has increased by 9 per cent and total length of bus lines by 17 per cent.

The scheduled tramway frequency is: 15 minutes for each line (most of the operation day time); since 1991, it has been 12 minutes. Bus frequency is between five and 90 minutes in rush hours (the average time being 12 minutes). There are 136 bus terminals and 1 885 stops, including 594 stops equipped with shelters.

Average travel time for 18 city districts ranges from 30-47 minutes; for the whole city, average travel time is 34 minutes (including access, waiting and transfer times).

Table 1. **Operating trends in Krakow public transport**

	1984	1986	1988	1990	1992	1993	1994	1995
Bus fleet in service	476	496	503	480	432	456	460	439
Tram fleet in service	434	442	421	407		356	366	374
Bus-km travelled (million)	42	44	44	42	38	37	38	37
Tram-km travelled (million)	34	36	34	32	26	26	25	26
Passengers (million)	741	740	724	468	399	508	564	-

Source: Urban Public Transport Company.

The passenger volume (ridership) has been estimated using the mobility rate of monthly ticket owners, provided by the Central Statistical Office (GUS).

In 1993, after five years of decreasing passenger volume (by 46 per cent!), demand rose by 27 per cent according to the GUS rate, but only by 10 per cent in real figures (Figure 1). The yearly vehicle-km run was reduced from 80 million in the late 1980s to 63 million from 1993 to 1995, i.e. by 21 per cent.

Table 2. **Operations and related data of comparable Polish cities (1994)**

City	Krakow	Gdansk	Lodz	Poznan	Szczecin	Wroclaw
Legal form of company	joint-stock	budgetary	joint-stock	budgetary	budgetary	budgetary
Urban population (000)	750.00	465.00	835.00	580.00	420.00	640.00
Tramway network (km)	80.00	50.00	113.00	57.00	44.00	90.00
Bus network (km)	515.00	259.00	334.00	258.00	230.00	370.00
Fleet inventory:						
tramways	520.00	260.00	472.00	322.00	285.00	449.00
buses	627.00	247.00	435.00	310.00	310.00	412.00
Vehicles in operation/(1 000)	1.07	0.77	0.84	0.78	0.93	0.93
Availability (%):						
tramways	69.20	65.00	74.50	68.60	64.60	67.20
buses (1)	71.30	77.00	79.70	75.20	66.80	71.20
Technical readiness (%):						
tramways	82.40	76.00	82.80	74.80	89.80	90.10
buses (2)	81.80	92.00	86.60	84.50	79.30	85.10
Annual veh-km (million)	63.10	27.20	54.40	33.00	32.00	47.30
Share of tramways in veh-km (%) (3)	39.00	46.00	46.00	45.00	38.00	47.00
Annual veh-km/person	84.00	58.00	65.00	57.00	76.00	74.00
Average daily duration for the operation [h]:	15.90	N/A	15.20	N/A	13.90	15.60
tramways	14.70	N/A	14.60	N/A	14.00	13.20
buses (4)						
Average operating speed [km/h]: tramways	14.10	15.60	15.10	14.20	14.30	14.70
buses (5)	17.90	17.90	18.70	16.40	20.30	20.10
No. passengers p.a. (million)	564.00	189.00	345.00	203.00	159.00	363.00
Annual trips/person	750.00	250.00	410.00	350.00	380.00	570.00

Notes :   Basic tariff data (31.12.1994);
        N/A.: data not available;
        (1) availability: vehicles in service/inventory vehicles;
        (2) technical readiness: vehicles technically ready for operation/inventory vehicles;
        (3) the rest (up to 100 per cent) is performed by buses;
        (4) excluding night service;
        (5) including stop over time at the terminals.

Source: Chamber of Urban Transport and author's calculations.

The low fleet availability rate (65 to 75 per cent) in comparison to over 90 per cent for western European operators is caused by:

-- a considerable number of vehicles which are technically out of order;
-- keeping the vehicle reserve in inventory:

- considering the poor reliability of old vehicles;
- fearing that the company will not get the money for purchase of new vehicles;
- substituting as quickly as possible a broken-down vehicle with an operating one; contracts stipulate fines for missing runs and lack of punctuality.

The rate: one (exactly 0.8 to 1.0) vehicle in operation per 1 000 inhabitants is a good figure for **medium**-sized cities (high-capacity vehicles). For big cities, this rate is higher (e.g. Krakow).

The tramway plays a very important role in the public transport service of large Polish cities, accounting for 37 to 48 per cent of total vehicle-km trips.

The average operating speed for buses is higher than for tramways because of the greater distances between bus stops, more routes outside of congested downtown areas, shorter lay-over time at termini. There is a slightly decreasing trend in operating speeds -- about 0.3 km/h a year, probably reflecting the influence of rising congestion and the requirement to maintain punctuality.

The number of passengers and the mobility rate (annual trips/person) are provided based on the data (considerably overestimated) of urban public transport companies (see Chapter 2.3). Compared to 1993, the number of passengers has increased in three cities studied and decreased in the remaining cities.

2.2 Car ownership

According to comprehensive transport surveys of Krakow households carried out in 1994:

-- 48.1 per cent do not own a car;
-- 37.2 per cent own one car;
-- 4.3 per cent own two cars;
-- 0.4 per cent own three or more cars.

It is interesting to note that in the centre of Krakow, households with three or more cars comprise 0.9 per cent of total household, i.e. three to four times as many as in other districts of the city. This is primarily due to car owners formally registering their vehicles in downtown areas, while living elsewhere; registering their vehicles downtown enables them to obtain special entry and parking rights downtown.

Table 3. **Changes in car ownership in Krakow**

	1970	1975	1980	1985	1990	1992	1994	2000	2005	2015
cars/1 000 population	32	54	104	143	198	212	249	315 to 335	340 to 400	345 to 445

Source: Official statistical data (the past) and author's estimation (the future).

Lower levels of future car ownership correspond to the lower level forecast (saturation level of motorisation -- 350 cars/1 000 population); the higher ones refer to the upper level forecast (saturation level -- 500 cars/1 000 population). The continued success of the approved transportation and physical planning policies should lead to the "pessimistic" scenario of motorisation development (Figure 2).

Estimated current car ownership as an extrapolation of trends in selected Polish cities is given in Table 4.

Table 4. **Current population and car ownership in selected Polish cities**

City	Population (000)	Cars/1 000 pop.
Warsaw	1 640	350
Lodz	830	180
Wroclaw	640	260
Poznan	580	320
Gdansk	460	210
Katowice	360	310
Bialystok	280	190
Nowy Sacz	80	180
Poland	38 600	185

Source: Yearbook of Central Statistical Office and author's estimation.

Car ownership levels in Polish cities range from 150 to 350 cars/1 000 population, and vary greatly according to the city. In general, car ownership is greater in large cities than in small cities. During 1990-1992, there was a remarkably high annual compound growth rate of 7 to 14 per cent; this trend is now decreasing, notably in large cities.

2.3 Mobility and modal split

Comprehensive traffic surveys are a dependable source of transportation behaviour data. In Krakow, these surveys were carried out in 1975, 1985 and 1994. It is particularly interesting to compare the data of 1985 and 1994:

The weekday mobility rate (trip/day/person) was 2.12 per inhabitant in 1985 and 1.87 in 1994. The decrease in this rate was caused by:

-- collapse of big industry and unemployment;
-- increase in numbers of retired persons;
-- better accessibility of goods and services;
-- increase in travel costs.

The current rate of 1.87 is composed of various groups of travellers: working people and students with a rate of 2.3; school children 1.8; unemployed 1.6; retired and non-working individuals 1.4. In motorised households the mobility rate is 13 per cent higher than in non-motorised households.

Recently, the daily mobility rate in Polish cities has ranged from 1.4 (in small cities) to 2.5 (Warsaw).

The percentage of private car journeys out of total motorised journeys increased from 5 to 15 per cent from 1975 to 1985. During this period, car ownership increased from 44 to 140 cars per 1 000 inhabitants. Now with about 250 cars/1 000 inhabitants the share of cars in motorised travel is estimated at 30 per cent (in rush hour approximately 27 per cent). The increase in the share of cars in overall travel is not only due to the growth of car ownership levels, but also the rationing of fuel in 1985 (Figures 3 and 4). This means that if in 1995 there was no rationing of fuel then the share of private cars in traffic would be greater (not 10.3 but e.g. 14 per cent); in consequence the growth in this share in the period 1985-94 would be smaller (instead of from 10.3 to 20.9 per cent it would be from 14.0 to 20.9 per cent).

Table 5. **Changes in modal split in Krakow**

Means of transport	Percentage of journeys	
Year	1985	1994
Pedestrian	30.3	28.2
Public transport	58.3	48.0
Personal transport (private car)	10.3	20.9
of which: drivers	7.6	15.9
passengers	2.7	5.0
Bicycle	0.4	1.6
Other (including: taxi, park-and-ride)	0.7	1.3
Total	100.0	100.0

Source: Comprehensive traffic survey in Krakow 1985, 1994.

The hourly travel variation for 1994 shows beneficial changes in comparison to the previous pattern (1975, 1985) from an efficiency standpoint. Share of rush hour in daily ridership is currently 9.3 per cent (7.00 to 8.00) and 11.1 per cent (15.00 to 16.00), a drop of about 2 to 3 per cent. The periods in between peak travel times are now more busy than previously (2/3 of maximum hourly volume in relation to 1/2). In the early morning (5.00-7.00), the travel volume is lower than in the 1980s. This has allowed for shorter work time for drivers.

Changes in travel demand should induce the transport operator to react by modifying supply (e.g. increasing service frequency in the period between peak travel time).

Interviews carried out in the context of a comprehensive traffic survey revealed the following reasons that individuals did not use a car:

-- car out of order -- 6 per cent;
-- car being used by another person -- 24 per cent;
-- lack of driver's licence or driver not available -- 30 per cent;
-- high cost of car use -- 13 per cent;
-- difficulty driving in the street network (i.e. congestion) -- 4 per cent;
-- difficulty finding a parking place -- 1 per cent;
-- other reasons -- 23 per cent.

To determine the mobility rate for Polish cities, a number of assumptions must be made. It can be estimated that for each percentage drop in motorisation degree falls from 0.8 (Warsaw) to 2.0 per cent (in small cities) of car share in non-pedestrian travels. E.g. in a small city with car ownership 250 cars/1 000 population (i.e. motorised society makes up 25 per cent of total) the estimated share of car travel is 2.0 x 25 = 50 per cent.

Assuming that:

--   the share of pedestrian travels is 30 per cent for large cities, 40 per cent for medium-sized cities and 60 per cent for small cities;
--   the mobility rate effected by public transport on Saturday is 2/3 and on Sunday 1/3 of that on a working day;
--   the transfer rate (average number of trips) ranges from 1.2 in small cities to 1.4 in big cities;

then the following mobility rate estimations can be made as follows in Table 6:

Table 6. **Estimated public transport mobility rate in Polish cities**

	Public transport mobility rate journeys/person/day	Average number of journeys/person/year	Average number of trips/person/year
Large cities	1.0	320	450
Medium-sized cities	0.8	240	320
Small cities	0.5	150	180

Source: Author's estimation.

3. TRANSPORT POLICY FOR KRAKOW

In January 1993, the City Council passed a resolution for a general transportation policy compatible with the recommendations of the OECD/ECMT Project Group (See OECD/ECMT, 1992). In the course of subsequent planning work, a detailed policy for improvement and development of transportation systems in Krakow was elaborated and completed in April 1994. This policy was integrated into the Master Plan for Krakow, which was approved by the City Council in November 1994. The author was the head of the team which worked out the transportation policy (see Friedberg, J. and Rudnicki, A., 1993) and solutions for the transport system within the Master Plan.

3.1 Transport policy objectives

The objectives of the policy were to:

-- improve accessibility of urban space;
-- improve the quality of transportation as an important component of quality of life in the city;
-- reduce transportation demand;
-- decrease absolute levels of car use and road freight;
-- equalise levels of transportation service among various urban zones;
-- improve accessibility to transport for disabled people;
-- increase occupancy of private cars;
-- favour less energy-hungry and more environmentally-friendly solutions;
-- promote public transport and non-motorised means of transport (pedestrian, bicycle);
-- reduce noise and vehicle exhaust emissions at source;
-- alleviate functional inconveniences of traffic (congestion, barrier effect, cutting neighbouring ties);
-- better traffic safety, mainly for pedestrians and cyclists;
-- stimulate spatial and economic development of the city;
-- protect natural and cultural values of the city;
-- co-create physical order of the city appearance;
-- influence on travel behaviour: mobility, choice of trip destination, choice of transport means, drivers' relationship to other transport system users;
-- more effective use of existing infrastructure;
-- zoning of areas accessible by car;
-- traffic regulations: priority for public transport, speed limits, traffic calming, sector accessibility schemes, pedestrian-only streets, strict enforcement of rules and regulations;
-- limiting degradation of rolling stock and infrastructure (street pavements, tramway tracks, bridges);
-- selected development of road network and parking facilities;
-- development of public transport; demonopolisation and improvement of operations;
-- integration of public transport system and individual traffic (park-and-ride, bike-and-ride)

-- making public transport more responsive to individual needs (small buses, taxis)
-- ensuring coherency within the transportation system at the local, regional, national and international levels;
-- constructing facilities for bimodal and intermodal transport of goods;
-- strengthening logistics of goods distribution in urban areas;
-- developing means of protection against noise and vibration; strict enforcement of emissions standards for vehicles;
-- improvements in transport sector management;
-- physical planning policy, including location decisions;
-- use of economic and fiscal instruments: (e.g. cost-benefit studies, tariff system, parking fees, tolls, taxes, subsidies);
-- encouraging public participation in transport policy development, choice of measures, acceptance of solutions.

3.2 Aims and measures for specific transport branches

Road network:

-- assure accessibility of development areas;
-- alleviate heavy through-traffic in the city and inter-district traffic in the business and commercial district (BCD);
-- improve the quality of service for inter-district traffic outside of the BCD area;
-- create new direct bus routes;
-- extend traffic calming zones to enhance public transport operations and conditions for pedestrians;
-- improve access to public transport stops, terminals and park-and-ride facilities.

Urban public transport:

-- improve the quality of service, or at least maintain the existing level of service quality (in the short term); render public transport more competitive with private car use, and fulfil the needs of city residents who do not own cars;
-- provide alternative means of transportation in zones with car traffic restrictions;
-- protect the urban structure and environment.

The OECD/ECMT Group recommends that the ratio of travel time using public transport compared to that using private car should not exceed 1 to 5; to date, this has only been achieved in the BCD. In the future, this requirement should be attained for 2/3 of all origin-destination pairs of travels. It is assumed that the standard of five persons per m² of standing space in a vehicle can be exceeded during rush hours on maximum 5 per cent of the network.

The main policy features concerning the development and operation of public transport are:

-- design the system to carry 75 per cent of non-pedestrian travellers during rush hours (more in the city centre, less in the outlying areas);
-- equalise the level of service amongst the different urban zones;
-- modernise the existing tramway and bus network as well as modifying the existing routes of both and improving traffic management;
-- construct a fast tramway network and separate bus streets/lanes;
-- improve accessibility for disabled people;
-- integrate the various modes of public transport with common time tables and common fares (one ticket will be valid for an entire trip, including transfers and parking at park-and-ride facilities);
-- develop the street network based on the needs of public transport, in order to assure good accessibility to terminals and improved bus operations;
-- put a water tramway into service along the Vistula river within the built up area.

Railway system:

-- adapt the railway network to provide service to urban areas (the decision was made that the branch-line used until now for industrial purposes only would be at once adapted to allow passenger transport from the city centre to the airport);
-- establish trains running at regular intervals on the two main radial lines with 20-minute frequency periods (in central areas -- 10 minutes);
-- develop express lines for domestic and international travel (express trains currently run hourly to Warsaw during busy periods).

Bicycle path network:

-- ensure convenient, safe and environmentally-friendly conditions for all potential bike users;
-- render the bicycle more competitive than a private car;
-- reduce investment and operation costs of the transportation system.

3.3 Co-ordinating urban planning and transport policies

Transport policy should be co-ordinated with general urban planning in order to:

-- maintain the density of current urban development;
-- diversify large-scale housing zones (e.g. by introducing small businesses, light industry, and service ventures);
-- balance travel demands locally, especially to and from home and work and to and from home and stores;
-- avoid urban sprawl (suburban areas should primarily develop based on railway station connections);
-- intensify land use along attractive corridors of public transport service; development policy should correspond to the capacity of road and public transport network (this issue is strongly linked to parking policy).

3.4 Future urban transport model

Transportation in the Master Plan of Krakow is typically intermodal and integrated, especially as concerns passenger transport. The structural model (Figure 5) for the future transport system in Krakow can be briefly described as follows:

An outer fourth ring road with a 17- to 20-km diameter will carry through-traffic and some outer traffic to and from Krakow. An alternative to this outermost ring road will be the crossover of the East-West motorway and the North-South expressway. A third ring road with a 6- to 8-km diameter will carry inter-district traffic away from the city centre. Park-and-ride sites will be located in the vicinity of this circle, with connections to efficient public transport ensuring (by radial routes) service inside this ring. The second ring will be comprised of collector streets with restrictions for private car traffic. Traffic calming zones will be located inside this ring. The first ring surrounds the Old City and is now cut at several points for inter-district through traffic.

3.5 Targeting modal split

Determining optimum modal split is a key part of transportation policy development. Recommended modal split options should ensure sustainable operation and development of the city. Modal split targeting should aim to:

-- maintain pedestrian travel at its current share of about 30 per cent of all inner-city trips;
-- significantly increase bicycle travel (up to 5 to 10 per cent more);
-- maintain public transport use at its current level of 75 per cent of non-motorised trips during rush hours;
-- hold the share of private car use at a level of 25 per cent on average in rush hours (in the distant future -- maximum 35 per cent) with the perspective of reducing car traffic in particularly busy zones and resisting increased car traffic in outlying areas:

Table 7. **Recommended share of car use in Krakow by zone**

	Share of private cars in non-pedestrian trips during rush hours
Old City	3 to 5%
Downtown area (nineteenth century)	8 to 18%
Heavily developed areas and other areas with profitable public transport service	20 to 35%
Remaining areas inside the city border	40 to 60%

Source: Author's analysis.

The percentages expressed for the Old City and Downtown areas reflect a policy with strong restrictions on private traffic (on average, only 25 per cent travel by car); those given the lower two categories reflect a more liberal policy (35 per cent travel by car); efficient "car pooling" could decrease this share.

Other options investigated have not been recommended, because they were too extreme. A proposal for complete freedom for private car users was rejected as being excessively expensive in terms of investment and environmental costs, with the potential to destroy the city structure. A pure "car-free city" option is now politically impossible, since it completely cancels the utility of a private car.

A reasonable level of accessibility to individual city areas by private cars is the starting point for zoning. The higher the land use density, the better the public transport service; the higher the share of public transport the greater the restraint on car traffic.

3.6 Future public transport system

The starting point for all public transport development strategies is to maximise efficiency of the existing system. This can be done by upgrading facilities and rolling stock, co-ordinating and synchronising time schedules, and using traffic priorities and dispatching control. For medium- and long-term strategies, rapid buses (with special lanes and streets) and fast tramways or LRTs are recommended. (A metro for Krakow has been considered and rejected on account of the very high capital investment required). Factors influencing the decision to primarily develop the fast tramway network, in spite of the higher investment costs as compared to a bus system, include the easier and more natural methods of traffic segregation for tramway tracks, the low sensitivity of trams to passenger overload as well as the traditional aspects of tramways.

The recommended public transport system (Figure 6) will include:

-- 36 km of new tracks for a fast tramway and 10 km of tracks for a traditional tramway cost about US$130 million;
-- 10 km of separate bus streets cost about US$10 million.

In the initial stages, the fast tramway will be connected to the existing tramway network, although they will eventually be separated. The network is shaped like a fork, has seven terminals, runs predominantly on a North-South axis, crosses the centre of the urban system, serves all new developing areas, and accesses previously poorly served residential districts. It will be constructed starting from the South and progressing towards the BCD. Bus service will dominate North-South routes in the West of the city, running on separate lanes and streets. All separate tramway tracks (especially those running independently from streets) will be adapted for bus traffic.

The system has the following features:

-- high-density network;
-- moderate investment expenditures (1/20 of the cost of constructing a metro);
-- extension of the current network instead of replacement of existing tracks with new ones;
-- immediate start of rapid tramway construction without waiting for all necessary capital to be acquired first;
-- installation of fast tram tracks as a additional to existing tram tracks
-- maximum integration of the current system, using the existing bus and tram network, and separate bus lanes and tram tracks;

--   convenient connections between the city systems mentioned above and the airport, railway terminals and stops, regional bus terminals and with individual traffic (park-and-ride facilities and bicycle paths);

--   adaptability for future development (contingencies for the transformation of the East-West track into an underground line);

--   limited range of underground sections for the fast tramway, using the constructed tunnel under the main railway station;

4. ORGANISATION OF THE PUBLIC TRANSPORT SYSTEM

4.1   Overview

Under the previous regime, all public transport company assets belonged to the State. With decentralisation, however, all vehicles, equipment and transport became municipal property. Most of the transport companies are still public -- owned by municipalities -- in one of three legal forms: budgetary unit, a public enterprise, or a corporate establishment. At the end of 1994 (see The World Bank, 1994), 83 out of 137 transport companies (61 per cent) chose to have mass transport activities carried out through a budgetary department of the city, among them, Warsaw, Poznan, Wroclaw, Gdansk; 25 companies (18 per cent) opted for the public enterprise status, including two as state enterprises; 28 (20 per cent) for the joint-stock company operating under the Commercial Code (including Krakow and Lodz). Only one company opted to become a large private enterprise. One of the reasons behind the decision to have a budgetary unit was the desire to avoid paying taxes on excess wages in the public sector.

The companies use the transport infrastructure, which remains the property of the city. Amortisation obligation is the responsibility of the municipality; however, the municipality does not operate the infrastructure directly and is not always aware of the current needs for renovation of particular vehicles and transport facilities. To increase the capital stock of the public transport company, a transfer of used property as an initial contribution was made.

Currently, the private sector does not play an important role in the mass passenger transport system. Most of the private operators have only one or very few microbuses. The exact number of private operators is unknown to the local transportation authority. In Krakow, the number is estimated at between five and 20 with the total number of microbuses between 20 and 50 and a few standard buses. Microbus companies compete with the urban public transport company in the most attractive transport corridors. Some of the small private operators service routes indicated by the contractor i.e. the urban public transport company; in this way, they have indirect access to subsidies. The other operators do not benefit from subsidies, but have full freedom to establish their fares. A single ticket usually costs 50 to 100 per cent more than that offered by the public transport company.

Private operators can positively influence efficiency, offering competitive costs and service quality. Currently, the private sector operates under more favourable conditions than public transport companies. Informal activities of private operators, however, should be replaced by obligatory invitations to tender and licensing of operators.

4.2 Organisational changes in Krakow public transport

In 1990, along with the changes in the political system came criticism of large enterprises and monopolistic structure. The Urban Public Transport Company in Krakow began to seek answers to this criticism. The question was whether to transform this company into a limited liability company or into a joint stock company. Separating backup facilities as financially independent entities while keeping the company's units together in the form of a holding was proposed. At the same time, demands concerning workers' wages and maintenance of public transport services were being made. A general strike was called at the end of 1991. Facing extended strike conditions, the City Council divided the urban transport company into six limited companies 100 per cent-owned by the City of Krakow, each handling:

-- mass transportation of passengers;
-- repair of buses;
-- repair of tramways;
-- construction, repair, and maintenance of tracks, contact lines and substations;
-- construction and repair of buildings;
-- transportation of goods and taxi service.

The reasoning behind this restructuring was to:

-- separate the transportation services function for passengers from other auxiliary activities (repair, construction);
-- create conditions to raise workers' wages without extra taxes;

-- limit the administrative staff;
-- lower total costs;
-- reduce the staff power (for political reasons).

In the beginning, all limited companies were linked by common materials procurement, store-rooms, and book-keeping departments and were overseen by one Supervisory Board. The Krakow City Government appointed five members to the Board and two were elected by the staff. The head of the Supervisory Board co-ordinated activities of all companies. Since 1992, each company has acquired its own Supervisory Board, which carries out exclusively statutory tasks. In Krakow, the Deputy Mayor is the head of the Supervisory Board of the Urban Public Transport Company.

Diminishing orders and competition with increasing numbers of private firms have led to the insolvency of two municipal companies: those overseeing building construction and repair in 1992, and taxis and transportation of goods in 1993. (In this case, the taxi drivers bought the cars from the City and created private taxi partnerships). Recently, an offer for privatisation of the company overseeing tracks, contact lines and substations was made.

Only the Urban Public Transport Company, Ltd. had guaranteed orders from the City of Krakow; however, even with these, the company was operating below potential. Other companies had to submit tenders, as orders from the City covered only a portion of their activity potential; the rest of the orders had to be sought on the market. Conversely, specialised companies located in other cities have expressed interest in bidding for track and vehicle maintenance. In 1994, the municipal tramway repair company made 85 per cent of its turnover from the Urban Public Transport Company Ltd. (in previous years from 65 to 87 per cent), but the municipal bus repair company made only 20 per cent. Lack of stability poses a major problem for the repair companies: numbers of ordered general overhauls from 1991-1994 were: 115, 45, 93, 73.

The separation of the repair companies from the transport company proved profitable (lower repair costs, higher quality) due to tough competition. The introduction in 1993 of a Value Added Tax in Poland made the global financial effect worse for the City of Krakow: the tax is charged by the repair company, but cannot be recovered by the operator. Transport companies are excluded from this debiting, in which repair works have not been separated.

4.3   The public transport authority

Specialised public transport authorities have been created in many Polish cities. At the end of 1994, there were 13 local transport authorities, compared to eight in 1993. Before a transport authority was established in Krakow, the Urban Public Transport Company Ltd. determined its operational activities, evaluated their implementation, and ordered repair work from other municipal companies. In 1993, the public transport section established the Krakow Transport Authority as a department of the City Infrastructure Office. In 1994, this Section joined the Department of the Municipal Economy at the City Hall.

The functions of the Public Transport Authority include:

-- investigating existing and future transportation demand;
-- preparing a development plan for the public transport system;
-- creating and updating the data bank for facilities and traffic;
-- establishing travel standards for public transport;
-- designing lines, location of stops and solutions for terminals and transfer nodes;
-- establishing guidelines and adjusting designs according to public transport requirements;
-- planning, inviting bids for and supervising construction of public transport investments;
-- preparing tariff systems;
-- planning revenues and expenditures;
-- distributing tickets; collecting revenues from the sale of tickets; controlling passenger ticket purchases;
-- determining reasonable levels of operations costs;
-- concluding contracts with operators;
-- supervising the state of municipal transport property committed to operators; responsibility for regeneration of this property;
-- determining subsidy levels for public transport;
-- designing a financial supply system for operators;
-- defining and implementing traffic priorities for public transport vehicles;
-- analysing traffic safety in public transport;
-- informing passengers and marketing public transport services;
-- co-ordinating overall public transport operations;
-- controlling quantity and quality of service performed by operators (checking adherence to contracts);
-- maintaining public transport facilities (technical state, lighting, cleanliness);

-- co-ordinating with other urban infrastructure entities (streets, energy supply);
-- fielding and investigating passenger complaints and requests relating to public transport services.

Before the creation of the Public Transport Authority, a number of these functions were carried out by operators. Some activities can be subcontracted to other service providers, but the Public Transport Authority should maintain final responsibility for their implementation.

4.4 Service agreements

Relations between the operator and the city are defined in an annual service agreement, with charges based on a rate per vehicle-km supplied.

In Krakow, the service agreement covers:

-- period of operation and frequency of each line;
-- total cost, projected revenues, operations subsidies including for maintenance costs;
-- repair plan and costs (rolling stock, tramway tracks);
-- an allowance in vehicle-km performance of a maximum 3 per cent each month; exceeding this value incurs penalties for the operator. The penalty means a decrease in subsidies equal to twice the amount of floating costs which have not been incurred;
-- a secured cost savings should be assigned: 50 per cent as a purse fund for staff; 25 per cent for additional investment tasks; 25 per cent for other purposes defined by the City;
-- a secured revenue surplus: 50 per cent as a purse fund for staff; 50 per cent for additional investment tasks;
-- general requirements relating to: information for passengers; cleanness of vehicles; terminals and stops, safety of passengers;
-- duties and liabilities of both parties.

The investment plan (for purchase of vehicles) is excluded from this agreement. Any changes in operation (lines, frequency) are possible during the year, if they lead to a better adaptation of supply to demand and if approved by the City Government. The objective of this agreement is to stimulate the company, save costs, and obtain additional revenues.

The operations evaluation is carried out on the basis of data provided by the public transport company -- a weakness in the existing system: at present, no measures for quality of service are specified in the contract.

A new evaluation system, now being tested in Krakow, should help to rectify this problem. The new system covers crossing points for tramways and buses. Each public transport line passes these points at least once, and the departure time and occupancy of vehicles are recorded. A set of measures is then calculated, including: factors for punctuality, regularity, comfort (based on the density of passengers in vehicles) and number of missed runs. The measures are calculated for each individual line and for a group of lines. All measures are optionally aggregated for a selected area, a week-day and for the whole network. The range of measurements covers all days, periods of days, months and measuring points. Each time, they are randomly put together. The operator knows neither the time nor place of recording, but is aware that the observation can be made at any moment and at any point.

The first results of these observations are promising. Testing will therefore continue and serve as a basis for estimating future public transport operations. The evaluation system will then be integrated into the contract.

The transport policy will correlate the level of subsidy to the level of service performed by the public transport company. Some general, as well as specific evaluation factors have been defined: a general evaluation factor includes a weighted average sum of access (walking) time, waiting time, time in the vehicle, and transfer time. Specific evaluation factors involve punctuality and regularity. Some time equivalents reflecting the fare system, passenger complaints about poor public transport operation, and the impact of road accidents on passengers are to be added. Some of the components will be adjusted to take travel conditions into consideration, for instance: quality of information for passengers, lack of service reliability, shelters and lighting at stops, operating standards (available places, overcrowded vehicles, and transfer convenience).

According to the contract, in Bialystok (population 280 000), the public transport authority imposes definite fines on operators in the following cases: missing a run, lack of punctuality, dirty vehicle, faultiness in vehicle equipment, menace to passenger safety, impoliteness of drivers. Bus departures are controlled by an electronic detection system.

4.5 Employment issues

The post-strike agreements between the Krakow City Authority and trade unions ensured jobs for all employees and a secured priority of orders from the City for all separate companies until the end of 1991. Since 1992, the company officials have formally had a free hand in their employment policy; however, the labour law, traditional prerogatives of workers, and the power of trade unions have made such loose policy difficult. (About 50 per cent of the Urban Public Transport Company staff are members of one of the six trade unions). In spite of these constraints, the company officials have succeeded in gradually reducing employment and changing its structure (Figure 7).

Table 8. **Changes in the employment structure of the Krakow Urban Public Transport Company**

Group of workers	Oct. 1990	End of 1990	End of 1991	End of 1992	End of 1993	End of 1994	1995 (est.)
Bus and tram drivers	2 021	1 851	1 790	1 786	1 810	1 681	1 700
Depot workers and traffic supervisors	3 969	2 108	1 959	1 865	1 621	1 602	1 550
Others (mostly administration)	1 173	867	809	803	815	775	740
Apprentices of the technical school	703	731	582	452	482	399	0
Total	7 866	5 557	5 140	4 906	4 728	4 457	3 990

Source: Data of Urban Public Transport Company.

Remarks: October 1990: *status quo* before separation.
The group of other workers includes: management, administration, traffic supervision and ticket inspection.
In 1995, the technical school attached to the company was to be taken over by the Board of Education.
In 1994, the number of drivers per vehicle (wagon) was: 2.62 for buses; 1.44 for tramways. In other big cities: 2.49 to 2.88 for buses; 1.30 to 1.98 for tramways.

The urban public transport company has divested itself of non-essential activities and reduced staff. However, following the first phase of action (end of 1990), part of the staff remained engaged in auxiliary activities. To avoid conflicts with trade unions, save compensation for dismissed workers, and economise its wage fund, the following measures have been taken:

-- old-age pensions and disability pensions for conflict-free end of work;
-- transfer of depot workers to other firms;
-- abandonment of overtime and four-brigade system for drivers and depot workers.

The transport company pays the retirement costs.

Pay raises in the Urban Public Transport Company parallel, or are even a few percentage points higher.

5. FINANCING OF THE PUBLIC TRANSPORT SYSTEM

5.1 Fare policy

Over the past ten years, fares have risen faster than wages. A resident of a Polish city could buy the following number of single public transport tickets for his average wage (a single ticket does not allow transfers):

Table 9. **Number of single public transport tickets per average wage in Krakow**

1980	1982	1984	1986	1988	1990	1992	1993
6 000	11 600	5 600	4 016	3 318	1 748	862	832

Source: Statistical Yearbook. Central Statistical Office, 1994 and earlier.

(See also Figure 8 prepared for Warsaw).

Over the last three years the trend has reversed. It must be noted, that in the 1980s, the relative ticket price was very low, even in comparison with other welfare states. The increases in ticket prices, progressively imposed because of very high

298

inflation, were very large, causing public discontent. The increase in monthly mass transport passes was lower than that of single tickets. The tariffs for a single ticket and for the whole network monthly pass in big Polish cities are given in Table 10.

The ticket prices in investigated cities vary greatly, especially as concerns monthly tickets. The time-limit tariff, introduced in a few big cities in 1993-94, satisfies passengers who travel for short instances. However, there are as yet no precise data demonstrating that time-limit tariffs have led to an increase in ridership or to any change in revenues of the public transport company. The Urban Public Transport Company in Krakow has equipped all vehicles with electronic fare-boxes; a precondition to introducing a time-limit tariff. The company is afraid that it will thus lose a part of its revenues. The time-limit tariff and the zone tariff are being studied. The former is simpler to implement; the latter helps to avoid a situation whereby the passenger is obligated to pay for standing in a traffic-jam. Some users of the transport system have criticised the tariff system as too complicated and lacking transfer and family tickets.

Table 10. **Public transport fares in large Polish cities**
(end of 1994)

	Krakow	Gdansk	Lodz	Poznan	Szczecin	Wroclaw	Warsaw
Price of single ticket Zl	6 000	time-limit 10' - 3 000 30' - 5 000 60' - 7 000 day-15 000	time-limit 30' - 3 000 90' - 9 000 120' - 2 000	time-limit 10' - 3 000 30' - 6 000 60' - 9 000 120' - 2 000	time-limit 10' - 3 000 40' - 5 000 120' - 10 000	6 000	6 000
Monthly ticket for whole network Zl (1 000)	220(a)	400(a)	280(a)	260(b)	300(a)	390(b)	240(a)

Notes: a) personalised ticket;
           b) ticket for bearer.

Source: Chamber of Urban Transport.

The Urban Public Transport Company in Krakow offers a variety of ticket options:

-- single or collective;
-- daily, weekly, monthly, quarterly, half-yearly, yearly;
-- for all days of the week or for working days only;
-- personal or bearer tickets;
-- one route or for the whole network;
-- full price and reduced price tickets.

The share of single tickets in overall ticket sales has been decreasing in Krakow as shown in Table 11 (see also Figure 9).

Table 11. **Changes in shares of ticket types (%)**

	1991	1992	1993	1994
Single tickets	60	44	27	21
Season tickets	40	56	73	79

Source: Urban Public Transport Company, Ltd.

This downward trend has been observed in other Polish cities which have applied a preferential policy for season tickets. The comprehensive traffic survey of 1994 showed that 37 per cent of the Krakow population owned season public transport passes: of these, the majority (63 per cent) purchased the pass for the whole network, and the rest for one route; 47 per cent purchased monthly tickets; 27 per cent, half-yearly (semester) tickets; and 43 per cent bought the pass at a discount tariff.

In 1994, the Krakow Urban Public Transport Company estimated the following average one-trip prices (without transfers) (see Table 12).

Even rejecting the prices calculated based on GUS rates (which are overestimated), the season ticket prices are very favourable for passengers.

Table 12. **Average one-trip prices in Krakow**

	Single ticket	Monthly for one route	Monthly for whole network	Half-yearly (or semester) for whole network
Full fare (Zl)	6 000 {$0.30}	1 820 (2 850)	1 000 (2 620)	760 (2 290)
Discount fare (Zl)	3 000 {$0.15}	920 (1 430)	590 (1 310)	380 (1 250)

Source: Urban Public Transport Company, Ltd., based on the Central Statistical Office (GUS) mobility rate, and the author's estimation (in brackets).

Since fares rose at rates above that of inflation, use of mass transport has become more expensive. In order to buy 50 single tickets in Krakow in December 1994, it was necessary to spend:

-- 6.7 per cent of the average wage (Zl 4.5 million, US$190);
-- 14.3 per cent of the minimum wage (Zl 2.1 million, US$90);
-- 21.4 per cent of the average income under the poverty line (Zl 1.4 million, US$60).

Krakow's all-inclusive monthly mass transport pass required:

4.9 per cent of the average wage;
10.5 per cent of the minimum wage;
15.7 per cent of the average income under the poverty line.

The State has established 50 per cent fare discounts for retirees, school children, students and the handicapped. Most cities have awarded cost-free journeys by public transport for the elderly (over 75). It is estimated that in Krakow, about 40 per cent of the population using public transport benefits from half-fare tickets; and about 12 per cent of all public transport trips are cost-free, including: 6 per cent of trips by the elderly, 3 per cent by drivers and their families, and 3 per cent by free riders.

At present, there are no special discount-fares for the unemployed and the poor in Poland. [Unemployment in 1995 was at 16 per cent of the labour force. Approximately 15 per cent of the population (about 6 million people) earns the minimum wage; and 25 per cent (10 million people) has income lower than the minimum wage.] The very important problem of special tariffs for the poor has been neither solved nor even considered by either the central or municipal authorities.

The recommendations of the World Bank on this issue (see The World Bank) are well-intentioned, but will be difficult to carry out. They include:

-- Mass transport discounts should be provided to:

- people who are under the poverty line;
- the unemployed and school children.

The fare, service quality and subsidies for designated categories of travellers should be linked.

The municipally-based Social Assistance Officers could be in charge of identifying eligible travellers and implementing the programme.

These and other recommendations will result in segmentation of the public transport market. The "jitneys" service type will probably magnify the disappointment among the economically weaker part of society. Special, heavily subsidised public transport for the handicapped has been introduced in some Polish cities, but it is still underdeveloped. Low-floor vehicles will be the future solution.

5.2 Fares and ridership

Assuming the rising trend in single ticket prices -- shown above in Table 9 -- as typical for the whole tariff system and all public mass transport companies, one can conclude that in the period 1986-1992:

-- the average price of transport increased 4.6 times (in relation to average wage);
-- the total annual number of passengers carried by urban transport operators dropped by 34 per cent.

These figures suggest that the average elasticity of demand coefficient is about 0.07. Since this estimation is somewhat unreliable, then it can be concluded that:

-- the single ticket price did not reflect the price of travel in urban public transport;

302

-- changes in transport behaviour were caused by other factors, i.e. car ownership growth, appearance of unemployment, more rational decisions of individuals;

-- hyperinflation may have influenced the investigated correlation.

More reliable and more instructive results, which show the correlation between the decrease in tariffs to the increase in ridership, were collected in Krakow.

In 1992, the price of an all-inclusive monthly mass transport pass was reduced (in nominal value) by 25 per cent and frozen for 1 1/2 years; relative to inflation, it became cheaper by 46 per cent. This pass, called the "Public Transport Promotion Card", allows free parking at the park-and-ride facilities. The prices of single tickets and monthly passes for a single route rose several times during this period; as a result, purchases of all-inclusive monthly passes increased considerably.

Generally, the price of one public transport trip decreased by 30 per cent (relative to inflation) between 1992 and 1993. Despite reduced interest in purchases of single tickets, revenues of the public transport company increased by 20 per cent in 1993 (in real prices) compared to 1992. In the same period, total public transport ridership in Krakow grew by 10 per cent -- notably given the context of the drop in passenger volume. These results were achieved thanks to courageous decisions and accurate tariff policy set by the Municipal Authority of Krakow and the Urban Public Transport Company. The effect was a 10 per cent increase in ridership, brought about by a 30 per cent decrease in prices, which has produced a fare price elasticity of demand of about 0.3. This is comparable to the results in many western countries (see Talley, 1983).

5.3 Revenues and expenditures

From 1988 to 1992, expenditures for development and maintenance of the Warsaw transportation system decreased: for roads, from Zl 2 050 billion to 450 billion (1992 prices); for public transport (excluding underground), from Zl 1 850 billion to 1 550 billion; for the underground, from Zl 1 900 billion to 700 billion; total drop in spending, from Zl 5 800 billion to 2 700 billion. (See Rozkwitalska C. *et al.*, 1993).

In the same period, ticket revenues increased by 50 per cent and maintenance costs by 17 per cent; subsidies were reduced by 42 per cent. This tendency had a negative impact on public transport use and strongly stimulated the development of private car traffic.

Table 13. **Revenues and related data for large Polish cities (1994)**

	Krakow	Gdansk	Lodz	Poznan	Szczecin	Wroclaw
Legal form of company	joint-stock	budgetary	joint-stock	budgetary	budgetary	budgetary
Urban population (000)	750.00	465.00	835.00	580.00	420.00	640.00
Revenues Zl (billion)	717.00	N/A	N/A	365.00	316.00	N/A
US$ (million)	33.30					
Ticket revenues only						
Zl (billion) (a)	679.00	272.00	607.00	350.00	296.00	297.00
US$ (million)	31.60					
Subsidies Zl (billion)	366.00	180.00	372.00	254.00	228.00	304.00
US$ (million)	17.00					
Subsides/vehicle-km						
Zl (000)	5.80	6.60	6.80	7.70	7.10	6.40
US$	0.27					
Subsides/person						
Zl (000)	488.00	387.00	445.00	438.00	543.00	475.00
US$	22.70					
Subsidies/passenger						
Zl (000)	650.00	950.00	1 080.00	1 250.00	1 430.00	840.00
US$	0.03					
Revenues/vehicle-km						
Zl (000)	10.70	10.00	11.20	10.60	9.30	10.50
US$	0.50					
Revenues/passenger-km						
Zl (000)	1.20	1.44	1.76	1.72	1.87	1.37
US$	0.06					
Funds for vehicle purchase - all sources						
Zl (billion)	77.00	78.00	189.00	37.00	74.00	55.00
US$ (million)	3.60					

Note: (a) Exactly: all revenues involved with transportation services.

Source: Chamber of Urban Transport and the author's calculations.

Ticket sales are the main revenue source for public transport companies. In Krakow, total revenues from transportation service in 1994 were as follows: 50.4 per cent from single tickets (falling trend); 46.0 per cent from season passes (rising trend); 2.3 per cent from hiring vehicles for tourist purposes; 1.3 per cent from subsidies from suburban communities. In 1994, actual revenues were lower than projected revenues (Zl 700 billion). This shortage was made up by greater revenues from auxiliary activities (Zl 38 billion, i.e. 5.3 per cent of total revenues), which included: advertising on vehicles and other objects (Zl 5.5 billion, US$250 000); spare parts and fuel sales; renovation of vehicle parts; repair services; apartment rental; parking and stops; bus stand-by services; medical services; income from financial transactions.

Subsidies are provided neither by the State nor the provincial administration. The funds, which come from the municipal budget, are to cover: direct operating costs, repair costs and depreciation as well as to supply more capital to the joint-stock company. In 1994, these funds totalled Zl 366 billion (US$17.0 million). The investment funds are created from depreciation charges and capitalisation; total funds amounted Zl 90 billion (US$4.1 million).

In 1994, investment in urban public transport in Polish cities totalled Zl 2965 billion (US$138 million). Since 1993, the investment funds (in constant prices) have increased -- a positive change following a ten-year decreasing trend. In 1993, as much as 70 per cent of these funds have been allocated for construction of the metro in Warsaw. The national rate of investment per city inhabitant for public transport fluctuates around Zl 150 000 (US$7). In Krakow, this rate was Zl 120 000 (US$5.6). The 1995 investment plan provided for a 12 per cent growth in funds based on real prices. Eighty-six per cent of all funds will be spent for the purchase of buses.

In 1994, most of the investment funds (Zl 90 billion) for Krakow were spent first on: buses (86 per cent) and computer hardware and software (5 per cent). No funds were spent for the construction of a new tramway track. Half of the funds for bus purchases were obtained from a depreciation fund, and half on credit. For the period 1995 to 2000, investment funds are projected according to three scenarios (See Suchorzewski, W. 1995):

--   **The survival scenario:**   yearly funds at the current level (US$140 million), allowing the purchase of 350 buses, 60 tramways, six trolley buses and five metro cars.

--   **The moderate development scenario:**   average yearly funds of US$200 million, allowing for the purchase of: 780 buses, 95 tramways, 15 trolley buses and six metro wagons and the spending of about US$24 million for construction of new tramway tracks until 2000.

-- **The considerable development scenario:** average yearly funds of US$270 million, allowing for the purchase of 1 200 buses, 110 tramways, 20 trolley buses and six metro wagons and the spending of US$ 35 million for construction of new tramway tracks.

The Krakow Urban Public Transport Company usually takes funds from current sources. About 5 per cent of the company's financial means comes from domestic bank loans (e.g. for purchase of buses). Leasing of buses has been determined to be unprofitable. The City of Krakow hopes to obtain World Bank loans for: repair of tramway tracks, construction of rapid tramway tracks and a traffic control system with priority for public transport vehicles.

The increasing level of depreciation and ageing fleets are proof of insufficient funds for new vehicles. In the period 1990-1993 there was a depreciation increase for vehicles from 65.3 to 69.8 per cent. The age structure of the fleet was as follows:

Table 14. **Age of fleet in 1994 (%)**

Buses	0-3 years	3-6 years	6-10 years	more than 10 years	Sum (%)
Country	10	19	45	26	100
Krakow	15	15	40	30	100

Tramways	0-5 years	5-10 years	10-15 years	15-20 years	20-25 years	25-30 years	more than 30 years	Sum (%)
Country	10	24	19	22	9	11	5	100
Krakow	7	34	16	14	18	1	10	100

Source: Chamber of Public Transport, 1994.

In 1994, the share of the newest and the oldest buses in Krakow was above average in the country. The average age of buses both nation-wide and in Krakow was eight years, while the nominal life of buses produced in Central Europe was six years. The average age of tramways both nation-wide and in Krakow was 15.1 years.

5.4 Costs

Operating costs per vehicle-km varied slightly among companies. Data are not fully comparable, because, for instance, budgetary units do not calculate depreciation costs. The average rate of about Zl 17 000 per one vehicle-km run (US$0.80) seems to be a reasonable value.

To avoid tax payments, a joint-stock company should not show a net income on its financial statement. This does not concern budgetary units, since they do not pay an income tax.

The changes in cost structure were the result of varied levels of inflation for particular materials and intended activities of the company management.

Table 15. **Costs and related data for large Polish cities (1994)**

	Krakow	Gdansk	Lodz	Poznan	Szczecin	Wroclaw
Total annual costs						
Zl (billion)	1 088.00	488.00	1 215.00	624.00	541.00	870.00
US$ (million)	50.60					
Operating costs						
Zl (billion)	1 049.00	453.00	995.00	617.00	524.00	N/A.
US$ (million)	48.80					
Operating costs/ vehicle-km : Zl (000)						
tramways	15.70	17.00	19.20	20.10	18.50	17.90
buses	17.30	16.40	16.60	17.50	15.00	15.40
average	16.60	16.60	18.30	18.70	16.40	16.20
Costs/passenger [Zl]	1 860.00	2 400.00	2 880.00	3 040.00	3 880.00	N/A.
US$	0.08					
Ticket revenues/ operating costs [%]	65.00	60.00	61.00	56.70	56.60	56.90
Subsides/ total costs [%]	33.70	36.80	30.60	40.70	42.10	34.90
Financial statement(a)						
Zl (billion)	-9.00	N/A.	+16.00	-5.00	+2.00	N/A.
US$ (million)	- 0.40					

Note: (a) Financial statement: revenue-costs.

Source: Chamber of Urban Transport and the author's calculations.

Table 16. Operations costs of the Krakow Urban Public Transport Company 1991-1995 (%)

	1991	1992	1993	1994	1995 (est.)
Personnel	49.50	52.20	51.70	49.20	50.90
Fuel	13.00	13.50	14.70	12.20	11.80
Energy	8.50	7.60	8.80	10.10	10.30
Tyres	1.70	1.80	1.50	1.60	1.90
Spare parts	15.60	12.90	12.10	13.70	12.30
Other costs (a)	11.70	12.00	11.30	13.00	12.40
Direct operating costs	100.00	100.00	100.00	100.00	100.00
Repairs (b)	23.60	14.40	20.10	8.30 c)	8.80 (c)
Depreciation (b)	-	- (d)	7.70	6.80	6.60

Notes: (a) Including leasing costs and loan interest.
(b) In relation to total direct operating costs.
(c) Excluding costs of maintenance/ repair of tracks and traction lines, financed directly by the City.
(d) Calculation of depreciation in joint-stock companies is obligatory since 1993.

Source: Urban Public Transport in Krakow and the author's calculations.

Comments:

There have been decreasing trends in the share of personnel costs. In 1995, they were fixed at one half of direct operating costs due to a reduction in administrative costs, e.g. 20.7 per cent to 17.7 per cent during the period 1993-1995. Share of fuel costs has slightly decreased and share of energy costs has slightly increased, because of the adjusting of energy prices to world prices. The share of the sum of fuel and energy costs is generally unchanging and constitutes 22 per cent of all direct operating costs. Tyre costs are steady at below 2 per cent. Spare parts costs are slightly decreasing to the level of 1/8 of operating costs. Share of fixed costs have been 37 per cent and in 1995 were slightly increasing.

Table 16 shows lack of stability in allocation of funds for repair purposes.

The cost increase in nominal terms was less than the inflation rate, despite a higher cost inflation rate for some components (e.g. unit costs of spare parts and energy). For example, in 1994, the inflation rate was 32.2 per cent and the growth of total operating costs in Krakow was 27.0 per cent. Comparable results were achieved in 1992 and 1993. This cost savings enabled municipal authorities to reduce the subsidies gradually and to soften the rate of ticket mark-up. During 1991-1994, the share of subsidies in operational cost financing was reduced from 35 to 19 per cent. The strain on the city's finances from subsidies for public transport has been reduced to about 15 per cent of the budget.

Table 17. **Changes in costs and subsidies of the Krakow Urban Public Transport Company and share of subsidies in the city budget 1991-1995 (in constant prices)**

	1991	1992	1993	1994	1995 (plan)
Costs	145.00	120.00	113.00	107.00	100.00
Subsidies	179.00	137.00	125.00	107.00	100.00
Share of subsidies in total expenditures of the City (%)	21.70	16.10	16.80	14.20	15.40

Source: Urban Public Transport Company in Krakow and the author's calculations.

(See also Figures 10 and 11).

5.5 Cost recovery in public transport companies

Table 18. **Urban public transport companies with specified cost recovery**

Cost recovery (%)	Percentage of companies in Poland (a)					Percentage of companies abroad (b)
	1990	1991	1992	1993	1994	1989
less than 30	5.60	2.40	-	-	-	16.00
30-40	9.90	8.30	2.80	0.80	0.80	12.80
40-50	36.60	21.40	17.00	4.20	5.30	17.60
50-60	33.80	25.00	18.90	14.30	9.10	12.80
60-70	12.70	23.80	29.20	23.50	22.90	8.80
70-80	1.40	13.10	19.80	26.10	29.00	8.80
80-90	-	3.60	10.50	16.80	16.80	3.20
90-100	-	2.40	0.90	9.30	11.50	4.80
more than 100	-	-	0.90	5.00	4.60	15.20
Total (%)	100.00	100.00	100.00	100.00	100.00	100.00
Average cost recovery in the country (%)	44.10	54.10	65.00	70.70	74.10	58.20
Number of companies investigated	71.00	84.00	106.00	119.00	131.00	125.00

Notes: (a) Chamber of Urban Transport.
(b) UITP.

Source: W. Suchorzewski Transportation Engineering Consulting.

(See also Figure 12).

Table 19. **Cost recovery of the Krakow Urban Public Transport Company**

Year	1989	1990	1991	1992	1993	1994	1995 (planned)
Cost recovery (%)	38	45	53	56	58	64 62 (a)	67 62 (a)

Note: (a) Including the maintenance and repair costs of tramway tracks and contact lines. Since 1994, these costs have not been incurred by the Urban Public Transport Company.

Source: Urban Public Transport Company.

Table 18 shows an increasing trend in cost recovery of an average of 10 per cent annually from 1990 to 1992 and 5 per cent annually from 1992 to 1994. In Krakow (Table 19), the average yearly cost recovery increase from 1989 to 1995 was 5 per cent. Including total tramway track costs, cost recovery was 62 per cent. Improvements in efficiency were possible thanks to revenue growth (mainly fare increases) and a relative decrease in operating costs. Since the latter factor has limited possibilities, a further increase in cost recovery would be risky for the public transport system (Figure 13).

In 1994, six public transport companies in Poland earned surplus revenues over operating expenditures. This result is not fully reliable, however, because some subsidies have not been included.

6. INITIATIVES FOR SUSTAINABLE TRANSPORT

The Urban Public Transport Company in Krakow has taken the following actions to improve transport-related environmental conditions:

-- replacement of buses with high air and noise emissions with lower-emission vehicles; this action has been applied to lines running inside city areas that are threatened environmentally (e.g. introduction of 22 Scania buses into the downtown ring; they emit ten times less carbon monoxide and hydrocarbons than buses produced in Central Europe with outdated technologies;
-- introduction of low-sulphur diesel fuel;
-- extension of natural gas and propane-butane gas use in bus engines;
-- purchase of smoke meters, which satisfied the most-recent requirements; instruction of bus drivers on how to reduce smoke emissions;
-- elimination of asbestos brake linings;
-- application of a vibro- and sound insulation during major repair of tramway tracks.

7. CONCLUSIONS AND RECOMMENDATIONS

7.1 Conclusions

General

A transportation policy based on municipal resolutions is essential to preserving the role of mass public transport. A complete transportation policy should include: an overall plan; performance objectives and measures; options for modal split and their consequences; development of the transport system; legal specifications; structure of transport management, sources of funding for operation and development of the transportation system.

In Poland, there is a long tradition of public transport use in urban areas. The opportunity now exists to maintain the high share of mass transport in overall urban and suburban travel; however, stopping unfavourable trends and taking action in favour of public transport is required.

Transportation behaviour and ridership

Diminishing ridership over the past few years has been primarily caused by a rise in car ownership, but it was also the result of the process which brought about changes in the political system (collapse of big industry, easier accessibility of goods and services, more sensible transportation behaviour). In a number of big cities, the decrease in public transport use has been stopped.

In spite of the drop in ridership, urban public transport in Poland still plays a key part in the service of non-pedestrian travel. Its share ranges from 50 per cent in medium-sized cities to 75 per cent in the largest cities. Unfortunately, public transport companies are slowly having to adjust their supply to evolving passenger behaviour.

Comprehensive travel surveys are rarely undertaken and only in few cities. There is an urgent need to create a system for monitoring changes in user behaviour. Central Statistical Office mobility rate figures for owners of season public transport passes (highly overestimated) produce a false perception of ridership.

Beneficial changes have taken place in hourly patterns of public transport volume: the peaks have been flattened out, and in the early morning rush hour, demand has dropped.

Polish cities, especially Krakow, are generally well-served by the public transport system. The standard of service (fewer number of passengers per vehicle) has been improved by a reduction in ridership and an only moderate decrease in vehicle-km run. The tendency towards increasing the number of lines at the expense of service headway extension should be stopped.

Future growth in motorisation will depend on the transportation policy carried out by state and particularly municipal authorities. The policy, which is liberal in relation to private car traffic, can produce high levels of car ownership (500 cars/1 000 population or more). A public transport-friendly policy with restrictions for private car use can stop car ownership at the level of 350 cars/1 000 population.

The current level of private car share in total non-pedestrian travel (25 per cent in the largest cities to 50 per cent in the smaller cities) should generally be frozen. One can allow an increase of this average level of car share in outer parts of cities, at the cost of further reducing the private car traffic downtown.

Considering urban development and car ownership growth forecasts, on the one hand, and the limited possibilities for extending the street and parking network on the other, one can assume that ridership will not change in the next five to 10 years. However, the decrease in passenger volume may reach 5 to 10 per cent in large- and medium-sized cities, and 15 to 25 per cent in small cities.

Organisation

The principal public transport company has been partitioned into smaller parts, with the separation of transportation functions and auxiliary activities (e.g. repair of vehicles and tracks). Such solutions have facilitated management, and thanks to market competition, costs of repairs have dropped and quality has improved. The maintenance of vehicles and tracks should be included in the tasks of the transportation company.

The transport administrator and the carrier should systematically be separated, thus promoting market relations in urban mass transport and improving efficiency. The administrator should organise the planning of routes and time-tables; establish (or stipulate) fares; plan investments; handle tendering of contractors; controlling service performed by operators. In large cities, the transport administrator should be a specialised institution, as in the case of Warsaw.

Public transport companies are subjected by the local authorities to increasing economic stress and inspection of services. Improvements in efficiency and quality

313

of service are apparent; however, in an undeveloped transportation market or -- worse -- a monopolistic carrier, it is difficult to establish real economic costs.

Co-ordination of transportation in urban and suburban areas has had a difficult start in Poland. It involves: the *voivode* (provincial seat of the central administration), municipal authorities, the state railway, the state bus company, and municipal and private operators.

There is a tendency to use the "budgetary unit" structure for transportation services because of the legal and financial benefits associated with this solution: for example, the lack of a depreciation calculation, by which taxation on excess wages can be avoided. This form is not satisfactory as a long-term development policy, however. High expectations are set on the "Municipal Enterprise Act", currently under preparation. A well-tested option would be a joint-stock company operating under the Commercial Code.

The power of trade unions and high compensations for discharged workers are major constraints associated with implementing a bolder employment policy.

Private operators can profitably influence efficiency, offering competitive costs and service quality. Currently the private sector operates in more favourable conditions than public transport companies. Informal activities of private operators should be replaced by an obligatory invitation to tender and licensing of operators.

Application of these recommendations will render public transport more attractive. Most initiatives do not require large financial means. Quality of service should be an integral part of the contract between the municipality and the operator -- a condition for the awarding of licences and a factor in the determination of subsidy levels for an operator. A special factor for assessing overall quality of urban public transport should be applied.

Finance

Public transport companies in Poland possess more fleet than necessary to meet demand. The fleet is comprised of old, worn-out vehicles. Such a situation increases maintenance costs, but the companies fear that they will lack resources to purchase new buses and tramways.

The share of personnel costs (mainly as a result of lower administrative costs) and spare parts costs in the cost structure have been reduced and remain at a level of 1/2 and 1/8 of operating costs, respectively. The cost increase in nominal terms was slower than the inflation rate, despite the higher inflation rate of cost components.

This indicates that the efficiency of public transport companies has improved. Operating cost savings have enabled municipal authorities to reduce subsidies gradually and to soften the rate of ticket mark-up.

The lack of adequate funds and stability in their allocation for repair purposes has resulted in infrastructure deterioration (mainly rolling stock and tramway tracks); the economic conditions of special repair companies have thus worsened.

The Urban Public Transport Company in Krakow has decreased its expenditures; first, by reducing the annual vehicle-km, then, by cutting operating costs by 6 to 7 per cent annually. These cost-cutting initiatives have accompanied a reduction in subsidies, initially considerable. The revenues of the company have fluctuated every year according to tariff changes.

A further economic upswing and an increase in municipal income has allowed a stable financial system for operation and development of urban public transport.

To improve the financial management of the public transport company, a computerised monitoring system should be designed and introduced. This system should be integrated into the cost control system -- particularly in a monopolistic company. Simple reserves from cost reduction have already been used up.

Insufficient funding for new vehicles and repair of tracks has caused a rapid depreciation of fleet and infrastructure, increasing unreliability of transportation services and higher operating costs. The average age of the operated fleet is: tramway 15 years, buses eight years (this exceeds the nominal life of buses produced in Central Europe).

There was an increasing trend in cost recovery in Poland, with average yearly increases of 5 per cent over the last three years. Five per cent of Polish companies have probably already acquired a surplus of revenues over operating expenditures. In 1994, the average rate of cost recovery was 74 per cent. Improvements in efficiency were possible thanks to the growth of revenues (mainly by fare increases) and the relative decrease of operating costs. In the current preconditions, using prices for a further increase in cost recovery could be risky for the existence of the public transport system.

Fares

Tariffs should be diversified and easy for passengers to understand. Passes for the whole network should be promoted through competitive pricing. The single ticket should enable cost-free transfers and, in big cities, the price should be linked to the length or duration of the trip. Further increases in ticket prices (in real prices) should not be considered.

Rising ticket prices make public transport less accessible to poorer persons. In spite of the detailed recommendations of the World Bank (see The World Bank), one cannot expect a quick solution to this matter from municipal authorities. The fare discounts for retirees, school children, students and the handicapped and free-of-charge transport overload the budget of public transport companies (and therefore, the city), causing income losses of 25 to 35 per cent. These reduced rates should be repurchased by the State, allowing virtually all companies to achieve profitable results.

The Krakow experiment has proved that it is possible to increase ridership in public transport by decreasing the price of the network pass. The coefficient of fare elasticity of demand has been estimated at 0.3, a value corresponding to that in western countries.

7.2 Recommendations

-- improve access to public transport stops and vehicles (e.g. reduce space and traffic collisions, lower vehicle floor);
-- achieve better punctuality and regularity;
-- equip stops -- especially terminals -- with shelters, commercial points, coin-box telephones, and other facilities;
-- improve information for passengers (in vehicles, at stops, in mass media);
-- provide cost-free time-tables to passengers for requested lines, stops;
-- introduce a common tariff (one ticket admitted by all operators);
-- facilitate purchase of tickets and season passes;
-- increase frequency of operation (maximum scheduled frequency -- 10 minutes in rush hours, 20 minutes in non-rush hours);
-- synchronise operation of lines creating clusters (groups of lines running together);
-- speed up vehicle operations (giving traffic priority to public transport means);
-- reduce vehicle noise and improve conveyance (reduce vibration, eliminate needless acceleration /deceleration manoeuvres and vehicle stops);
-- eliminate overcrowded vehicle conditions;
-- provide seats for a majority of passengers in non-peak hours;
-- provide transport without transfers for all main travel connections;

-- facilitate passenger transfers at nodes of the public transport network (common platforms, co-ordination of schedules for individual lines);
-- improve cleanliness of vehicles and stops;
-- provide passengers with a feeling of personal safety;
-- improve behaviour of drivers and inspectors towards passengers.

FIGURES

Figure 1. Changes in public transport passenger volume in Krakow

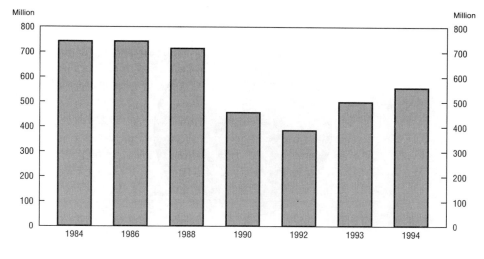

Source: Central Statistical Office.

Figure 2. Changes in car ownership in Krakow

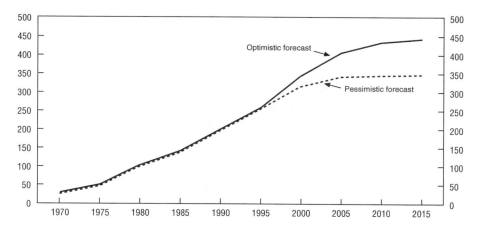

Source: Central Statistical Office and author.

321

Figure 3. **Modal split in Krakow (1985)**

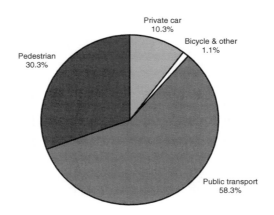

Source: Traffic Survey of Krakow, 1985.

Figure 4. **Modal split in Krakow (1994)**

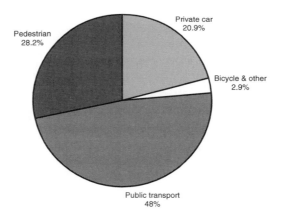

Source: Traffic Survey of Krakow, 1994.

Figure 5. **Model of future Krakow transport system**

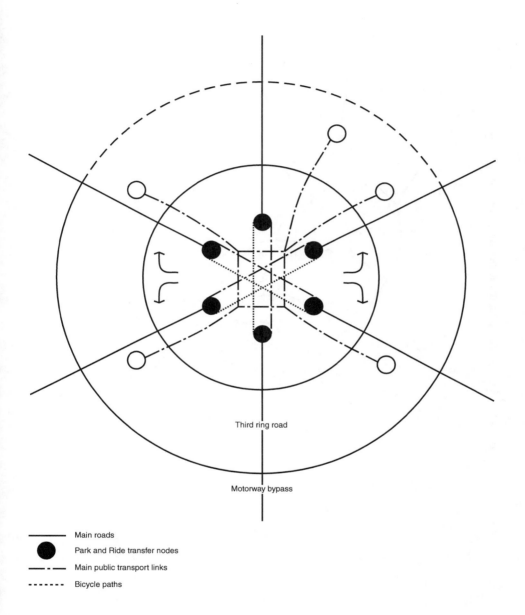

Third ring road

Motorway bypass

—————— Main roads

● Park and Ride transfer nodes

—·—·— Main public transport links

- - - - - Bicycle paths

323

Figure 6. **Future rail and tramway network**

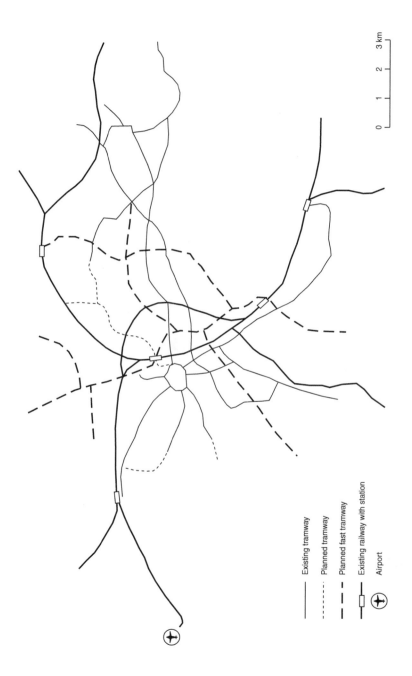

——— Existing tramway

·········· Planned tramway

– – – Planned fast tramway

Existing railway with station

⊕✈ Airport

0 1 2 3 km

Figure 7. Changes in the employment structure of the Krakow Urban Public Transport Company

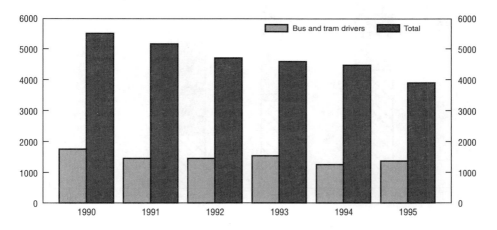

Source: Krakow Urban Public Transport Company.

Figure 8. Single public transport tickets per average monthly wage in Warsaw

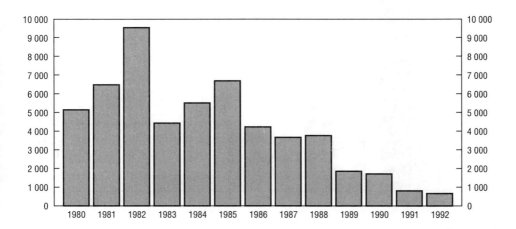

Source: Central Statistical Office.

325

Figure 9. **Changes in shares of ticket types in Krakow**

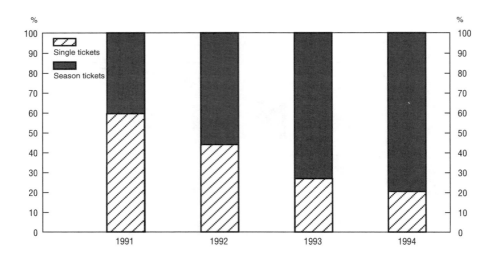

Source: Krakow Urban Public Transport Company.

Figure 10. **Changes in costs and subsidies of the Krakow Urban Public Transport Company**

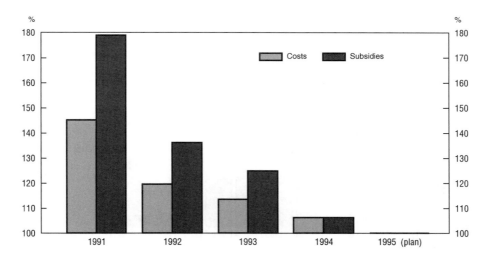

Source: Krakow Urban Public Transport Company and the author.

Figure 11. **Share of public transport subsidies in the Krakow city budget**

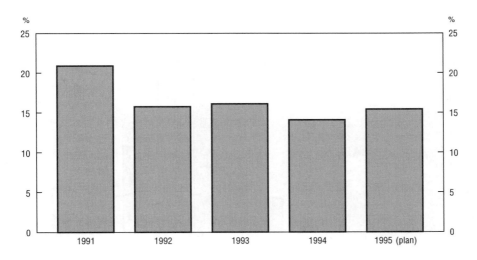

Source: Krakow Urban Public Transport Company and the author.

Figure 12. **Percentage of cost recovery in Polish urban public transport companies (1994)**

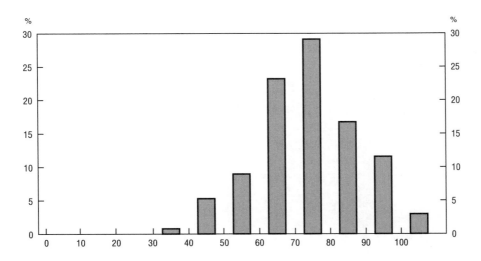

Source: W. Suchorzewski Transportation Engineering Consulting.

Figure 13. **Cost recovery of the Krakow Urban Public Transport Company**

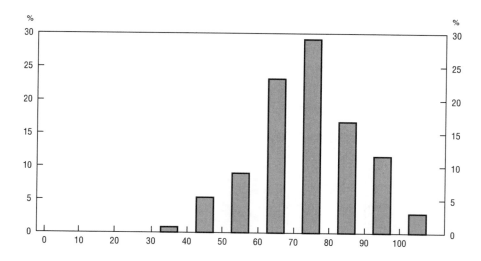

Source: W. Suchorzewski Transportation Engineering Consulting.

BIBLIOGRAPHY

1. Annual Report of Urban Public Transport Company in Krakow. Krakow, 1991-1994.

2. CENTRAL STATISTICAL OFFICE: Statistical Yearbook. Warsaw, 1994 and earlier.

3. CHAMBER OF URBAN TRANSPORT IN POLAND: Urban Public transport in numbers. Warsaw, 1994 and earlier.

4. Comprehensive traffic surveys in Krakow. 1975, 1985, 1994.

5. FRIEDBERG J., RUDNICKI A.: Transport policy for Krakow. "Urban Transport". No. 6, 1993.

6. OECD/ECMT Project Group: *Urban travel and sustainable development.* Paris, 1992.

7. ROZKWITALSKA, C. *et al.*: "System of organisation, operation and financing for urban public transport in preconditions of market economy and self-government". Institute of Physical and Municipal Economy. Warsaw 1993.

8. RUDNICKI, A. *et al.: Transportation service in urban areas in Poland.* Expertise of the Polish Academy of Science, Committee of Transport. Research and Technical Papers of Association for Transportation Engineers. Series: Monographs, No 1 (vol.30). Krakow 1994.

9. SUCHORZEWSKI, W., Transportation Engineering Consulting: *Development of urban mass transport in Poland in the period 1995-2000 and assumption for its development after 2000.* Warsaw 1995.

10. TALLEY, W.K.: *Introduction to Transportation.* South-western Publishing Co. Cincinnati, 1983.

11. THE WORLD BANK: Poland -- Urban Transport Review. Rapport No. 12962-POL. October 1994.

Remark: Items 1 to 5 and 7 to 9 were edited in Polish.

Organising and Financing Urban Public Transport in Budapest

Katalin Tánczos
Technical University of Budapest
Hungary

TABLE OF CONTENTS

LIST OF TABLES

LIST OF FIGURES

SUMMARY

Hungary is moving from a highly centralised state control of transport planning to a more decentralised market-led approach. Budapest, the capital, is struggling to cope with a rapid increase in motor vehicle traffic, resulting in more congestion, road accidents, air and noise pollution, and leading to serious economic, financial and social problems. At the same time, a favourably high ratio of public transport use -- 82 per cent in the 1980s -- has dramatically decreased to 60 per cent as a result of economic and social changes. Servicing the huge debt inherited from the previous regime has made it very difficult for the government to take the right long-term macroeconomic steps. To maintain the balance necessary for development of the national economy in the near future, officials and residents of the capital will have to face severe budget constraints.

New, innovative solutions are being sought to the problems of adapting the Budapest public transport system to changing public demand. Adoption of new approaches to the organisation and financing of urban public transport will significantly influence passenger transport demands, as well as the environment and the socio-economic conditions of the city. Therefore, it is important to learn from the experiences of others and -- considering the special circumstances of the country and the city itself -- to introduce changes under which the rate of use and level of service of the urban public transport system can be preserved.

This paper examines the main features of the existing public transport system; provides an overview of the transport development policy of the city; evaluates the organisations operating in the conurbation; describes the structure of financial sources and their use; summarises the main issues involved in restructuring the organisation and financing systems; and determines the necessary steps for creating a co-ordinated regional public transport system.

1. INTRODUCTION

Hungary is moving from a highly centralised state control of transport planning to a more decentralised market-led approach. Within the city of Budapest, the Municipality is now solely responsible for providing public transport services. The Budapest Transport Company (BKV) provides multi-modal services throughout the capital and beyond the municipal boundaries. Two other companies, VOLANBUSZ, the state-owned bus company, and MAV, the Hungarian State Railway, operate the main lines in the Budapest region.

A much higher proportion of Budapest residents use public transport than private means. For many years, the city's public transport users have been accustomed to fare stability; now they are faced with continuously rising fares. The budget can no longer provide the enormous subsidies of the past, and the aim is to increase BKV's cost recovery ratio to 50 per cent over the next few years. At the same time, BKV and the Municipality are facing major problems due to the need for replacement of worn-out vehicles, buses, underground stock, trolley-buses and trams.

Given this critical situation, transport economists must assist policy-makers, planners, and all those involved in urban public transport -- including consumers, workers and managers -- in understanding the dynamics of public transport in market-oriented countries. The challenge facing Hungarian transport planners is how to combine the advantages of public control and co-ordination with greater flexibility and consumer responsiveness.

This paper describes the main features of the urban public transport system in Budapest as it was inherited from the past regime; examines the effects of changing demands linked to the new market economy; and details the characteristics and performances of transport networks and companies operating in the Budapest area.

2. KEY URBAN TRANSPORT ISSUES IN CENTRAL AND EASTERN EUROPE

Central and Eastern European Countries (CEEC) and their western European neighbours face different challenges in the area of urban public transport. In western European countries, where there is a relatively low rate of public transport use, improving public transport has been the main focus for encouraging sustainable development. In these countries, developing public transport systems is seen as a way to render city life more pleasant and to preserve the environment.

In CEEC, the majority of passenger transport demands have been provided by the public sector over the last 40 years. The inhabitants of large conurbations have relied to a relatively high degree on public transport services, which have been provided at a relatively low price compared to average individual income. Under the former regime, the provision of urban public services was considered more a political than an economic question. Appropriate connections for commuters from the suburbs to the capital (more than 300 000 people per day) were considered an important and necessary factor for production. Passenger satisfaction with public transport services was seen as a determining element in the lifestyle of the population.

Today, officials of large and medium-size cities face the problem of rapid growth in motor vehicle traffic, resulting in increased congestion, air pollution and other environmental, economic and social problems. Because of a lack of adequate transport capacity in these cities (expressed in available road surface) transport managers must fit the size and service parameters of the public transport system to the changing requirements of their potential passengers. This new demand structure reflects higher levels of motorisation. At the same time, the local authorities must struggle with the serious problems of limited financial resources, considering other financing requirements (e.g. schools, hospitals, cultural centres).

After evaluating the different situations in western and eastern European cities, it can be concluded that the main objective of cities in more-developed western European countries is to maximise the increase in public transport use, while in CEE cities, the goal is to optimise the size and quality of services as public transport use decreases. These differences call for special approaches, which sometimes require a combination of "western" and "eastern" strategies.

3. URBAN PUBLIC TRANSPORT IN BUDAPEST PRIOR TO TRANSITION

Budapest has had a relatively well-developed urban public transport system since before the transition period. Under the previous regime, the system's policy-making and power structures were organised in a centralisation-redistribution mechanism, whereby the State, and later the City Council, collected and then redistributed taxpayer revenues for urban public transport, education, healthcare and other needs according to the fixed rules of the planned economy. In other sectors of the economy, market mechanisms had already begun to play a considerable role during the second half of the 1980s. The population of the Budapest agglomeration, including the inhabitants of the settlements around Budapest (who constituted the daily commuting workforce for the capital) was about 2.5 million. The social well-being of these people, which represented more than 20 per cent of the total population of the country, was considered an important political factor.

In addition, the service level of the urban public transport system was considered more a political than an economic question. The operational efficiency of the Budapest Transport Company (BKV) was evaluated on a macroeconomic level: the indirect social effects of providing a relatively high level of urban public transport service for the citizens was considered first, instead of the direct financial results of the firm. Maintaining this financially inefficient system required a huge amount of subsidisation which had to be covered by the taxpayers.

In respect to quantitative supply, public transport in Budapest could be considered acceptable, compared with other large cities of the world, with excellent accessibility and frequency of service and a relatively high ratio of public/private use of transport facilities. The quality of the rolling stock and facilities is less favourable, however: most of the vehicles in operation were built in the 1960s and 1970s, according to the technical standards of that time. The underground trains, outdated already at that time, could be considered as an exception. In general, the urban public transport system has aged, with both the train park and the equipment out-of-date. The composition and age of the train park contributed to the high rate of operational failures, fuel consumption, environmental pollution and operation costs.

In addition, because of the lack of Danube bridges and the radial structure of the road and rail network of the country, the transport problems of the capital were exacerbated by considerable transit freight traffic. Difficulties in loading and parking in the inner zones of the city also caused significant problems.

Under the former regime, BKV had to operate within the structure and general rules of the centrally planned economy. The lack of real market forces and competition meant that there was little incentive for managers to operate efficiently. The principle direction was, in fact, contrary to market dynamics. An example of the kind of company behaviour prevalent in the second half of the 1970s is the staggering of shift schedules in different factories located alongside the routes of tram or bus lines to avoid -- or at least reduce -- overloading of transport vehicles. Also contributing to the inefficiency of operations was the hierarchical and overstaffed structure of the organisation, which contained many units linked to the non-basic activities of the company.

Moreover, the low fare-box revenues necessitated a considerable amount of subsidisation that had to be provided by different financing sources. Numerous conditions were placed on possibilities for obtaining additional funding (the object was to hold to the planned budget as much as possible), but allocation of financing was more a political than an economic decision.

4. URBAN PUBLIC TRANSPORT IN BUDAPEST FOLLOWING TRANSITION

4.1 Change in demand linked to the new market economy and their effects on urban transport

After the democratic changes in 1989, the trends of the second half of the 1980s continued in urban passenger transport. The number of individual vehicles on the road was steadily rising, even though the increase in specific cost of car usage significantly reduced the yearly operation of vehicles. Traffic congestion increased, and use of public passenger transport dropped.

Passenger car ownership in Hungary is on average 200 vehicles per 1 000 inhabitants, and 250 per 1 000 in the capital. These figures are considerably lower (by about 50 per cent) than those of more-developed European countries. The composition of vehicle types and their average age present serious problems on technical, environmental and energy levels.

The change in economic life over the last few years has made its effect felt in urban transport; the demand for urban public transport is continuously falling. Rush-hour traffic is less distinguishable from traffic during the rest of the day, since daytime traffic has intensified as a result of growth in private business and the travel of unemployed people, among other reasons.

Regarding urban traffic safety, contrary to the decreasing trends in most West European countries, accident data in CEEC showed increasing trends until 1990, both in respect of their number and severity. When examining changes in traffic safety over a longer period of time, it can be concluded that after a period of stability between 1980 and 1987 when the number of personal injury accidents and fatalities was constant in spite of the continuous growth of the vehicle fleet, traffic safety started to decline rapidly, mainly as a consequence of changing social phenomena: in 1993, the introduction of the 50 km/h speed limit in urban areas resulted in significant improvement in this area, and the frequency of urban traffic accidents with personal injury decreased by nearly 25 per cent.

By comparing the emissions data and characteristics of motor vehicle transport in Budapest and other large cities with similar data in other European cities, it is clear that, despite of the lower degree of motorisation, the vehicle fleet produces an output of harmful emissions similar to that of other cities where motorisation is more developed. The air pollution caused by motor vehicles is decisively influenced by the structure of the private cars and their average age of over ten years. The poor air quality of the capital is also a consequence of infrastructure deficiencies, including lack of by-pass roads, and traffic attenuation facilities. Vibration and noise are much less significant pollution problems than that of air pollution in Budapest, although noise in almost one-third of the apartments in the capital is of traffic origin. The growth rate of noise pollution, however, has decreased.

4.2 Principal characteristics of the Budapest urban public transport system

With the changes in demand for transport has come an evolution in modal split. Over the last several years, the trip distribution of public and individual transport was 70 per cent and 30 per cent respectively in Budapest. In 1995, the value of this ratio is estimated to be 60 and 40 per cent. Compared to the 1985 figures of 80 and 20 per cent, a significant and rapid change in the modal split can be recognised.

As stated earlier, the role of public transport in the transport system of Budapest is very important. The present public transport network of Budapest satisfies the quantitative demands, but its quality is open to question.

Several key problems can be identified:

- low travel speed on some main lines;
- conditions of transfer between the different public transport modes and between private and public transport (inadequate park-and-ride system);
- poor reliability of services, (e.g. irregularity, unkept schedules) with the exception of underground lines;
- the inconvenience and lack of travelling comfort (crowded vehicles in peak hours, inadequate passenger information at stops and on vehicles).

The daily commuting traffic from the 43 settlements of the agglomeration zone to Budapest is about 300 000 persons, 200 000 of which use public transport facilities. 22 per cent of these passengers arrive by coaches (VOLANBUSZ); 30 per cent of them by railway (MAV) and the remaining 40 per cent by BKV services.

The total length of the public transport network of Budapest is 1 020 km, 810 km of which are BKV routes and 210 km VOLANBUSZ and MAV routes. The latter two companies serve only suburban travel; local transport is provided by BKV.

The density of the public transport network in Budapest is 2 km/km^2 in densely populated areas and 4 km/km^2 within the boundaries of Budapest; 95.5 per cent of the stops can be found within 400 m, and 99.4 per cent within 500 m of the city. The average operating (round-trip) speed is 17.6 km/h.

The total length of BKV services is 1 165 km (133 km in the vicinity of Budapest) of which 72 per cent is bus service; 12 per cent tram, 5 per cent trolley-bus, 10 per cent rapid transit (underground and suburban railways) and 1 per cent other means of transport (cog-wheel railway, funicular, chair-lift, ship, ferry-boat).

The number of passengers carried by BKV has been decreasing over the past years. Daily trip distribution has changed recently, with traffic decreasing in the morning peak hours and increasing in the off-peak hours. The total patronage in the afternoon peak period has not changed significantly over the past few years.

The detailed characteristics of BKV's network are summarised in Table 1.

Table 1. **Detailed characteristics of BKV's 1993 network**

Branch	Construction length (km)	Number of stops	Round-trip speed (km/h)
Tram	158.5	681	14.2
Trolley-bus (network)	68.5	287	12.7
Bus (network)	766.5	3 519	17.3
Suburban railway	109.2	137	23.7
Underground railway	34.5	78	24.5
Ship (route)	19.7	15	6.7

About 15 per cent of public transport in Budapest comes from interurban traffic, (origin of trips outside of Budapest) 82 per cent is commuter traffic.

In 1993, the registered number of passengers carried by BKV vehicles was 1 471 billion, 11 million less than the previous year. There was no significant change in the division of passengers among the branches. The number of passengers per branch is shown in Figure 1:

Figure 1. **Number of passengers carried in 1993**

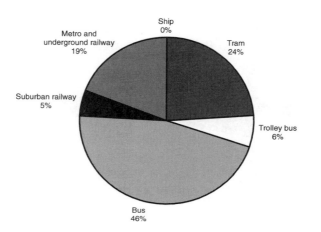

In order to satisfy public transport demand, BKV vehicles completed 26 149 billion place-kilometres. The breakdown among the branches is shown in Figure 2.

Figure 2. **Place-kilometres in 1993**

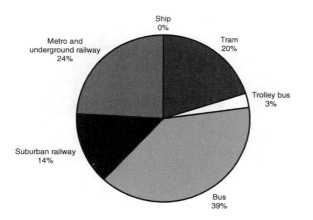

Total passenger transportation measured in passenger-kilometres amounted to 6 407 billion, 33 million less than in 1992. The distribution of passenger-kilometres among branches only slightly changed in comparison with the previous year (Figure 3).

Figure 3. **Passenger-kilometres in 1993**

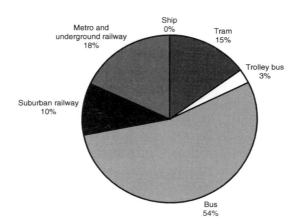

The distribution of car operating hours in 1993 is shown in Figure 4.

Figure 4. **Distribution of operating hours in 1993**

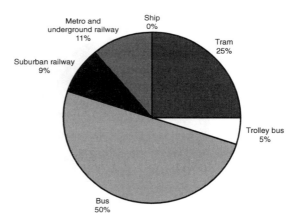

Average vehicle load factor (ratio of passenger-kms and place-kms) evolved favourably in 1993 (Figure 5). The utilisation ratio was between 20 and 35 per cent.

Figure 5. **Load factor of vehicles**
(and the change from the previous year)

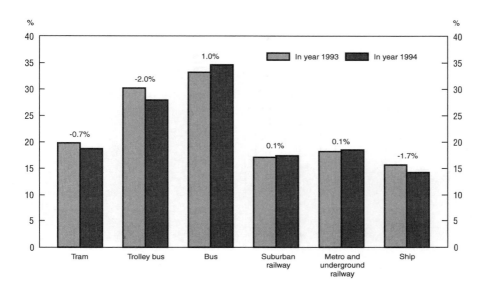

The BKV vehicle fleet and passenger place capacity available for passenger transport at the end of 1993 are shown in Figure 6. The number of vehicles and the passenger place-kilometres have gradually decreased over the past few years.

Figure 6. Distribution of the number of operating vehicles and the availability factor in 1993

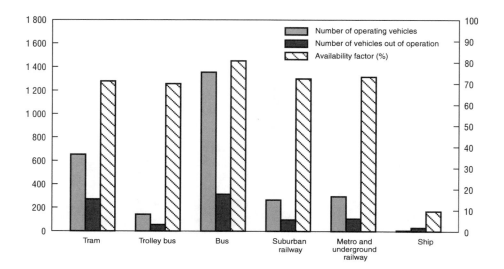

On a daily average, 2 756 vehicles were operated during peak hours. The percentage of the vehicle fleet available for traffic is shown in Figure 7, and the average passenger places available for traffic is shown in Figure 8.

Figure 7. **Percentage of number of vehicles available for traffic in 1993**

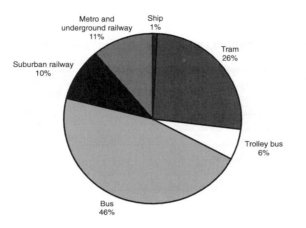

Figure 8. **Percentage of passenger places available for traffic in 1993**

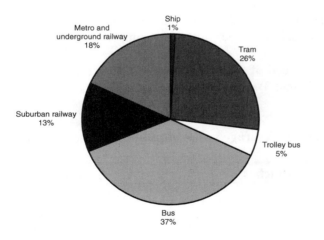

MAV (the Hungarian State Railway) operates on 11 suburban lines, providing railway connections between the settlements surrounding Budapest and the city centre (Table 2):

Table 2. **Railway connections to the capital and their characteristics**

Line	Length (km)	Number of settlements reached	Total population reached	Number of stops or stations
Budapest - Vac	26	5	78 003	9
Budapest - Veresegyhaz	19	4	20 666	7
Budapest - Isaszeg	13	2	20 145	2
Budapest - Mende	15	4	26 694	5
Budapest - Monor	22	4	51 062	5
Budapest - Ocsa	13	3	31 759	3
Budapest Kunszentmiklos - Tass	44	9	57 085	8
Budapest - Erd	7	7	46 500	2
Budapest - Tarnok	8	2	63 00	3
Budapest - Bicske	35	3	48 020	6
Budapest - Dorog	32	6	40 976	8

The majority of the VOLANBUSZ lines run parallel to the railway. Considering the higher comfort level of the bus service, the modal spilt is changing continuously in favour of the bus company.

The average speed of the public transport vehicles is similar to other large European cities (Table 3).

Table 3. **Average speed of public transport vehicles**

Branches	Average speed (km/h)
Tram	15 - 16
Bus	21 - 22
Trolley-bus	17 - 18
Underground	32 - 33
Suburban railway	30 - 31

The condition of the tram tracks along with heavy traffic on the bus and trolley-bus lines significantly influence the speed of public transport vehicles. There seems to be a continuous decrease in average speed on all means of transport, except Metro and suburban railways.

The assessment of the rolling stock can be summarised as follows: there are a total of 1 300 vehicles in the fixed rail network. About one third of these vehicles has reached their planned operational life. The average age of the rail rolling stock of BKV is as follows (Table 4):

Table 4. **Average age of rail rolling stock in 1993**

Branch	Average age in years
Tram	25
Trolley-bus	13
Metro, underground	14
Suburban railway	18

One third of the buses has exceeded their planned lifetime, the technical condition rate (actual age compared to the amortisation norm) of these vehicles is 25 per cent for buses and 45 per cent for trolley-buses. The condition of the vehicles of the VOLANBUSZ and MAV is similar.

The condition of tracks is also comparable. The average age of the tram tracks and suburban railways is 16 years, however, some sections are 50 to 60 years old. The technical conditions rate of the tracks is as follows (Table 5). The conditions of the track and other infrastructure assets of VOLANBUSZ and MAV are generally worse.

Table 5. **Technical condition rates of the tracks in 1993**

Branch	Condition rate (%)
Tram	25
Underground	35
Metro	70
Suburban railway	30

Because of the poor condition of the tracks, speed limits have been imposed to prevent accidents and to decrease noise and vibration.

BKV has a significant number of depots and service buildings. The average technical rate of the depots and the industrial buildings is 35-40 per cent. The condition of the safety equipment is better, with an average technical rate of 35-50 per cent. The capacity of the vehicle maintenance workshops does not meet the demand; as a result, the lack of capacity leads to delays in the maintenance schedule.

The public transport traffic control system is traditional, but is undergoing modernisation. In most cases, the traffic controller receives information from the vehicles at one of the two termini of the lines, but only ten per cent of the vehicles are equipped with radio telephone. At present, an automatic vehicle monitoring system is being installed which will provide all the necessary information for the controllers to enable them to make quick and appropriate decisions. Only nine of the 270 termini are equipped with computers containing time tables for certain disorders and emergencies in public transport traffic.

In March 1995, the Hungarian government launched a radical reform programme to reduce the state budget deficit. Implementation of the promised budget reform will require determined steps from the government, including: acceleration of the privatisation process; strong reduction of wide social supports; and rigorous selection of investment projects financed by the state budget. These steps may influence the main policy issues in organising and financing urban public transport in Budapest.

Proposals for reorganisation of BKV were to be made by a consulting company in the second half of 1995. The non-core activities of the company will most likely be separated and privatised, and a shareholding company (BKV Rt.) will be formed with a reduced number of employees. As an important part of this transformation process, the value of BKV's assets will be re-evaluated and increased.

A call for tender has been made for proposals to create a co-operative regional public transport system before 2000. In the first phase, a common tariff system among the three operating companies (BKV, VOLANBUSZ, MAV) is to be established. In the second phase, the integrated public transport system is to provide for harmonized transport planning and traffic management.

4.3 Development plans for urban transport infrastructure

A 1994 BETS consortium study, financed by Phare and carried out by TRUTH Ltd., identifies infrastructure improvements as well as technologies and management practices that will support medium- and long-term planning for an environment-friendly transport system in Budapest. Options for transport network developments, examined in the BETS study, are based on the following requirements:

-- avoiding environmental degradation in the city;
-- improving traffic conditions;
-- securing the maximum degree of mobility for the inhabitants of Budapest compatible with environmental requirements.

The planning process will be based on a broad set of data, including:

-- socio-economic information about the population, reflecting the characteristics of the social structure:

  • population (number, age, sex, educational level);
  • housing (number, number of rooms/flat, types of ownership, year of construction, comfort, number of buildings, number of flats/building);
  • household (size, number of children);
  • economic activity (income by zones, employment levels, car ownership by zones);

-- traffic data from two sources:

  • origin-destination matrices;
  • traffic counts at specific counting stations;

-- additional data to be used in the planning process to calibrate the modal split models.

In the first phase of the planning process, TRUTH Ltd. used a computer model to develop three test networks using the following parameters:

-- with the existing situation;
-- with a road infrastructure development-oriented transport system;
-- with a public transport development-oriented system.

351

According to pre-assessment of these development alternatives, the public transport-oriented development provided best results; the objectives of this option are to improve the public transport network through the introduction of new or extended public transport lines. Furthermore, minor road infrastructure construction would accommodate traffic volumes and improvements in the connections of road transport networks, without attracting more traffic and causing additional delays. This development alternative is summarised as follows:

-- increased public transport capacity;
-- higher accessibility;
-- more-efficient transport mode connections.

With this development path, the following results are projected:

-- the public transport network will accommodate the majority of the trips originating in the suburbs;
-- a significant increase in ridership will be noticed in rapid public transport originating in the suburbs;
-- congestion will decrease considerably in the city centre and on the Buda side;
-- environmental pollution will tend to decrease due to traffic bypassing the city centre.

4.4 Financing development of the urban public transport system

After the democratic changes in 1991, the Municipality of Budapest prepared a plan for the development of the capital's transport system. Projects linked to rationalisation of the public transport system were given high priority in the ranking process, primarily because the annual budget and required subsidisation of BKV had been increasing for years. Recently, the Municipality of Budapest, as the owner of BKV, has provided a significant amount of subsidisation (36 per cent of total revenue) to offset operating costs not covered by fare-box revenues. The state budget also provides capital (7.6 per cent of total revenue) for the development of infrastructure and renovation of vehicles. The plan illustrates that the main goal of the local authority was to stop the increase in required annual financial support of BKV, while maintaining operability of the system.

Because of the lack of domestic financial resources, discussions on credit opportunities were undertaken with the international financing institutions: The European Bank for Reconstruction and Development (EBRD), The World Bank (WB), European Investment Bank (EIB). Following lengthy talks, foreign bank credits became available for financing the development of the public transport system. In early 1995, an agreement was reached on a credit contract based on acceptable conditions for Budapest officials.

Under the terms of the agreement, the EBRD provides a credit framework of ECU 53 million based on current price levels with a concession interest rate for transport development. One part of the credit (54 per cent) carries a fixed interest rate for 15 years; another part (23 per cent) has a LIBOR+1 per cent; and the third part (23 per cent) has a fixed interest rate for four years. These sums can be called during the grace period until the end of 1997.

By combining these resources with those of the state budget, the construction of three large infrastructure development projects for the public transport system of BKV has been started.

In 1994, approximately ECU 6.5 million, from government sources, was spent on the reconstruction of the first phase of tram track on Great Avenue. In 1995, the second phase of the 47-km tram track reconstruction will be finished using about ECU 30 million of WB credit.

The second project, reconstruction of Tram line No. 2, which carries a significant public transport traffic flow on the Pest side of the Danube, required a total of ECU 4.4 million. The preparatory phase of this construction was carried out in the second half of 1994; completion is scheduled for 1995. This project has been partially financed by the Municipality of Budapest, and about ECU 1.4 million has been paid by BKV.

With an investment cost of ECU 17 million, the third project concerns the reconstruction of the first underground line. EBRD is providing ECU 10 million of funding for this initiative, and commercial banks will lend the remaining sum to the Municipality.

The renovation of the vehicle park has also been financed by international bank credits. 170 articulated buses and 92 minibus have been purchased and 500 bus engines reconstructed. An on-board monitoring system has been installed on 200 BKV vehicles providing detailed information for more efficient traffic management. Preparation of a feasibility study for a new underground line is being financed by the EIB.

In addition to these development projects, which have been started over the last two years, the alternatives of a medium-term master plan for Budapest have been evaluated as well. Forecasts predict further increase in individual car use, reaching a 50-50 per cent balanced ratio of public and private transport use by the beginning of the next decade. These trends will require intensive development of the city road network, along with the introduction of a new parking plan, which will determine four types of zones based on different parking rates and conditions.

Also included in the medium-term master plan is a description of four basic land uses: residential, office, shopping and industrial. The privatisation process taking place in the capital will be subject to constraints as a result of the application of a public transport-friendly land use policy.

4.5 Tariff changes and their effect on subsidy rates

Launched in 1946, the public transport ticket system in Budapest was valid for 20 years with only minimal adjustments. In 1966, public transport tariffs rose by one third. In the 1970s, tariffs did not change. In mid-1982, however, the suburban railway (HEV) increased its fares by 100 per cent and in 1985 the prices of all tickets doubled.

A new public transport tariff system was introduced in 1989 as a part of the economic policy aimed at reducing subsidies. As a result, fares sharply increased by an average of 85 per cent. The new tariff system preserved the unified tariff inside the administrative boundaries of Budapest. Outside the boundaries of the capital, two zones were formed for season bus tickets, and the zone tariff system was preserved in the suburban railway (HEV) lines.

There were two further tariff hikes in 1990 and 1991 by an average of 60 per cent and 50 per cent respectively. Small tariff modifications of 6 per cent were introduced in the first quarter of 1993 in compliance with new value added tax regulation, and a further increase of 22 per cent was approved in July 1993 by the Central Assembly of Budapest. In 1994, the price of a single ticket increased to HUF 25, and a combined monthly pass to HUF 1 150. The most recent fare increase of an average 35 per cent was introduced in March 1995. Single ticket prices subsequently rose to HUF 35 and combined monthly passes to HUF 1 500. (The average inflation rate has been 20 to 30 per cent per year in the past few years.)

These significant tariff changes over the past five years were unavoidable given the increase in the prices of energy sources and the increase in social insurance and profit taxes. The decrease in subsidisation (in real terms) resulted in a reduction in place-km performance of about 10 per cent. All these issues have contributed to the increase in the cost of urban passenger transport.

Significant changes have occurred in the subsidisation rate. The cost recovery rates between 1989 and 1995, calculated as (farebox+other operating revenues)/(total net costs-depreciation), reveals the following values: 38.2 per cent in 1989; 39 per cent in 1990, 37.9 per cent in 1991, 38.5 per cent in 1992, 35.2 per cent in 1993, 34 per cent in 1994. The estimated value for 1995 is 40 per cent and the required value in 2000 will be 50 per cent.

Given the requirements of the international banks, which include raising the cost recovery ratio to 50 per cent, a further increase will have to be introduced at the tariff level. According to estimations, tariffs will increase by 40 per cent in 1996; 20 per cent in 1997; and 20 per cent in 1998.

The structure of the BKV budget on the revenue side (in billion HUF) was as follows in 1994 (Table 6):

Table 6. **Revenue structure in 1994**

Type of revenue	HUF in billions	Percentage (%)
Fare-box revenue	8.4	32
Support from the state budget (for concessioned passengers)	5.8	22
Subsidisation from the Municipality	9.2	35
State contribution to development	2.0	7
Revenues from advertisement	1.0	4
Total revenue	26.4	100

The estimated values for 1995 are as follows in Table 7:

Table 7. **Revenue structure in 1995**

Type of revenue	billion HUF	Percentage (%)
Fare-box revenue	11.4	37
Support from the state budget (for concessioned passengers)	5.0	16
Subsidisation from the Municipality	11.0	36
State contribution to development	2.3	7
Revenues from advertisement	1.3	4
Total revenue	31.0	100

5. CONCLUSION

According to public opinion and expert evaluations, BKV has been able to perform its task on a European level: its public transport network is extensive; frequency of vehicle passage is maximum every 10-15 minutes; and vehicles are not overcrowded. A lack of capital injection, however, along with existing financing pressures and the accelerated deterioration of vehicles will sooner or later render public transport less competitive relative to private cars. To maintain the relatively high ratio of public transport, further development of the system with a strong emphasis on the quality of public transport services is necessary. Because of the significant amount of the international financing used for the planned developments, the Municipality will have to sell some of its properties to repay the loans. This means that radical changes are necessary in the organisation and financing system to guarantee the best management of available capital.

Simply adopting solutions from foreign countries is not the right answer to the problems. The top management of the capital must examine the best structures for financing the system's operations. Privatisation can take place only in particular subsystems of the urban public transport system. The rationalisation of staff has to be supported by sound human resource management policy. The integrated system of urban public services and the unified "image" of BKV must be maintained.

Systematic solutions to parking problems will help to manage urban passenger transport demand. A parking plan has been already prepared, according to which car traffic will be restricted in the inner zones and the castle district of the capital. Weekends are already car-free in the recreational areas of the city, and serious penalties are assessed for illegal parking. Furthermore the number of pedestrian zones has been gradually increased in the sub-centres of the capital.

The system for monitoring environmental pollution (measuring devices for air and noise pollution) has priority in the development plan. Different traffic control strategies have been defined to manage special cases of environmental damage.

Modifications of the privatisation law have been discussed and accepted by Parliament. It has become clear that privatisation would contribute to increasing the productivity and efficiency of operations, but that it cannot solve the problem of self-financing for the whole urban public transport system. Subsidisation will have to be maintained, but in a more rational and controlled way.

Possible alternative revenue sources must be examined in detail. Along with modest increases in tariff levels, new financing sources must be identified. These types of sources include travel taxes on companies with more than ten people; shared income from park-and-ride services; and revenues from increased advertisement and marketing activity.

The restructuring of the large BKV organisation into smaller and more homogeneous parts (such as bus, tram, underground and other groups of operation) would facilitate a more clear cost-control mechanism and help to monitor the efficiency of the different "profit" centres. Principles behind the restructuring of BKV include:

-- formation of a share-holding company;
-- separation of the non-core activities (e.g. track building and maintenance, vehicle maintenance shops, printing and publishing services, etc.) from the organisation;
-- building a supplier-consumer system based on profit and/or cost centres;
-- development of a management information system;

-- creation of a new zone-based tariff system taking into account the longer-term objectives of a unified tariff federation with MAV and VOLANBUSZ;

-- privatisation of transport services on a few side lines;

-- integration of a regional co-operative transport system by the end of the decade;

-- identification of new ways to finance losses (e.g. contribution to revenues by selling off the unnecessary assets of the BKV).

BIBLIOGRAPHY

TANCZOS, K., "Experience of deregulation and privatisation of urban public transport in the UK" (in Hungarian), *Urban Transport* (*Varosi Kozlekedes*) Vol. 1991, No. 6.

TANCZOS, K., "Market oriented strategy in the development of urban public transport", OECD/CEMT Conference, Budapest, 1994.

TANCZOS, K., (with co-authors), "The fare system of urban public transport in Budapest", 20th Annual Public Transport Symposium, 1989. Newcastle-upon-Tyne.

Budapest Public Transport Fare System Restructuring Study, SOFRETU, 1993.

BETS Study 2nd Interim Report, TRUTH Ltd, 1994, Yearbooks of Budapest Transport Company.

IV. IMPLEMENTING URBAN TRANSPORT POLICIES

Achieving Public Approval for Innovative Transport Policies

Bo E. Peterson
Stockholm Transport
Sweden

TABLE OF CONTENTS

SUMMARY

The expansion of car traffic has led to increasing strain on the environment and growing problems in connection with accessibility on the roads and streets in the three main metropolitan areas of Sweden: Stockholm, Gothenburg and Malmö.

In 1988, the Swedish Minister of Transport appointed a committee -- the Metropolitan Traffic Committee -- to prepare comprehensive data on which to base decisions aimed at limiting the effects of traffic on public health and the environment in metropolitan areas.

The committee began its work by establishing five steps for action to serve as a framework for its report to the minister:

1. agreement on the problems;
2. acceptance of the objectives;
3. support for a package of interacting measures;
4. determination of sources of financing;
5. suggestions for constitutional changes.

The work carried out by the committee, embodied in the so-called "Dennis Agreement", can be summarised as the identification of five necessary interacting measures:

1. reinforced regional and municipal planning;
2. upgraded and expanded public transport;
3. new traffic routes to solve local problems;
4. restrictions on car traffic;
5. more stringent exhaust requirements for cars and heavy vehicles.

An agreement was signed in January 1991 by the Social Democratic, Conservative and Liberal parties of the City and County of Stockholm. The agreement covers investments in public transport and major traffic routes, totalling approximately SKr 28 billion during the period 1991 to 2005.

The agreement is monumental in several respects: its goals, its means, its financial scope, its time frame, the dimensions of its constituent projects, its holistic character (no "plucking out the plums"), its requirement for broad political support, its geographic purview, its inclusion of public transportation as well as roads and car tolls, and the large number of interested parties it subsumes.

Even though much information was made available to the public from the very beginning, it was not until concrete construction plans were finalised that public opposition began to be heard. Suddenly, opponents of the agreement began to lobby the media, writing letters to newspapers, organising protest meetings and circulating petitions. These opponents often had differing viewpoints: some found the plan undemocratic, charging that it had been agreed on behind closed doors; others were opposed to specific parts, or parts of parts. There were objections to the plan's environmental impact from the proposed extensions of both road and rail. It was also feared that the extension of the road and highway system would bring an increase in traffic.

Many now say that confidence in politicians has been eroded, and that they have betrayed the trust of the voters. But the 1991 and 1994 elections for parliament and county and local councils show no evidence of this. Only 1 per cent of voters changed their allegiance to parties that had expressed opposition to the agreement.

Perhaps more work should have been done -- before the negotiations and in their early stages -- to construct a shared vision of the problems regarding the environment, congestion and the region in general. Subsequently, further resources could have been used to achieve a broad consensus for goals in these problem areas.

Nevertheless, both the government and the opposition have proclaimed the 1990s as "Sweden's Transportation Infrastructure Decade". It is to be a decade in which Sweden creates the conditions for growth and faith in the future on the eve of this country's integration into Europe. Investments in the country's transportation systems will help make that possible. Environmental impact will thereby also be limited. The Dennis Agreement can be seen as a symbol of this optimistic view of the future. In the current period of economic recession and budgetary constraint in Sweden, it is interesting to note that investments in infrastructure are not questioned, although their implementation will take more time than planned due to financial problems.

1. INTRODUCTION

The expansion of car traffic has led to increasing strain on the environment and growing problems in connection with roads and street accessibility in the three main metropolitan areas of Sweden: Stockholm, Gothenburg and Malmö.

Traffic is now the single main source of environmental disruption in the three cities. Air pollution is the worst problem, coupled with high noise levels along certain traffic routes and busy streets. Exhaust fumes and noise in the cities constitute major local health problems. At the same time, exhaust fumes contribute to air pollution problems on a regional and global scale.

This paper presents the decision-making process in the Stockholm region concerning measures to solve traffic problems. It describes the political negotiations, the resulting agreement as well as the content of the package agreed upon. Primarily, however, it focuses on the problems of assuring acceptance from the whole political community, all interested organisations, and residents affected by the measures.

2. THE FIRST POLITICAL APPROACH: THE METROPOLITAN TRAFFIC COMMITTEE

In 1988, the Swedish Minister of Transport appointed a committee known as the Metropolitan Traffic Committee to prepare comprehensive data on which to base decisions aimed at limiting the effects of traffic on public health and the environment in metropolitan areas. The committee was made up of 12 politicians from six political parties representing the Parliament as well as the county councils and the municipalities in the three regions.

2.1 Framework for action

The committee began its work by identifying five necessary steps to serve as a framework for action in the preparation of its report to the minister:

1. agreement on the problems;
2. acceptance of the objectives;
3. support for a package of interacting measures;
4. determination of sources of financing;
5. suggestions for constitutional changes.

It was also agreed that car traffic in large cities creates:

-- air and noise pollution;
-- congestion.

2.2 Setting the objectives

When drafting its proposals, the committee's most important objectives were to:

-- Decrease traffic-related air pollution in metropolitan areas in order to improve public health and minimise the damaging effects of pollutants on buildings, plant life, soil and water.

-- Reduce interference caused by traffic noise. In the first instance, conditions shall be improved for those people who are exposed to excessively high noise levels and for whom the noise constitutes a serious health risk.

-- Lower congestion levels on the road network.

Specifically, the following objectives for the year 2000 were established for air and noise pollution and congestion:

- NO_x reduced by 50 per cent from 1980 levels;
- CO_2 reduced to 1988 levels;
- noise level, maximum 30 dBA indoors;
- noise level, maximum 60 dBA outdoors;
- congestion reduced by 30 per cent from 1987.

One conclusion from analyses performed by the committee was that traffic and environmental problems in the three cities must -- in order to achieve these objectives -- be combated through a large number of interacting measures comprising, for example: improvements in public transport; the extension and construction of traffic routes; economic, administrative and traffic engineering control instruments; and environmental control measures. No one measure alone can solve all the problems.

2.3 Measures targeted

The Metropolitan Traffic Committee identified five necessary interacting measures:

1. reinforced regional and municipal planning;
2. upgraded and expanded public transport services;
3. new traffic routes to solve local problems;
4. restrictions on car traffic;
5. more stringent exhaust requirements for cars and heavy vehicles.

Reinforced regional and municipal planning

It is extremely important that building development be planned and located in such a way that it alleviates the need for travel and favours public transport. In order for this to be possible, it is necessary to reinforce general planning at both the municipal and regional levels.

Upgraded and expanded public transport services

A significant upgrading and development of public transport services is essential. In order to ensure that such development gives rise to both attractive and environmentally compatible public transport, it should first take the form of fixed-track and trolley services, or alternatively low-emission diesel, ethanol or natural gas-driven bus services in their own segregated lanes to safeguard a high level of accessibility.

Improved modal change terminals and attractive new park-and-ride facilities are other examples of the investments that need to be made in public transport.

371

New traffic routes to solve local problems

The existing road network must be supplemented by traffic routes that can relieve some of the pressure on the network and help to reduce local environmental problems.

The construction of main traffic routes can have both a positive and a negative impact on the environment. The positive aspect is that some traffic route developments can lead to reduced traffic in central city areas. The street space freed by this development can be used to assure the accessibility of public transport services and improve conditions for commercial traffic, pedestrians and cyclists.

Among negative aspects of road development is the fact that car traffic often increases as a result of greater road capacity. One criterion for any decision to pursue road construction should be that expected overall environmental impact is positive.

Other measures designed to improve traffic flow and reduce environmental interference include: modernisation of traffic signal techniques; extension of the car-free pedestrian street system; more loading zones and other improvements in commercial traffic; and better street maintenance.

Restrictions on car traffic

It is not enough to simply develop and improve public transport and/or the roads in order to achieve established objectives. Measures must also be introduced that restrict the amount of car traffic. In the inner-city areas, this is necessary in order to meet targets for exhaust fumes and congestion, and in the metropolitan regions as a whole, to meet objectives for reduced NO_x and CO_2 emissions.

Financing

The committee considered that car tolls are an important control instrument in metropolitan traffic for reducing congestion and improving the environment, particularly in central areas that suffer the heaviest environmental impact. At the same time, tolls provide substantial revenue which can be ploughed back into the traffic system. A car toll within Stockholm's inner-city area of SKr 25 per day would give an annual net income of approximately SKr 650 million.

More stringent exhaust requirements for cars and heavy vehicles

Calculations indicate that the development of public transport, the construction and extension of major traffic routes, and the introduction of car tolls are not sufficient to achieve the objective of reducing NO_x emissions by 50 per cent between the years 1980 and 2000. Therefore, additional measures that have an effect on vehicle exhaust emissions will need to be introduced.

Changes in the Constitution

In conclusion, the committee submitted the following proposals for constitutional changes:

-- car tolls, currently not legal, are to be proposed in bill to Parliament in 1996;
-- more stringent exhaust requirements for cars and heavy vehicles;
-- temporary ban on car traffic;
-- special environmental labelling of vehicles.

3. THE POLITICAL PROBLEM: ROAD PRICING SCHEME

The Metropolitan Traffic Committee's comprehensive road pricing scheme, proposed for the city of Stockholm, was deferred due to political problems. Faced with opposition from the Conservative party, the Social Democrats, the main party behind the proposal, were unable to convince the Minister of Transport that the scheme was feasible from a legal point of view.

The plan was to restrict an area in the centre of Stockholm, where motorists would have to pay to take their cars. Cars on two through-roads would be exempted from paying. The scheme was to have begun with simple cardboard licences displayed on car windscreens and checked by traffic wardens, eventually becoming an electronic system, which would check moving cars for the presence of smart cards; the rear number plates of offending cars would be photographed and their owners billed.

4. THE SECOND POLITICAL APPROACH: APPOINTMENT OF NEGOTIATORS

After opposition thwarted development of the above scheme, a decision was made by the Government in April 1990 -- as a second approach to solving the problems -- to appoint a negotiator for each of the three metropolitan regions (Stockholm, Gothenburg and Malmö) who would present proposals -- together with regional representatives -- for improved traffic systems. One of the reasons for the governments decision was the conclusion reached by the Metropolitan Traffic Committee that activities in the three cities were being hampered by shortfalls in the traffic systems, and that this was in turn having a bad impact on the environment.

The negotiator for the Stockholm region, Bengt Dennis, who at the time was Governor of the Bank of Sweden, started with a presentation to all six political parties in the City and County. He presented a package with almost the same five interacting measures as suggested by the Metropolitan Traffic Committee. Three parties accepted no new roads in the package and were asked by Bengt Dennis to leave the negotiations.

An agreement was signed in January 1991 by the Social Democrat, Conservative and Liberal parties in the City and County of Stockholm. The agreement covers investments in public transport and major traffic routes amounting to a total of approximately SKr 28 billion during the period 1991 to 2005. The agreement assumes additional agreements on particular issues during 1992.

The Social Democrat Party, the Conservative Party and the Liberal Party agreed on 29 September 1992 to the following addendum to the agreement signed on 23 January 1991 concerning co-ordinated measures to improve the environment, increase accessibility, and create better conditions for development of the Stockholm Region. The measures referred to are also intended to contribute to increased housing construction.

The agreement covers the period 1992-2006 and comprises programmes and plans for investments of approximately SKr 15.8 billion in public transport, 18.2 billion in traffic routes and 1.9 billion in other road-related facilities, totalling SKr 35.9 billion (all sums based on January 1992 prices).

Additional contracts among concerned parties and principals will be prerequisite to the complete implementation of the investment projects included in the agreement. Subject to certain conditions, the Swedish National Road Administration has declared itself prepared in principal to finance and implement the construction of a complete ring road (the Ring) around inner Stockholm and an Outer By-pass Route. It is intended that these traffic routes be financed entirely by fees imposed on vehicle traffic. The agreement further provides that the Swedish National Road Administration will be responsible for maintaining the Ring and the Outer By-pass Route -- and that the funds freed through these routes being financed by vehicle-user fees can instead be used to finance investments in public transport facilities.

4.1 Infrastructure financing system

Figure 1. **Infrastructure financing system for Stockholm**

The existing system for financing infrastructure in the Stockholm Region is illustrated below:

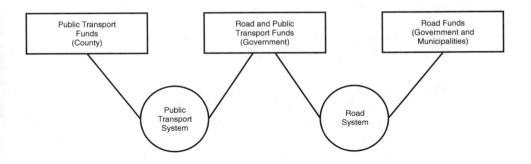

The proposed new financing system is as follows:

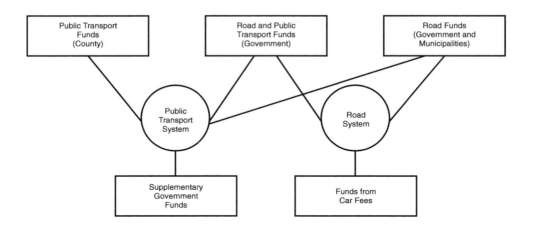

4.2 Public transport projects agreed

The agreement provides for the following public transport projects:

--   The underground railway will be modernised. A total of almost SKr 7 billion will be invested in the underground railway system;

--   The capacity of the railway network will be increased by the addition of a third track over Riddarholmen (south of Stockholm Central Station) and some new double track sections north and south of Stockholm. A total of SKr 4 billion will be invested in capacity improvements in connection with the railway system;

--   A rapid transit tram line will be built from Gullmarsplan via Älvsjö to Liljeholmen and then be extended to Alvik for a total of SKr 2 billion. A further extension to the north and east is planned for a total cost of SKr 2.1 billion.

-- A trunk network will be laid for the public transport system in Stockholm's inner city. Public transport will be given reserved street space and priority in the traffic signal system to the greatest extent possible. Every attempt will be made to speed up the changeover to environmentally adapted vehicles. SKr 700 million will be invested.

-- Park-and-ride facilities will play an increasingly important role in the future traffic system. Special funds (SKr 2 billion) have been allocated for the extension and construction of such facilities.

Road investments to be financed by road pricing include:

-- Additional sections of "the Ring", a ring road around Stockholm, as well as a future "Outer By-pass Route" are being financed by fees levied on car traffic. The Swedish National Road Administration is the body responsible for these projects at a total cost of SKr 18 billion.

-- When car traffic in the inner city can be reduced in step with the completion of different sections of the Ring, improvements will be made in the street environment. SKr 1.2 billion has been earmarked for street environment improvements in the region, including measures for the reduction of traffic noise in existing residential properties.

5. "OFFICIAL" COMMENTS ON THE DENNIS AGREEMENT

The secretary for the negotiations, Bo Malmsten, Director of the Stockholm Region Planning Office, prepared a "white paper" on the plan, which includes the following more-or-less "official" comments on the negotiated agreement.

-- The Dennis Agreement is unique in structure as well as in content and scope. It is the result of major political efforts.

-- The agreement is interesting from a public law perspective, as it is a pact -- not among representatives of public agencies -- but among political parties.

-- The agreement comprises the kind of investments in new public transport and road traffic facilities that have been deemed necessary for the long-term development of the Stockholm area into a well-functioning metropolitan region.

-- The accord was made possible in large part by the leader of negotiations, Bengt Dennis. No other person enjoyed such great public authority at that time as the Governor of the Bank of Sweden; his public profile most certainly had a major influence on the negotiations.

There was, however, considerable receptivity on the part of the political parties, as well. All parties understood the gravity of the situation and recognised that vigorous measures would have to be taken to ensure the overall development of the Stockholm region.

The political parties assigned their foremost representatives to the negotiating group, all of whom were prepared to regard the matter from a broad perspective and with an outlook on the future. They all realised, too, that an agreement would require compromises.

The Dennis Agreement was set forth in three stages:

1. preliminary agreement in January 1991;
2. final agreement on 29 September 1992;
3. checkpoint in 1996.

The agreement is "monumental" in several respects: its goals, its means, its financial scope, its time frame, the dimensions of its constituent projects, its comprehensive nature (no "plucking out the plums"), its requirement for broad political support, its geographic purview, its inclusion of public transportation as well as roads and car tolls, and the large number of interested parties it concerns.

The agreement's major road-investment projects are the Ring and the Outer By-pass Route. Its biggest public-transportation projects are the light-rail system, railroad enhancements, subway investments, and improvements to the Roslag Line.

The pre-negotiation brief called for an agreement that would yield a better environment, improved accessibility, and greater potential for economic growth. Does the Dennis Agreement, then, satisfy that brief? A number of studies have been carried out to analyse the consequences of the various measures called for.

As far as the environment is concerned, the environmental impact analyses of the entire package reveal that the Dennis package will result in a reduction in both traffic and exhaust emissions. Calculations show that the national economic gains will be 11/2 times the investment costs.

Both the government and the opposition have proclaimed the 1990s as "Sweden's Transportation Infrastructure decade". It is to be a decade in which Sweden creates the conditions for growth and faith in the future on the eve of this country's integration into Europe. Investments in the country's transportation systems will help make that possible. Environmental impact will thereby also be limited. The Dennis Agreement can be seen as a symbol of this optimistic view of the future. In the current period of economic recession and budgetary constraint in Sweden, it is interesting to note that investments in infrastructure are not questioned, although their implementation will take more time due to financial problems.

It should be noted that since the plan was signed, it has been formally approved by the Swedish *Riksdag*, or parliament, the Stockholm County Council and 19 concerned municipalities. This means that at all political levels, a majority of representatives have backed the plan. There are, nonetheless, details that various municipalities have not yet accepted.

6. IMPLEMENTATION OF THE PLAN

Since the Dennis Plan was finalised in 1992, work on its various components has been proceeding according to schedule. Officials in the relevant administrations and consultants are developing plans, and subcontractors are building. The state has provided investment funds to improve features of public transport along with guarantees to allow the Swedish National Road Administration to borrow on the financial market pending the revenue from the proposed toll gates ringing the city. The entire process is supervised by a political negotiating group with representatives from the county and city councils. Every second month, the group meets with senior administration officials.

Throughout the planning and negotiation stages for the Dennis package, information campaigns were held, whereby for the most part, ideas and proposals were presented to regional political representatives and then discussed. There were also special hearings for stakeholder groups affected by the proposals. After publication of the studies, press conferences were held, inciting strong interest on the part of the mass media. The trade press and special interest television programmes also became involved.

A special unit was established to disseminate information to stakeholder groups and to the general public based on the studies that have been carried out. The unit also arranges information meetings. Since 1987, a great number of reports have been published on the various components of the Dennis plan. A database containing all the information, including every official report and comprising over 3 000 documents was set up. For every component project, information brochures have been prepared and distributed at meetings and conferences with stakeholders and interested residents in the Stockholm region. There have been press conferences at every stage of the approval process. During the work of the Metropolitan Traffic Committee on the actual negotiations, the media were given the background, the reasoning. According to the media, no other regional issue has ever aroused as much attention as the Dennis Plan.

As with building construction, every road construction project has to go through a formal urban planning process. This involves obtaining approval for development plan details from the local councils of those areas affected. It also involves providing access to the plans for property owners affected, other stakeholders and the general public so that they may not only study the plans but also have an opportunity to comment on them, in part or in their entirety. The plans can be appealed up to government level.

6.1 Opposition from the Public

Even though considerable information was made available to the public from the very beginning of the Dennis Plan process, it was not until concrete construction plans were finalised that public opposition began to be heard. Suddenly, opponents of the agreement began to lobby the media, writing letters to newspapers, organising protest meetings and circulating petitions. These opponents often had differing viewpoints: some found the plan undemocratic -- charging that it had been agreed on behind closed doors -- while others were opposed to specific parts -- or parts of parts. There were objections to the plan's environmental impact from the proposed extensions of both road and rail. It was feared as well that the extension of the road and highway system would bring an increase in traffic.

A number of environmental organisations are in the forefront of the protests. *Ad hoc* groups have been formed -- often fronted by celebrities, including writers, actors, and economists. Individuals have also protested on their own. Group protests are most frequently against the entire plan, while individuals generally focus on specific elements of the project that affect them directly. In this case, rail tracks or motorways have been accepted if they are situated at some distance from the protester's home.

When Bengt Dennis launched negotiations with the parliamentary political parties, six parties were involved. When it became apparent that the final agreement would have to be a compromise between public transport aims and the needs of private vehicles, three parties announced that they would not be able to back a plan that involved building new motorways. The Dennis Plan was thus approved by only three parties (which still represent more than 80 per cent of franchised votes both locally and in national parliament).

Many now say that confidence in politicians has been eroded, and that they have betrayed the trust of the voters. But the 1991 and 1994 elections for parliament and county and local councils show no evidence of this. Only 1 per cent of voters changed their allegiance to parties that had expressed opposition to the agreement.

It is also difficult to understand criticism that the plan was reached through undemocratic means, ignoring the need to base support on local party cadres. The democratic system is based on decisions being made by elected representatives-politicians. There is no other way, short of referendum. There have, in fact, been demands for a referendum on the plan, backed by several critics and even endorsed by a few politicians. However, the Stockholm City Council decided in November 1995 that a referendum would not be held.

There are indeed many difficulties associated with a referendum. Voter eligibility would have to be determined: e.g. would only those residents of the urban area or all those who inhabit the region participate? In addition, wording of the questions would have to be addressed: would the referendum cover the entire plan or one or several of its components? In the first case, there would be a problem in presenting voters with comprehensive yet easily understood basic data. At the same time, the ramifications of a "no" would have to be made clear: would any investments be allowed, given that all traffic projects agreed on in the last ten years are included in the plan? If voters were given the opportunity to approve or disapprove components of the plan, there would be a problem of demarcation, since several projects are interconnected. For example, if there were to be improvements in traffic lane access for buses and in the overall environment of central Stockholm, then car traffic would have to be diverted to motorways and constrained by toll barriers.

A second type of criticism is directed at specific components of the plan and even parts of components. On this level, two groups of critics can be distinguished: one group is comprised of those who are personally affected because of property expropriation, the risk of noise nuisance, visually unacceptable changes from construction or projected traffic flow. The other group is made up of those whose opposition is based on principle. Examples of this latter group include those against a surface rail track, lobbying instead for a tunnel; those opposed to toll barriers; those against a specific stretch of motorway; those who do not want a high-speed tram link, and so on.

Opposition to the Dennis Plan manifests itself in different ways -- most often, through letters to the newspapers. There are also items in local television and radio broadcasts. Meetings and demonstrations are also organised, as well as delegations calling on leading politicians and government leaders to take action against the plan. These opponents are not numerous and the same people often turn up in different circumstances; however, they are very vocal and attract considerable media attention, especially when the statements are made by celebrities.

Supporters of the plan are less visible and more moderate in tone. They primarily comprise politicians in the parties backing the plan and various business groups. They also include individuals concerned that nothing is being done about the traffic situation. The rationale for supporting the plan is that attempts to improve the traffic situation has for decades been fruitless, and that Bengt Dennis has been able to unite over 80 per cent of the region's political representatives. It is argued that the plan's measures are integrally linked and that cancelling parts of the plan would reduce its desired effects radically. It is further asserted that the plan is, *per se*, a compromise, in which the three parties were forced to accept certain aspects as trade-offs against others. For example, the Moderate Party wants new motorways but not toll barriers; the Social Democrats want tolls but are against one of the proposed stretches of motorway, and the Liberal Party wants measures promoting public transport, but does not want one of the other motorway sections.

7. PERSONAL REFLECTIONS

Between 1988 and 1990, I was the Secretary of the Metropolitan Traffic Committee.   Between 1991 and 1992, I was one of several officials at Stockholm Transport responsible for drafting the basic facts supporting the Dennis Plan negotiations and since 1993, I have been one of several people charged with overseeing implementation of the plan's proposed measures for public transport.

Within this context, some of my personal reflections on the process leading up to the finalisation of the Dennis Plan are as follows.

In hindsight, one might wonder whether there was any other way to research and negotiate the plan and/or whether presenting the background and final content differently would have won over more politicians, more stakeholders and individuals to the necessity and justification of the measures chosen. As regards the politicians: it is evident that the three parties that did not take part in the final negotiations -- the Centre Party, the Green Party and the Left Party Socialists -- were unable to accept the extensive road construction that the other three believed necessary to improve transport access. On the other hand, long drawn-out political discussions might have been avoided if support for the issues had been sought and gained earlier and on a broader basis.

As far as stakeholder organisations go, it must be clearly understood that they are for or against various measures according to whether these measures clash or harmonize with the organisation's basic values. Motorist organisations cannot be expected to support toll barriers; nature conservation groups cannot be expected to accept construction in parklands; tenant organisations cannot be expected to look kindly at increased noise levels, and so on. Thus, political decisions can never satisfy all of these diverse groups. What is of greater interest is whether deterioration in one area can be acceptable if the action facilitates improvement in another. For example, can intrusion into a parkland area be justified by resulting improvement in traffic safety? Can raised noise levels from rail traffic be compensated by reduced travel time for passengers? Neither experts nor laymen can agree.

The final arbiter is the general public, and the question is how much information the public has absorbed and how well it has understood all the information provided before, during and after the finalisation of the plan. A limited investigation shows that:

-- most people are aware that the Dennis Plan is named after Bengt Dennis;

-- the majority of those interviewed judge the main purpose of the plan to be "to improve the environment";

-- people do not see the whole picture;

-- knowledge about the plan is related to the degree of personal involvement;

-- on a superficial level, motorists have greater knowledge of the plan than regular users of public transport;

-- one of the most commonly quoted sources of information is advertising on buses and trains;

-- most residents of Stockholm can name three or four components of the plan;

-- no more than one in five people interviewed have more than a vague idea of what the Dennis Plan means in concrete terms;

-- people are suspicious and tired of information provided by politicians and journalists.

Three years after the finalisation of the Dennis Plan, there is still intense debate in the media over some of the plan's components. Wide public discussion about such large and complex issues is naturally unavoidable. But would the discussion have been calmer and more fact-based if information had focused from the start on common problems and goals rather than on the chosen solutions? There is much evidence to support this. Many people say they do not understand the reasons for all the proposals. Many cannot understand that traffic problems will become worse with population growth -- more cars, greater demands for freedom of movement and so on. Many do not recognise the negative effects of traffic on health and the environment.

Perhaps more work should have been done before the negotiations and in their early stages to construct a shared vision of problems regarding the environment, congestion and the region in general. Additional resources could therefore have been used to achieve a broad consensus for goals in these problem areas, thus rendering the discussion more subtle. In this way, the plan would not have been branded by some individuals as a technocratic product with little consideration of human values.

8. RECOMMENDATIONS

Recommending technical solutions to urban transport problems on the basis of one city's experience is relatively simple: cities and countries have for many years shared this kind of knowledge with one another.

Recommending solutions concerning the political decision-making process and handling public awareness is considerably more complicated. Differences on both cultural and political levels render the transfer of knowledge in these areas more complex. "Receiving" cities can, however, study the experience of "donor" cities and extract information relevant to the design and development of their own models.

In general, three elements of advice can be given regarding the implementation of integrated urban traffic projects:

1. make sure a thoroughly elaborated basis for decision-making exists and is in place;
2. create broad support for the idea and establish it firmly among politicians;
3. inform the general public at an early stage of the process in an easily understandable manner.

V. THE CASE OF BUCHAREST

The Metro: An Essential Part of the Bucharest Public Transport System and its Future

Octavian Udriste
Metrorex
Romania

TABLE OF CONTENTS

LIST OF FIGURES

1. INTRODUCTION

Public transportation is considered by many today the most convenient option for travel in large urban areas. Among public transport systems, electric power traction stands out, with its high performance record in terms of capacity, safety, space economy, low energy consumption, and importantly, its non-pollutant quality. Although infrastructure needs require above-average initial capital costs and specific operating cost subsidies, electric power traction's positive features are widely recognised: such systems are built in economies in recession, applying advanced solutions based on recent technologies. It is important to note that subsidies are not granted for the public transportation operator's benefit; but instead, for that of the community.

If capital and operational costs are impressive in figures, the results are difficult to quantify, because they include a variety of improvements concerning the social activities of the serviced area. Public transport plays a structural role in the economy and serves as a vector for development in the serviced areas. This effect is important in satisfying present and future demands at low costs. For this reason, it is essential to have an "aggressive" planning policy and not wait until it is too late for a decision, or until the decision is based on demand pressure. The attractiveness of residential, commercial and industrial areas may be enhanced just by adding this essential public transport service.

In its efforts to be considered as a major European city, Bucharest needs to adopt an integrated urban transport policy -- supported by adequate financial resources -- to address the city's transportation problems in a timely fashion. In this context, the Metro is and will continue to be an essential part of the public transportation system of Bucharest.

2. HISTORICAL FRAMEWORK

The idea to build a metro system in Bucharest is not a recent one. Records kept by the Romanian Engineers Association show that the first studies for a metro were made immediately after the First World War. At that time, the city was growing rapidly and trying to gain recognition as one of Europe's modern cities. The results of the studies were inconclusive due to the economic and political conditions at that time. Economic crisis followed by the Second World War meant that studies on metro development were only considered again in the mid-1950s, this time, in the context of a joint venture with the USSR. This initiative was one of the so-called "SOVROM" enterprises, which were created in a variety of sectors during the years of Soviet dominance, with the specific objective of using Romanian resources to build Soviet strength. The project was eventually abandoned, as the financial commitment was considered to be too great for Romania. In the following period, railroad systems were considered obsolete, which also affected the initiative to build a Metro system; as a result, the project was again postponed.

It was only in the early 1970s that the idea was again examined and approved. Construction ensued at a sustained pace of 4 km of double track and two stations per year (the reasoning behind this pace will not be discussed in this paper). As all large investments made over the last decades in Romania, a mixture of economic, social and political factors and an unrealistic concentration of financial and human resources resulted in the construction of large, impressive structures, some of which have proven to be useful to society. However, errors were made as well, notably in the case of the metro: the faulty conception and planning of the lines and stations -- the consequences of which are felt today -- the completion of the work, and other problems could have been avoided if experts in metro design and systems development had been allowed to work freely without the interference of strictly political pressures.

3. INSTITUTIONAL AND ORGANISATIONAL ASPECTS

The Bucharest Metro was initially organised as a railroad transport system under the Ministry of Transportation's Railroad Department. Today, the Metro is an autonomous administration under the Ministry of Transportation. The main features of the rolling stock and installations, the administrative structure of the staff, and the stringent safety requirements in effect require that this status be maintained. Under these circumstances, good co-ordination with the surface public transportation operator -- RATB -- and with the transportation and urban planning services, is feasible. These organisations are currently co-operating well together, even though they fall under the authority of different administrative entities.

Experience in dense urban areas has demonstrated the necessity of having an institutional organisation with a mandate to ensure the coherent development and operating policies of all organisations concerned with urban transport. We are demanding that such an entity be established in Romania, in order to bring together all responsible groups involved in the urban transport sector. The organisation should be opened up to the membership of architects, urban planners, sociologists, and specialists from research institutes or universities, as well.

We have before us as examples the paths followed by other countries; although lessons can be learned from their experiences, we must avoid their mistakes. In this context, the organisation proposed above may be instrumental in facilitating the search for solutions to existing and future problems.

4. CURRENT SITUATION

The Bucharest Metro has operated satisfactorily with no major accidents for over 15 years, despite: political interference from the Communist regime under Ceaucescu (including an almost total interdiction on imported equipment) during the design and construction phases; pressures to start operation of incomplete lines; and a lack of subsidies for two consecutive years. This favourable operations record can be exclusively attributed to the monumental efforts put forth by the Metro staff. Today, we are confronting lower transport capacity due to the poor quality, decreased numbers, and reduced availability of the rolling stock, as well as poor service of the installations. The *status quo* can be characterised by technically and physically worn-out equipment -- some of which was in inferior condition at the beginning of its use -- resulting in poor reliability of service and high operating costs.

In 1975, three main metro lines were put into operation, comprising 60 km of double track, 40 stations, four depots and a central control centre. Considering the length of the lines, which covers only 3.4 per cent of the length of public transport lines in Bucharest, the subway today provides 25.2 per cent of the total trips made in Bucharest, more than 200 million trips per year (see Figures 1 and 2).

The principal objective established for the Bucharest metro was to link the industrial zones of the city with the residential areas. If this objective was achieved, the lines and the stations placements did not always respond to real transport demand. The city centre was especially at a disadvantage due to a limited number of stations. The average distance between stations -- 1 500 metres -- is too great, and in the densely populated areas this has resulted in an incomplete utilisation of the transport system. By comparison, the Budapest subway, with a total of 50 km of track, is able to assure 5.6 million trips per km and year. Under virtually the same conditions, the Bucharest subway is covering 3.6 million trips per km and year.

The drop in the number of users after 1989 (as shown in Figure 3) is a normal consequence of the specific social and economic conditions in Romania compared to other countries in this part of Europe. After 1989, private car use and gasoline consumption were no longer restricted and surface public transport was improved. The psychological element associated with recently found mobility has maintained pressure for use of individual transport means, even though the ratio between gasoline price per litre and public transport ticket price is 3:1. Recovering public transport users is therefore a difficult challenge, which can only be met by offering a higher quality service. If we do not act in this direction, the road network will be suffocated by cars in a very short time.

5. EXPECTATIONS FOR FURTHER DEVELOPMENT

The increase in attractiveness of public transport is determined by the system's features (network and station configuration, frequency, comfort and safety, accessibility and fare structure) and their correlation. Regarding the Metro, some features can be modified, some not. For example, as regards the existing network, the placement of routes and stations is fixed; therefore, an improvement in quality could only be obtained by modifying other elements. New lines will only be able to be considered if there is financing for construction. In recent years, technological decline has been halted and a complete rehabilitation strategy supported by comprehensive feasibility studies has been established. Required resources, however, are greater than the internal capital investment funds available under the current austerity budgets (for example, just completing the work already under way on construction lines will take over 15 years). Therefore, the only reasonable solution today is to apply for a foreign loan. We consider that investment in the country's infrastructure is imperative for normal development of overall economic activity. It encourages development of industry and services through improvements in essential facilities and equipment.

It is also necessary to promote the idea (new in this country) of a "multi-modal transport system", a concept that provides through design and construction the co-ordination of routes, commuting and a unique fare structure, despite the transport system's ownership (privately or publicly owned) or type of operator's authority (local or national).

Unlike the majority of the large European cities, Bucharest does not have a regional railway network such as the *S-Bahn* or RER systems, which are able to cross the city and link it with populated suburban areas and the airports. This situation has persisted in Bucharest, although studies conducted at the turn of the century recommended such a system (Figure 4). Railroad development has taken into account only the main routes of the country until now, and the typical passenger trains are long-distance trains with infrequent intervals or commuter trains available only at rush hours. Moreover, Bucharest's railroad stations, with the exception of Gara de Nord, are accessible only with difficulty by the city's public transportation.

A possible solution to this situation would be to extend the current and future metro lines to residential areas outside the city on the surface, using existing railroad lines wherever possible. In this way, the problematic long distances between stations -- characteristic of the regional system -- would be rectified by a mixed regional railroad and urban metro system. A feasibility study recently conducted on this problem proposes as a first step the construction of a branch from the future Gara de Nord line, LAROMET, to Baneasa and Otopeni airfields and even further to the Snagov resort area (see Figure 5). This line would cover 59 km, 24 km of which will comprise already-existing railroad line.

6. FINANCIAL ASPECTS

The existing subsidy for Metro operations accounts for a normal portion of the budget. However, the balance rate of the subsidy, which reaches around 70 per cent of total operational costs, exceeds normal budget share. This situation is a product of Romania's transition economy, which is characterised by a low technological level, requiring considerable financial and human support, and the technical difficulty of adapting fare prices to exterior economic conditions. Even if the technical obstacles are resolved this year through a new fare collection system based on magnetic stripe tickets, social and economic problems will continue to influence fare policy. It should be noted that subsidies come from one source in Romania -- the central budget. A financing system able to bring in contributions from the local budget or from specific taxes, as is the case in other countries, is possible under certain conditions and could alleviate some of the burden on the central budget.

Recent studies on the economic and financial rehabilitation programme for the Bucharest Metro demonstrate the continued necessity of the subsidy, due to the social protection policy and the high costs of maintenance and safety for the rolling stock and installations.

On the other hand, obtaining higher levels of efficiency is possible only with a considerable rehabilitation effort. Following are three possible scenarios for this initiative:

-- low levels of investment activity;
-- forced organisational and financial rehabilitation without the required technical support;
-- a daring and realistic rehabilitation project.

The first scenario leads to stagnation, an unsatisfactory technical status and an abnormal financial situation. The second copes with major safety risks regarding the rolling stock and the installations, but compromises operations. In our opinion, which is sustained by the completed studies, there are no other rational alternatives to rehabilitation. The only remaining problem is to find the financial resources with the best possible conditions.

7. CONCLUSION

Today, the Bucharest Metro has a medium-sized network with a satisfactory level of operations, but with a great number of technical and financial problems. Its staff is well trained, but excessive in number. A radical improvement in quality of service and a better financial situation can only be achieved through intense and sustained technical efforts, internal re-organisational measures, and an adequate legal and institutional framework. These are initiatives that must be taken in order to achieve an efficient, non-pollutant and high-quality public transportation system.

Parts of the rolling stock rehabilitation programme have already begun: the technical degradation of the fleet has been stopped and the required annual subsidy has been cut by around 7 per cent in one year. It is essential that this plan be continued and extended in accordance with adopted strategy in order to facilitate the administrative reorganisation of the system and produce the financial results necessary to put the Bucharest Metro on solid grounds for future development.

The Bucharest subway must maintain and develop its role in the city's public transportation system in order to be able to extend its service to suburban areas. It is therefore mandatory that decision-makers better understand the current situation and put forth the necessary financial commitment to meet this end.

FIGURES

Figure 1. **The structure of public transport in Bucharest (1994)**

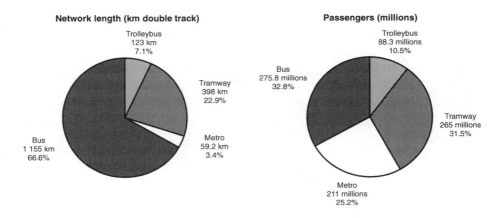

Network length (km double track)

Trolleybus
123 km
7.1%

Tramway
398 km
22.9%

Bus
1 155 km
66.6%

Metro
59.2 km
3.4%

Passengers (millions)

Trolleybus
88.3 millions
10.5%

Bus
275.8 millions
32.8%

Tramway
265 millions
31.5%

Metro
211 millions
25.2%

Source: Metrorex.

403

Figure 2. Network of the Bucharest Metro

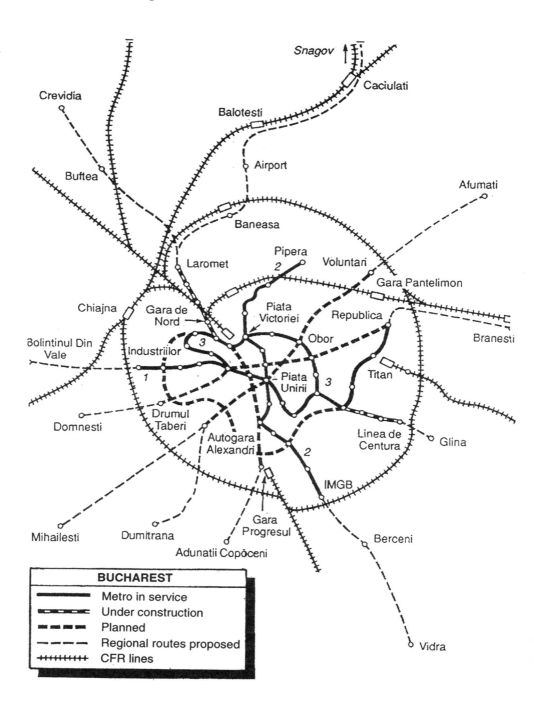

Crevidia

Snagov

Caciulati

Balotesti

Airport

Buftea

Afumati

Baneasa

Pipera
2

Voluntari

Laromet

Gara Pantelimon

Chiajna

Gara de
Nord

Piata
Victoriei

Republica

Branesti

Bolintinul Din
Vale

Industriilor
3

Obor

1

Piata
Unirii
3

Titan

Domnesti

Drumul
Taberi

Autogara
Alexandri

Linea de
Centura

Glina

2

Mihailesti

Dumitrana

IMGB

Gara
Progresul

Berceni

Adunatii Copăceni

Vidra

BUCHAREST

▬▬▬▬▬	Metro in service
▭▬▭▬▭	Under construction
▬ ▬ ▬ ▬	Planned
— — —	Regional routes proposed
+++++++	CFR lines

Figure 3. **Annual number of passengers in the Bucharest Metro**

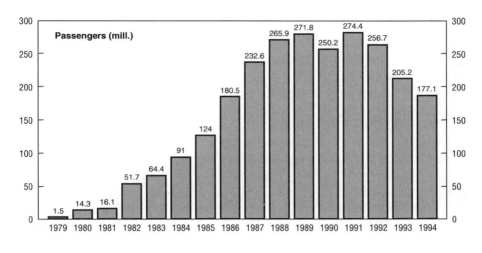

Source: Metrorex.

Figure 4. **Bucharest railroads with proposed diameter line**

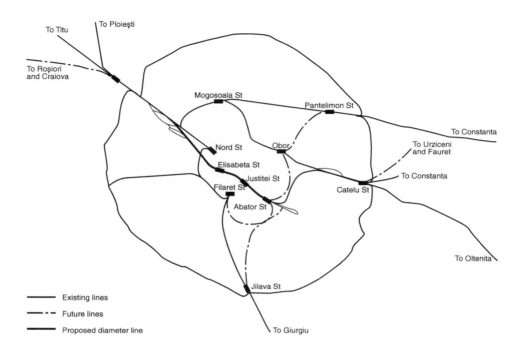

Figure 5. **Projected extension of the Bucharest Metro**

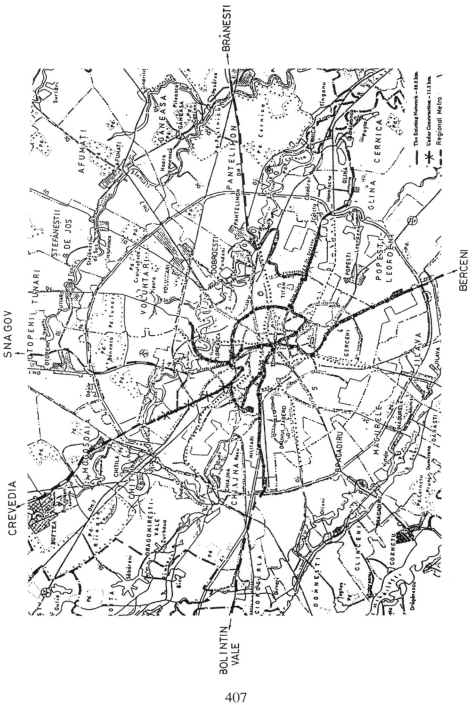

Integrated Public Transport in the Municipality of Bucharest and Agro-industrial Suburbs

Constantin Popescu
Regia Autonomă de Transport Bucuresti
Romania

TABLE OF CONTENTS

LIST OF TABLES

LIST OF FIGURES

1. INTRODUCTION

The transportation system is one of the main components of a city's social and economic life; it is, in fact, an extension of the production processes within the serviced area. A vital public service for a city, public transport ensures optimum functioning of the urban system and provides dynamism, unity and coherence for all its elements.

A performant urban public transport service provides mobility for persons who cannot financially afford individual transportation. It facilitates fluidity in overall traffic flow and is less harmful to the environment. Moreover, the operating cost per passenger is much less than that of individual transportation.

In Bucharest, public transport is under pressure due to the difference between the rates of demand and supply (20 per cent), and the high wear-and-tear on infrastructure and the vehicle fleet (approximately 70 per cent of fleet affected). Substantive institutional and legislative measures must be taken and a general model suitable for other cities in Romania must be designed. The goal of these measures is to promote growth in operating efficiency in public transport by introducing decentralisation and deregulation mechanisms.

Investment policy is of great importance to public transport. The macroeconomic effects of infrastructure investments, including costs of alternative options, must be evaluated if government finances are to be invested in further development. It is becoming increasingly clear that the successive positive effects of investment in public transport present greater macroeconomic advantages than other public costs. For example, investment in social protection produces important social effects in the short term, but in the long term, produces negative macroeconomic results due to individual preference for consumption and sustenance rather than for entrepreneurial investments. In this case, an economic cost-benefit analysis is most-often advised for establishing the feasibility of an infrastructure project. This must take all elements into account, including macroeconomic effects in the long term.

Of utmost importance -- and difficulty -- for urban public transport decision-makers is the determination of an optimum modal split to serve the present and the future needs of the urban area in the most-efficient way. The final choice should always be based on demand for services, and not on the system itself and its existing network. At the same time, the decision must be made free from all political or commercial pressure.

Even with all the recent examples of mistakes made in other European cities over the last 20 years, which concern neglect of public transport, we can persuade neither officials nor decision-makers of the need for and utility of a well-organised public transport system. Given the positive effects of public transport on the population, environment and city as a whole, creating a well-structured urban transport system seems to be the only way for halting a decrease in mobility of the urban population.

The adoption of minimum European standards would prevent further differences between Bucharest and other European cities concerning public transport problems, and could be used by authorities as an argument for the integration of Romania in European structures, as well.

A firm policy to encourage public transport use requires not only an endowment of sufficiently modern vehicles, but also methods that develop favourable public transport access routes in traffic. Moreover, an integrated public transport system with reasonable fares must be designed and implemented. Indeed, a high-quality, integrated, public transport system is considered to be the cheapest and the most agreeable solution for the public at large and the right solution for the city of Bucharest.

The present situation in Bucharest is complicated, due to the lack of a specific public transport law establishing passenger rights to mobility and the responsibilities of authorities. There are also problems in the regulation of local taxes and a lack of formal co-ordination between public transport operators and local authorities.

New trends in journey structure are appearing, namely an overall movement away from residential zones to the suburbs (in the future, many neighbourhoods will be built in the suburbs). Moreover, an increase in the area served by public transport and an important modification of passenger flow directions and levels is foreseen.

The problem with improving public transport is not a financial one, as it would initially appear, but rather, its absence from the priorities list of authorities. The reason for this could be the lack of a proper approach in establishing long-term objectives for an efficient public transport system. Although investments in public transport are without exception of great value and in long terms, neither local authorities nor public transport operators can plan even three to four years ahead because of poor annual budget results.

2. PRESENT SITUATION IN BUCHAREST PUBLIC TRANSPORT

The public transport network in Bucharest is served by the following independent operators:

a) Regia Autonomă de Transport Bucuresti (R.A.T.B.): provides surface transport services (trams, trolleys, buses) for the city and its suburbs;

b) METROREX R.A.: provides the underground transport for the city;

c) Societatea Natională a Căilor Ferate Romane (S.N.C.F.R.): provides urban and suburban underground railway transport to and from the capital;

d) the public inter-city transport company ("Intertrans"): provides suburban and inter-city transport, using part of the urban public road network.

Dynamics of the Bucharest surface public transport system in 1994 include the following:

-- The average fleet rate grew 5.6 per cent in daily service compared to 1993, due to purchase of new DAF buses, modernisation of trams, and transfer of second-hand trams from Germany (see Table 1).

-- The length of the surface public transport network totalled 1 676 km in both directions, an increase of 1.7 per cent compared to 1993 due to placement of new lines and extension of old lines -- primarily bus lines (see Table 4).

-- The average route length for trams was 9.2 km in both directions, 7.6 km for trolleys and 10.4 km for buses, representing a 1 per cent increase compared with 1993 (see Table 5).

-- The number of vehicle-km travelled grew by 9.4 per cent compared with 1993, primarily due to the increase in bus vehicle-km travelled. (see Table 6).

-- The daily average service time per vehicle was: 13.5 hours for trams (down from 1993), 13.6 hours for trolleys and 11.6 hours for buses (see Table 8).

-- The operating speed of public transport vehicles increased by 2.8 per cent for trams, due to improvements in the infrastructure; for buses and trolleys, these indexes were lower than in 1993 because of poor road conditions (see Table 9).

-- The number of place-km offered by public transport vehicles (assuming 8.5 passengers/m2) increased by 5.5 per cent, mainly due to an additional tram service (6.8 per cent). For trolleys, this figure decreased by 1 per cent in 1994 compared to 1993, because of the old age of the trolleys (see Table 10).

-- The number of passenger journeys decreased compared with 1993; the drop was most dramatic for trolleys (down 20 per cent in 1994) (see Table 11).

-- Fare-box revenues were set at 208.38 lei/journey for trams (the maintenance of which is more expensive than for other vehicles), 204.85 lei/journey for buses, 203.05 lei/journey for trolleys (see Table 13).

-- Subsidies for the entire R.A.T.B. activity amounted to 77.86 per cent of total revenue, increasing in 1995 to 79.40 per cent (see Table 14).

-- The approved subsidy for 1995 (119.6 billion lei) was not sufficient to meet total needs, predicted to reach 173.6 billion lei. Funds necessary to cover operating costs for the last three months of the year were expected to be granted. Approved investment funds were also below the required level of 256.3 billion lei (see Table 14).

As neither a specific law nor political decision-making process exists for public transport, the increases in the operational indexes above were not the results of any involvement of central or local authorities, but rather the outcome of efforts on the part of transport operators. Public transport policy should be developed for the long-term. Although subject to political tendencies, transport policy cannot be modified every year in function of these tendencies, as the effects of some investments designed to affect the behaviour and mentality of people need time to materialise.

3. CONCLUSIONS AND RECOMMENDATIONS

With the objectives of establishing an integrated transport system, the Municipality of Bucharest commissioned an urban transport rehabilitation study from TRANSURB Consult in BELGIUM. Following analysis of the situation, the consultancy made a number of recommendations, most of them beyond the Bucharest transport company's competence. These recommendations include the following:

a) Define national urban transport strategies.

b) Clearly outline public transport policy at both the national and local levels by:

- establishing the position of authorities towards public transport and their role within the economy of the city;
- establishing well-defined objectives related to the service, environmental, social protection.

c) Draw up and approve a public transport law setting the organisational framework for the establishment of a Public Transport Authority which will:

- co-ordinate the unitary methodology of the whole transport activity (service, maintenance-repairs, strategy-tactics);
- integrate urban transport services by developing and organising them around a unitary concept;

- geographically integrate the transport modes (e.g surface transport stations should be nearer to those of the metro, railway, inter-city), with the aim of facilitating transfers among modes and provide connection facilities favourable to the passengers);
- give some priority on public roads to surface public transport vehicles (e.g. full priority for the primary network when leaving the stations, and exclusive corridors);
- discourage individual (private) transport in very crowded areas using partial hour restrictions or even total restrictions in some areas and on some primary roads;
- correlate the interest of each transport subsystem with the general interest of the urban public system, and stimulate fair competition in the sector.

d) Establish a fair policy for subsidising public transport, including the conclusion of the Local Budget Law provisions, having the following goals:

- sustain the public transport system through government and local authority support: from resources needed for development (new technologies, updated transport means) to operations subsidies;
- equitably granted investments for and economic co-ordination of Bucharest public transport, its development and rehabilitation; a substantial improvement in street furnishings necessary to organise and develop public transport and update passenger information media.

e) Gain new economic leverage when distributing material, human and financial resources among the transport systems by:

- designing fare structures and policies that will allow easy transfer from one transport mode to another;
- correlating presentation of schedules, routes and transfers (folders, maps indicating transfer possibilities, clear signs and orientation panels for the public in the main traffic junction) in order to obtain a larger number of passengers.

We believe that achieving an integrated transport system will lead our country to a new concept of city organisation, its place and importance, and to visible improvements in the urban structure, offering the capital a greater dynamism and sound possibilities for a better quality of life.

TABLES AND FIGURES

Table 1. **Average fleet in daily service**

Modes	1993	1994	per cent ±
Motor tram cars	362	373	+3.0
Trolleys	180	184	+2.2
Buses	775	834	+7.6
TOTAL	1 317	1 391	+5.6

Figure 1. **Average fleet in daily service**

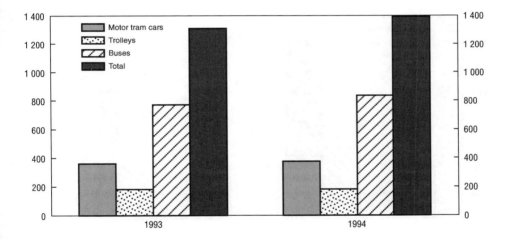

Source: RATB.

Table 2. **Average fleet in operation on a weekday (peak hour)**

Modes	1993	1994	per cent ±
Tram cars	410	426	+3.9
Trolleys	199	199	-
Buses	824	842	+3.3
TOTAL	1 424	1 467	+3.0

Figure 2. **Average fleet in operation on a weekday**

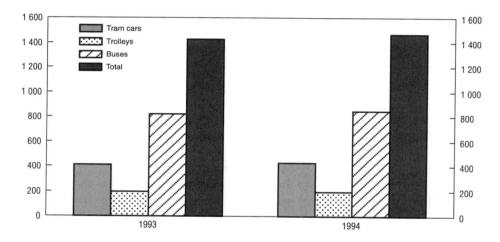

Source: RATB.

Table 3. **Length of public transport network (km)**

Modes	1993	1994	Per cent ±
I. TRAMS	381.8	369.7	-3.2
-- on streets[1]	320.4	307.3	-4.0
-- on concrete slab sleepers	235.8	229.7	
• railway type	24.5	19.8	
• normal rail (grooved rail with channel)	60.0	57.8	
-- in depots	36.5	37.6	+2.7
-- length equivalent of special rail pieces	24.8	24.8	
II. TROLLEYS	130.1	134.1	+3.1
-- on streets	119.2	123.2	
-- in depots	10.9	10.9	+3.3
III. BUSES	730.0	756.0	+3.6

[1]   Tram tracks on Sos. Panduri, bd. T. Vladimirescu and str. Odoarei were discontinued.

Table 4. **Length of urban transport routes (as of 31 December 1994)**
(km round trip)

Modes	1993	1994	Per cent ±
Trams	395	398	+0.7
Trolleys	122	123	+0.8
Buses	1 130	1 155	+2.2
TOTAL	1 647	1 676	+1.7

Table 5. **Average route length (km round trip)**

Modes	1993	1994	Per cent ±
Trams	9.4	9.2	-2.1
Trolleys	7.2	7.6	+5.5
Buses	10.4	10.4	-
TOTAL	9.8	9.9	+1.0

Table 6. **Vehicle-km travelled (millions)**

Modes	1993	1994	Per cent ±
Trams	27.4	29.6	+8.0
Trolleys	11.5	11.7	+1.7
Buses	54.8	61.2	+11.6
TOTAl	93.7	102.5	+9.4

Figure 3. **Vehicle-km travelled**

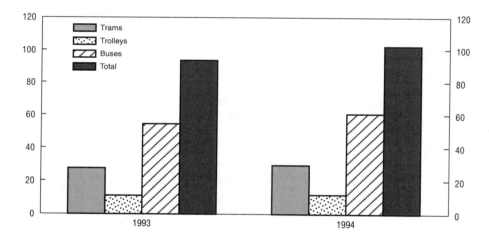

Source: RATB.

Table 7. Average distance travelled daily by one vehicle in operation (daily veh-km)

Modes	1993	1994	per cent ±
Trams (motor cars)	207.5	217.2	+4.6
Trolleys	175.7	174.8	-0.1
Buses	193.8	201.2	+3.8
Average	194.9	201.8	+3.5

Table 8. Average daily operating time per vehicle (hours)

Modes	1993	1994	Per cent ±
Trams	14.6	13.5	-7.5
Trolleys	13.4	13.6	+1.5
Buses	11.3	11.6	+2.6
TOTAL	12.1	12.4	+2.5

Table 9. Operating speed (km/h)

Modes	1993	1994	Per cent ±
Trams	14.2	14.6	+2.8
Trolleys	13.0	12.9	-0.8
Buses	17.2	17.3	-0.6
TOTAL	15.6	15.9	+1.9

Table 10. **Place-km offered by public transport vehicles (assuming 8.5 passengers per m2) (millions)**

Modes	1993	1994	Per cent ±
Trams	7 499.00	8 010.1	+6.8
Trolleys	1 911.14	1 890.6	-1.0
Buses	6 390.70	6 767.5	+5.9
TOTAL	15 801.10	16 668.2	+5.5

Figure 4. **Place-km offered by public transport vehicles**

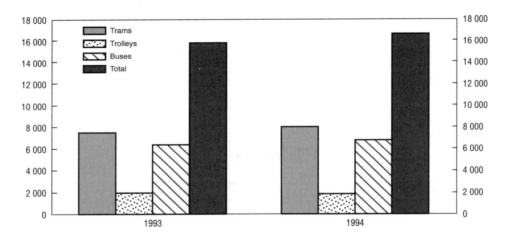

Source: RATB.

426

Table 11. **Passenger journeys (millions)**

Modes	1993	1994	Per cent ±
Trams	281.9	264.9	-6.0
Trolleys	111.4	88.3	-20.0
Buses	289.6	275.7	-4.8
TOTAL	682.9	628.9	-7.9

Table 12. **Revenues and subsidies for public transport (millions)**

Specification	1993	1994
Revenues	48 990.7	129 415.6
of which, Subsidy	38 112.7	88 674.0

Table 13. **Revenues per transport mode (millions)**

Modes	Lei per veh-km		Lei per journey	
	1993	1994	1993	1994
Trams	133.08	464.03	15.90	208.38
Trolleys	115.40	452.67	15.80	203.05
Buses	84.79	280.04	16.70	204.85

Table 14. **Revenue structure**

Type of revenue	1994 billion ROL	Per cent	1995 (approved) billion ROL	Per cent	1995 (necessary) billion ROL	Per cent
Fare-box revenue	40.70	22.14	45.00	20.60	45.00	9.48
Subsidisation from the budget	88.60	48.21	119.60	54.77	173.60	36.55
State allocation for development	54.50	29.65	53.80	24.63	256.30	53.97
Total	183.80	100.00	218.40	100.00	474.90	100.00

Table 15. **Costs per transport mode (millions)**

Modes	1993	1994
Tram	21 210.60	56 408.10
Trolley	6 235.20	18 844.30
Bus	21 544.80	54 466.00
Total	48 990.60	129 718.40

Table 16. **Specific costs based on transport mode performance**

Modes	Lei per veh-km		Lei per journey	
	1993	1994	1993	1994
Tram	627.5	1 559.10	74.50	212.90
Trolley	490.9	1 567.40	67.30	213.50
Bus	374.0	842.90	73.70	197.90
Total	494.3	1 149.80	71.70	206.20

Table 17. Cost breakdown for surface public transport
(millions lei)

Elements of primary cost	1993				1994			
	Trams	Trolleys	Buses	Total	Trams	Trolleys	Buses	Total
Raw materials	1 499.40	909.60	3 524.50	5 933.50	8 368.3	2 737.00	9 224.90	20 330.20
Per cent to total	7.07	14.59	16.36	12.11	14.83	14.52	16.94	15.67
Combustible, electric power	3 959.90	1 264.90	4 396.20	9 621.00	11 431.50	3 547.90	10 375.00	25 354.40
Per cent to total	18.67	20.28	20.40	19.64	20.27	18.83	19.05	19.55
Amortisation of fixed means	183.50	96.10	2 236.70	2 516.30	2 384.60	938.8	3 993.50	7 316.90
Per cent to total	0.87	1.54	10.38	5.14	4.23	4.98	7.33	5.64
Repairing works and services	7 392.90	521.10	2 537.20	10 451.10	15 835.30	2 043.90	7 905.00	25 784.20
Per cent to total	34.86	14.36	11.78	21.34	28.07	10.86	14.51	19.88
Wages	7 148.80	3 128.90	7 790.90	18 068.60	17 814.80	9 363.90	22 343.40	49 522.10
Per cent to total	33.70	50.18	38.16	36.88	31.58	49.68	41.02	38.18
Tax and other expenses	27.70	12.80	37.70	78.20	573.60	212.80	624.20	1 410.60
Per cent to total	0.13	0.20	0.18	0.16	1.02	1.13	1.15	1.08
Revenues expenditures	998.40	301.90	1 021.60	2 321.90	-	-	-	-
Per cent to total	4.70	4.85	4.74	4.74	-	-	-	-
Total	21 210.60	6 235.20	21 544.80	48 990.60	56 408.10	18 844.30	54 466.00	129 718.40
Per cent to total	100.00	100.00	100.00	100.00	100.00	100.00	100.00	100.00

MAIN SALES OUTLETS OF OECD PUBLICATIONS
PRINCIPAUX POINTS DE VENTE DES PUBLICATIONS DE L'OCDE

ARGENTINA – ARGENTINE
Carlos Hirsch S.R.L.
Galería Güemes, Florida 165, 4° Piso
1333 Buenos Aires   Tel. (1) 331.1787 y 331.2391
                                        Telefax: (1) 331.1787

AUSTRALIA – AUSTRALIE
D.A. Information Services
648 Whitehorse Road, P.O.B 163
Mitcham, Victoria 3132   Tel. (03) 9210.7777
                                        Telefax: (03) 9210.7788

AUSTRIA – AUTRICHE
Gerold & Co.
Graben 31
Wien I   Tel. (0222) 533.50.14
                                Telefax: (0222) 512.47.31.29

BELGIUM – BELGIQUE
Jean De Lannoy
Avenue du Roi 202 Koningslaan
B-1060 Bruxelles   Tel. (02) 538.51.69/538.08.41
                                        Telefax: (02) 538.08.41

CANADA
Renouf Publishing Company Ltd.
1294 Algoma Road
Ottawa, ON K1B 3W8   Tel. (613) 741.4333
                                        Telefax: (613) 741.5439
Stores:
61 Sparks Street
Ottawa, ON K1P 5R1   Tel. (613) 238.8985
12 Adelaide Street West
Toronto, ON M5H 1L6   Tel. (416) 363.3171
                                        Telefax: (416)363.59.63

Les Éditions La Liberté Inc.
3020 Chemin Sainte-Foy
Sainte-Foy, PQ G1X 3V6   Tel. (418) 658.3763
                                        Telefax: (418) 658.3763

Federal Publications Inc.
165 University Avenue, Suite 701
Toronto, ON M5H 3B8   Tel. (416) 860.1611
                                        Telefax: (416) 860.1608

Les Publications Fédérales
1185 Université
Montréal, QC H3B 3A7   Tel. (514) 954.1633
                                        Telefax: (514) 954.1635

CHINA – CHINE
China National Publications Import
Export Corporation (CNPIEC)
16 Gongti E. Road, Chaoyang District
P.O. Box 88 or 50
Beijing 100704 PR   Tel. (01) 506.6688
                                        Telefax: (01) 506.3101

CHINESE TAIPEI – TAIPEI CHINOIS
Good Faith Worldwide Int'l. Co. Ltd.
9th Floor, No. 118, Sec. 2
Chung Hsiao E. Road
Taipei   Tel. (02) 391.7396/391.7397
                                        Telefax: (02) 394.9176

**CZECH REPUBLIC –
RÉPUBLIQUE TCHÈQUE**
Artia Pegas Press Ltd.
Narodni Trida 25
POB 825
111 21 Praha 1   Tel. (2) 242 246 04
                                        Telefax: (2) 242 278 72

DENMARK – DANEMARK
Munksgaard Book and Subscription Service
35, Nørre Søgade, P.O. Box 2148
DK-1016 København K   Tel. (33) 12.85.70
                                        Telefax: (33) 12.93.87

EGYPT – ÉGYPTE
Middle East Observer
41 Sherif Street
Cairo   Tel. 392.6919
                                Telefax: 360-6804

FINLAND – FINLANDE
Akateeminen Kirjakauppa
Keskuskatu 1, P.O. Box 128
00100 Helsinki
Subscription Services/Agence d'abonnements :
P.O. Box 23
00371 Helsinki   Tel. (358 0) 121 4416
                                Telefax: (358 0) 121.4450

FRANCE
OECD/OCDE
Mail Orders/Commandes par correspondance :
2, rue André-Pascal
75775 Paris Cedex 16   Tel. (33-1) 45.24.82.00
                                        Telefax: (33-1) 49.10.42.76
                                Telex: 640048 OCDE
Internet: Compte.PUBSINQ @ oecd.org
Orders via Minitel, France only/
Commandes par Minitel, France exclusivement :
36 15 OCDE
OECD Bookshop/Librairie de l'OCDE :
33, rue Octave-Feuillet
75016 Paris   Tel. (33-1) 45.24.81.81
                                        (33-1) 45.24.81.67
Dawson
B.P. 40
91121 Palaiseau Cedex   Tel. 69.10.47.00
                                        Telefax : 64.54.83.26

Documentation Française
29, quai Voltaire
75007 Paris   Tel. 40.15.70.00

Economica
49, rue Héricart
75015 Paris   Tel. 45.78.12.92
                                Telefax : 40.58.15.70

Gibert Jeune (Droit-Économie)
6, place Saint-Michel
75006 Paris   Tel. 43.25.91.19

Librairie du Commerce International
10, avenue d'Iéna
75016 Paris   Tel. 40.73.34.60

Librairie Dunod
Université Paris-Dauphine
Place du Maréchal-de-Lattre-de-Tassigny
75016 Paris   Tel. 44.05.40.13

Librairie Lavoisier
11, rue Lavoisier
75008 Paris   Tel. 42.65.39.95

Librairie des Sciences Politiques
30, rue Saint-Guillaume
75007 Paris   Tel. 45.48.36.02

P.U.F.
49, boulevard Saint-Michel
75005 Paris   Tel. 43.25.83.40

Librairie de l'Université
12a, rue Nazareth
13100 Aix-en-Provence   Tel. (16) 42.26.18.08

Documentation Française
165, rue Garibaldi
69003 Lyon   Tel. (16) 78.63.32.23

Librairie Decitre
29, place Bellecour
69002 Lyon   Tel. (16) 72.40.54.54

Librairie Sauramps
Le Triangle
34967 Montpellier Cedex 2   Tel. (16) 67.58.85.15
                                Tekefax: (16) 67.58.27.36

A la Sorbonne Actual
23, rue de l'Hôtel-des-Postes
06000 Nice   Tel. (16) 93.13.77.75
                                Telefax: (16) 93.80.75.69

GERMANY – ALLEMAGNE
OECD Publications and Information Centre
August-Bebel-Allee 6
D-53175 Bonn   Tel. (0228) 959.120
                                Telefax: (0228) 959.12.17

GREECE – GRÈCE
Librairie Kauffmann
Mavrokordatou 9
106 78 Athens   Tel. (01) 32.55.321
                                Telefax: (01) 32.30.320

HONG-KONG
Swindon Book Co. Ltd.
Astoria Bldg. 3F
34 Ashley Road, Tsimshatsui
Kowloon, Hong Kong   Tel. 2376.2062
                                Telefax: 2376.0685

HUNGARY – HONGRIE
Euro Info Service
Margitsziget, Európa Ház
1138 Budapest   Tel. (1) 111.62.16
                                Telefax: (1) 111.60.61

ICELAND – ISLANDE
Mál Mog Menning
Laugavegi 18, Pósthólf 392
121 Reykjavik   Tel. (1) 552.4240
                                Telefax: (1) 562.3523

INDIA – INDE
Oxford Book and Stationery Co.
Scindia House
New Delhi 110001   Tel. (11) 331.5896/5308
                                Telefax: (11) 332.5993
17 Park Street
Calcutta 700016   Tel. 240832

INDONESIA – INDONÉSIE
Pdii-Lipi
P.O. Box 4298
Jakarta 12042   Tel. (21) 573.34.67
                                Telefax: (21) 573.34.67

IRELAND – IRLANDE
Government Supplies Agency
Publications Section
4/5 Harcourt Road
Dublin 2   Tel. 661.31.11
                                Telefax: 475.27.60

ISRAEL – ISRAËL
Praedicta
5 Shatner Street
P.O. Box 34030
Jerusalem 91430   Tel. (2) 52.84.90/1/2
                                Telefax: (2) 52.84.93

R.O.Y. International
P.O. Box 13056
Tel Aviv 61130   Tel. (3) 546 1423
                                Telefax: (3) 546 1442

Palestinian Authority/Middle East:
INDEX Information Services
P.O.B. 19502
Jerusalem   Tel. (2) 27.12.19
                                Telefax: (2) 27.16.34

ITALY – ITALIE
Libreria Commissionaria Sansoni
Via Duca di Calabria 1/1
50125 Firenze   Tel. (055) 64.54.15
                                Telefax: (055) 64.12.57
Via Bartolini 29
20155 Milano   Tel. (02) 36.50.83

Editrice e Libreria Herder
Piazza Montecitorio 120
00186 Roma   Tel. 679.46.28
                                    Telefax: 678.47.51

Libreria Hoepli
Via Hoepli 5
20121 Milano   Tel. (02) 86.54.46
                                    Telefax: (02) 805.28.86

Libreria Scientifica
Dott. Lucio de Biasio 'Aeiou'
Via Coronelli, 6
20146 Milano   Tel. (02) 48.95.45.52
                                    Telefax: (02) 48.95.45.48

JAPAN – JAPON
OECD Publications and Information Centre
Landic Akasaka Building
2-3-4 Akasaka, Minato-ku
Tokyo 107   Tel. (81.3) 3586.2016
                                    Telefax: (81.3) 3584.7929

KOREA – CORÉE
Kyobo Book Centre Co. Ltd.
P.O. Box 1658, Kwang Hwa Moon
Seoul   Tel. 730.78.91
                                    Telefax: 735.00.30

MALAYSIA – MALAISIE
University of Malaya Bookshop
University of Malaya
P.O. Box 1127, Jalan Pantai Baru
59700 Kuala Lumpur
Malaysia   Tel. 756.5000/756.5425
                                    Telefax: 756.3246

MEXICO – MEXIQUE
OECD Publications and Information Centre
Edificio INFOTEC
Av. San Fernando no. 37
Col. Toriello Guerra
Tlalpan C.P. 14050
Mexico D.F.
                    Tel. (525) 606 00 11 Extension 100
                            Fax : (525) 606 13 07

Revistas y Periodicos Internacionales S.A. de C.V.
Florencia 57 - 1004
Mexico, D.F. 06600   Tel. 207.81.00
                                    Telefax: 208.39.79

NETHERLANDS – PAYS-BAS
SDU Uitgeverij Plantijnstraat
Externe Fondsen
Postbus 20014
2500 EA's-Gravenhage   Tel. (070) 37.89.880
Voor bestellingen: Telefax: (070) 34.75.778

**NEW ZEALAND –
NOUVELLE-ZÉLANDE**
GPLegislation Services
P.O. Box 12418
Thorndon, Wellington   Tel. (04) 496.5655
                                    Telefax: (04) 496.5698

NORWAY – NORVÈGE
NIC INFO A/S
Bertrand Narvesens vei 2
P.O. Box 6512 Etterstad
0606 Oslo 6   Tel. (022) 57.33.00
                                    Telefax: (022) 68.19.01

PAKISTAN
Mirza Book Agency
65 Shahrah Quaid-E-Azam
Lahore 54000   Tel. (42) 353.601
                                    Telefax: (42) 231.730

PHILIPPINE – PHILIPPINES
International Booksource Center Inc.
Rm 179/920 Cityland 10 Condo Tower 2
HV dela Costa Ext cor Valero St.
Makati Metro Manila   Tel. (632) 817 9676
                           Telefax : (632) 817 1741

POLAND – POLOGNE
Ars Polona
00-950 Warszawa
Krakowskie Przedmieácie 7   Tel. (22) 264760
                                Telefax : (22) 268673

PORTUGAL
Livraria Portugal
Rua do Carmo 70-74
Apart. 2681
1200 Lisboa   Tel. (01) 347.49.82/5
                                    Telefax: (01) 347.02.64

SINGAPORE – SINGAPOUR
Gower Asia Pacific Pte Ltd.
Golden Wheel Building
41, Kallang Pudding Road, No. 04-03
Singapore 1334   Tel. 741.5166
                                    Telefax: 742.9356

SPAIN – ESPAGNE
Mundi-Prensa Libros S.A.
Castelló 37, Apartado 1223
Madrid 28001   Tel. (91) 431.33.99
                                    Telefax: (91) 575.39.98

Mundi-Prensa Barcelona
Consell de Cent No. 391
08009 – Barcelona   Tel. (93) 488.34.92
                                    Telefax: (93) 487.76.59

Llibreria de la Generalitat
Palau Moja
Rambla dels Estudis, 118
08002 – Barcelona
                    (Subscripcions) Tel. (93) 318.80.12
                     (Publicacions) Tel. (93) 302.67.23
                                    Telefax: (93) 412.18.54

SRI LANKA
Centre for Policy Research
c/o Colombo Agencies Ltd.
No. 300-304, Galle Road
Colombo 3   Tel. (1) 574240, 573551-2
                      Telefax: (1) 575394, 510711

SWEDEN – SUÈDE
CE Fritzes AB
S–106 47 Stockholm   Tel. (08) 690.90.90
                                    Telefax: (08) 20.50.21

Subscription Agency/Agence d'abonnements :
Wennergren-Williams Info AB
P.O. Box 1305
171 25 Solna   Tel. (08) 705.97.50
                                    Telefax: (08) 27.00.71

SWITZERLAND – SUISSE
Maditec S.A. (Books and Periodicals - Livres
et périodiques)
Chemin des Palettes 4
Case postale 266
1020 Renens VD 1   Tel. (021) 635.08.65
                                    Telefax: (021) 635.07.80

Librairie Payot S.A.
4, place Pépinet
CP 3212
1002 Lausanne   Tel. (021) 320.25.11
                                    Telefax: (021) 320.25.14

Librairie Unilivres
6, rue de Candolle
1205 Genève   Tel. (022) 320.26.23
                                    Telefax: (022) 329.73.18

Subscription Agency/Agence d'abonnements :
Dynapresse Marketing S.A.
38 avenue Vibert
1227 Carouge   Tel. (022) 308.07.89
                                    Telefax: (022) 308.07.99

See also – Voir aussi :
OECD Publications and Information Centre
August-Bebel-Allee 6
D-53175 Bonn (Germany)   Tel. (0228) 959.120
                                    Telefax: (0228) 959.12.17

THAILAND – THAÏLANDE
Suksit Siam Co. Ltd.
113, 115 Fuang Nakhon Rd.
Opp. Wat Rajbopith
Bangkok 10200   Tel. (662) 225.9531/2
                                    Telefax: (662) 222.5188

TUNISIA – TUNISIE
Grande Librairie Spécialisée
Fendri Ali
Avenue Haffouz Imm El-Intilaka
Bloc B 1 Sfax 3000   Tel. (216-4) 296 855
                                    Telefax: (216-4) 298.270

TURKEY – TURQUIE
Kültür Yayinlari Is-Türk Ltd. Sti.
Atatürk Bulvari No. 191/Kat 13
Kavaklidere/Ankara
                           Tel. (312) 428.11.40 Ext. 2458
                                    Telefax: (312) 417 24 90
Dolmabahce Cad. No. 29
Besiktas/Istanbul   Tel. (212) 260 7188

UNITED KINGDOM – ROYAUME-UNI
HMSO
Gen. enquiries   Tel. (171) 873 8242
Postal orders only:
P.O. Box 276, London SW8 5DT
Personal Callers HMSO Bookshop
49 High Holborn, London WC1V 6HB
                                    Telefax: (171) 873 8416
Branches at: Belfast, Birmingham, Bristol,
Edinburgh, Manchester

UNITED STATES – ÉTATS-UNIS
OECD Publications and Information Center
2001 L Street N.W., Suite 650
Washington, D.C. 20036-4922   Tel. (202) 785.6323
                                    Telefax: (202) 785.0350

Subscriptions to OECD periodicals may also be placed
through main subscription agencies.

Les abonnements aux publications périodiques de
l'OCDE peuvent être souscrits auprès des principales
agences d'abonnement.

Orders and inquiries from countries where Distributors
have not yet been appointed should be sent to: OECD
Publications Service, 2, rue André-Pascal, 75775 Paris
Cedex 16, France.

Les commandes provenant de pays où l'OCDE n'a pas
encore désigné de distributeur peuvent être adressées à :
OCDE, Service des Publications, 2, rue André-Pascal,
75775 Paris Cedex 16, France.

                                               1-1996

OECD PUBLICATIONS, 2, rue André-Pascal, 75775 PARIS CEDEX 16
PRINTED IN FRANCE
(75 96 01 1) ISBN 92-821-1211-X – No. 48454 1996